A CHRISTIAN THERAPY
FOR A NEUROTIC WORLD

A CHRISTIAN THERAPY
FOR A
NEUROTIC WORLD

BY

E. N. DUCKER

FOREWORD BY
FRANK LAKE, M.B., D.P.M.

LONDON
GEORGE ALLEN & UNWIN LTD
RUSKIN HOUSE MUSEUM STREET

PRINTED IN GREAT BRITAIN
in 11 point Janson type
BY SIMSON SHAND LTD
LONDON, HERTFORD AND HARLOW

In gratitude to my teacher
The Reverend E. W. P. Ingham
without whose
profound knowledge and skill
this work might never have been
undertaken

Canst thou not minister to a mind diseased,
Pluck from the memory a rooted sorrow,
Raze out the written troubles of the brain,
And with some sweet oblivious antidote
Cleanse the stuffed bosom of that perilous stuff
Which weighs upon thy heart?

MACBETH V. 3

FOREWORD

THIS book represents a remarkable personal achievement. Its author is one of the regular parochial clergy, deeply involved in the care of a city parish, and the administration of a large Rural Deanery. Having a small population within the parish and ministering to a 'gathered' congregation, Canon Ducker has been able to step aside from the common pattern of house-to-house visiting. Instead, his days are occupied almost wholly from morning till night in the cure of souls, or, to give it its Greek synonym, in psychotherapy.

When every Bishop is handed the Bible at his consecration, he is commanded, among other tasks, to 'heal the sick'. These tasks he delegates to his vicars. Here is a vicar who takes seriously this delegacy and who has a Bishop who supports him in it.

Any psychiatrist who has worked for some years within the National Health Service, knows, as I do, that the resources of psychiatry, though considerable, are limited. Our professional resources are limited, both as to the number of diseases for which we have effective remedies, and as to the time the psychiatrist can spend with any one patient. In many mental hospitals this is limited on the average to about five minutes a patient per week. There is a popular fallacy that psycho-therapy of an analytic kind is generally available for indi-viduals under the National Health Service. On the contrary, as Dr Michael Balint of the Tavistock Clinic has written, 'It is no exaggeration to say that to obtain psychotherapy for an adult under the National Health Service is nearly as difficult as winning a treble chance in a football pool.' From a leading University Department in Psychiatry, a professor wrote to me recently in answer to a request for a student to be put on the list for psychotherapy, that 'our resources are very slender, we can take on about two or three new patients a year'.

Within British psychiatry there has always been a powerful undercurrent of resistance against psychoanalytical theory and therapy. Recent extensions of the effectiveness of physical therapy, especially in relieving the symptoms of depression through electroplexy, and very recently through a new series of drugs, have given encouragement to this natural scientific desire to be able to treat the patient at a safe and comfortable emotional distance, rather than by personal involvement. There is no likelihood in the near future of any appreciable extension of psychotherapeutic services from consultant psychiatrists. Since the number of referrals of neurotic patients are increasing, and few new appointments of consultant psychiatrists are made, the time available to talk with any patient is steadily decreasing.

In psychotherapy the essential 'vehicle' in which any 'medicine' is given, is the doctor's own personality. This, and the wisdom gathered in his training, constitute the medical psychotherapist's resources. With these he contrives to meet the disorders of the human spirit. Before he can begin to use these resources he must make a diagnosis. About three-quarters of all patients referred to psychiatrists could be labelled 'depressive'. Such patients are filled with gloom and guilty feelings, often with apprehension. The spirit is at a low ebb and there is neither power nor joy.

Most of the remainder of neurotic illnesses could be diagnosed as anxiety states, phobic states, conversion reactions (nothing to do with religious conversion) or hysteria. In all these there is a basic fear of separation from the sources of personal Being. Anxiety is accompanied by a threat of death to the spirit or some other unmentionable horror. Apprehension rises to panic at the approach of this inner threat to 'Being' itself. The patient feels on the edge of an abyss of dereliction and dread, or that he is falling into nothing, nothing but mental pain and terror. The obsessional and schizoid personality patterns prove also to be, in part, defences against this same dread of identification with non-being. This second group of psychoneuroses, in which the peace of the human spirit is shattered by perpetual inner panic, is not one which, as psychiatrists, we can do a great deal fundamentally to help, much less to cure. Psychoanalysts would be diffident, and think in terms of long treatment of doubtful effectiveness in the majority of these cases. Drugs can alleviate and tranquillize, but tend to cause addiction. Our psychiatric resources are most inadequate to the healing task for such people.

A third category of emotionally disturbed persons who are referred to psychiatrists, comprises those who suffer from personality and character disorders of a psychopathic kind.

They suffer, but they make society suffer too. These patients cannot make or sustain good personal relationships. The normal capacity to love and be loved has been shattered in the earliest years of life and distorted patterns of hate and distrust persist. Here too, as mental hospital psychiatrists, we find our personal resources of little avail. Only love with firmness, in a suitable family group, can, in time, heal such people. We often do little more than establish a diagnosis and hope that our hospital community can give the acceptance and care which is required to enable these socially maladjusted persons to learn to love again and to exercise the restraints of responsible living in their dealings with society. Yet their illness makes them initially disruptive of any therapeutic group. Our psychiatric resources are so strained by psychopathic patients that we tend to avoid either taking them into our care, or admitting them to our hospitals.

The fourth category comprises those whose minds have lost contact with reality. They are of 'unsound mind'. For the most part these suffer from schizophrenia. They too need not only the tranquillizing of the disturbed layers of the unconscious mind, they need loving community and understanding care. It is in providing these that psychological medicine is at its best, its resources now wonderfully enhanced by an ancient drug put to modern uses, and by the move to turn the mental hospital into a therapeutic community.

Here then, we have the four major categories of mental pain and disorder, in which what are lost are, successively, joy of spirit, peace of heart, power to love, and the sound mind.

Are there any resources for the replenishment of these spiritual and emotional deficiencies other than those administered by psychiatrists, the Health Service, and the Home Office? Recognizing, as a psychiatrist, my own very limited resources for the care and cure of these ubiquitous disorders of the human spirit, if my concern is rather for my patient's good than for the defence of my own professional omnicompetence, must I not be eager and willing to work with any other professional person who has at his command any resources of the kind my patients need?

For nearly 2,000 years the Church has been drawing attention to the fact that there are resources of love, joy, peace and a sound mind given by God to individuals within her fellowship, through her worship, prayer, and Sacraments, and in response to what God is offering to men through the work of the Holy Spirit. The consistent claim of the Church has been, that when people come to an end of their own resources and look away from themselves to what God has been doing in the earthly life, death, and the life beyond death of His Son, they receive, as an inexhaustible resource of personal being and well-being, the Spirit of Jesus within themselves.

The constitutive fact of Christian life is acceptance into a new relationship with God which can never be earned or deserved, but which is His own Gift. To those who are poor in spirit is given the Holy Spirit. It is He who relates God the Father to God the Son. He is given to us, to relate us in an entirely new way to the Divine life, to ourselves, to others who share this New Being through the new relationship, and to all other created beings. It does not rest on the adequacy of our previous human being. This New Being consists in right relatedness to Christ, and Christ accepts us in every kind of moral mess or personality disorder, or delinquency that He may find us in. What He never can accept are our delusions of adequacy, our pride in the things we do or think or suppose ourselves to possess. These being broken, as they usually are in those who have fallen so low in their estimate of their social adequacy as to consent to visit a psychiatrist, the way is open to that full acceptance to which Christ, Who is God's Good News, invites us.

This moment of brokenness is not only a psychological end-point. It is a precious moment of spiritual truth. To have arrived at this verdict about one's self is the pre-condition of entry into the New Being. Yet the present state of affairs is such that neither psychiatrists nor clergy are using this crucial moment, with all its potentiality for rebirth and new-being, as it could be used, as it is indeed being used, for instance, by the members of 'Alcoholics Anonymous'. No class of patient humbles the psychotherapist or the psychiatrist, or the parson for that matter, with a sense of the poverty of his own re-sources to arrest compulsive behaviour as does the alcoholic. No organization known to the psychiatrists is one-tenth as effective in conveying this entirely new spirit to broken people, as A.A. is. Before A.A. can make any headway at all with an alcoholic, he must have 'touched bottom'. He must have come to the acknowledged end of his own resources. In this brokenness he is urged to look to a Power higher than his own, and to a fellowship that accepts him as God accepts him. He enters, through a new and creative relationship into an experience of a new personal Being, and discovers within himself a powerful personal dynamic. In the power of this personal transformation not only does he obtain control over his compulsive drinking, but we observe that he no longer behaves neurotically. Joy and good spirits characterize his fellowship, and, losing all his self-pity and resentment he becomes an active rescuer of others in the same boat.

In all neurotic sufferers, not only in alcoholics, this moment of brokenness is potentially, like the death of the Phoenix, a moment when new life can arise out of the ashes of the old. In practice, few outside the fellowship of the A.A. recognize this. As psychiatrists we do our utmost to prevent people 'touching bottom'. Our treatment is to reassure the patient that all is not lost, if only thereby to reassure ourselves. As Jules Masserman suggested in his Presidential Address to the American Psychiatric Association, 'Is it possible that psychotherapy actually consists in the re-establishment of certain delusions necessary to all mankind?' Our therapeutic aims are modest. We work to establish the patient in his status quo, to get him back to his familiar illusion of egocentric independence and self-sufficiency. Since, for the most part, this is all the patient wants us to do, we may be excused as psychiatrists for limiting ourselves to these palliative measures, our words and our drugs alike placebos. This A.A. talk of brokenness, 'touching bottom', 'admitting that we were powerless' against our problem, and looking to God for strength and new life, with a confidence born of experience of hundreds of thousands that God does work in this way, so that wrecked lives are transformed, all this is too heady and heroic stuff for psychiatrists. Our patients would not thank us for pricking the human bubble. Our task is to blow it up where it sags, or reduce the tension if it strains to bursting. We are in danger of saying 'Peace' when there is no peace.

The psychologist is more accustomed to leading the patient towards painful insight, but few specimens of this rare bird ever nest much north of the Thames.

What of the clergy and the cure of souls entrusted to them

for many generations? They are not new boys as we psychiatrists are, in this business. AD 30 not AD 1930 marks their entry into this profession.

The fact is, that popular opinion as to what the parson is for, does not usually include the idea that he is a person to go to with a personal problem. If you have a troubled mind or gloomy spirits, fears or frustrations, uncontrollable impulses to rage or resentment or even (in Protestant England) a guilty conscience, you don't think first of talking it over with the vicar, you feel it would be easier to talk to the doctor. It possibly would be! At least he has been taught to listen, and knows that, if he has time, he ought to. He may not know what to do about it, but he has spent the last three years of his training in clinical studies, in bedside learning, watching and listening to individual patients. The clergyman, though appointed to a cure of individuals in need, is at present given no such training. It often seems that he is taught to be at home with books, not persons, with the abstract rather than the concrete, with the congregation in mass communication without feed-back, rather than with the individual. He may have had no opportunity to learn, by the process of doing it, under supervision, how to become a knowledgable listener to individuals, a diagnostician of their hidden disorders, and a physician of souls with specific and effective remedies for particular needs.

All this makes Canon Ducker's work more remarkable. He was determined to come by whatever training was available, and he was fortunate in his teachers. His own constant practice and reading, of Jung, Stekel and Freud, principally, have equipped him to a greater level of expertness in the practice of psychoanalytic therapy than most run-of-the-mill psychiatrists could aspire to. He uses the resources of analytic wisdom, not only in understanding the patient's problem in depth and in its unconscious roots, which is part of what every psychiatrist and psychoanalytically orientated case-worker would hope to do, and which all parsons could be taught to do. Canon Ducker also employs the therapeutic techniques and resources of the psychoanalyst. These he is well qualified to use, and does so with splendid effectiveness. In this he is a pioneer, and though the number of clergy who could follow him into this full orthodox practice of psychotherapy must probably remain limited, it would be an excellent thing for God's people if every Diocese had at least two such men.

As Eric Ducker so movingly shows in this book, he is not limited to psychoanalytic diagnosis, or to psychoanalytic resources for his therapy. He takes the patient down to the spiritual roots of the human predicament, to re-experience for instance, the dread of death by separation from the source of being, in forsakenness and dereliction. Only at this depth of need does the depth of Christ's redemptive resourcefulness become apparent. Here, where the full agony of mental pain is felt, the agony of the cry of Christ upon the Cross, emerging from the hell of forsakenness, assures the sufferer that though he has gone down into hell, Christ is there in the same hell with him. Moreover, Christ's forgiveness of those whose rage murders Him, is assurance to all those depressives whose unconscious aggression against life would slay right and left if it dare, that even His murderers are beloved. By this mighty resource of the Gospel, Christian therapy can give assurance that the divine love outlives and out-manoeuvres all that hate can do.

In all his work with patients, this psychotherapist is conscious of the presence and the workings of the Holy Spirit. It is difficult to write on this subject without arousing anxieties and we shall need the same spirit to give us a right understanding in reading this book. Its thought-forms may be unfamiliar and we shall need humility to be willing and wisdom to be able to see its truth.

I would suggest that if at any point, the reader feels disturbed or put out of good humour by it, that it should not be thrown down in annoyance. This, dear reader, is probably the moment of truth for you. It is as if the surgeon's hand, palpating the abdomen, has unwittingly come upon a sore spot. We are unaware, for the most part, of our most painful conflicts, but the discussion of them, by a kind of resonance, is apt to make us feel strangely ill at ease.

You can go back over this passage deliberately, and know that even if all this worst were true of you, if all the strange evil and perversion of which the human heart is capable were found in yours, this would only qualify you to be the next person whom the dying and risen love of Christ is welcoming, through brokenness, to New Being by His life within you.

As you continue to live in fellowship with Him, you will find His character reproduced in you.

St Paul lists the results of this Holy Spirit's life in you. They are love, joy, peace, patience, kindness, generosity, fidelity, adaptability and self-control. Elsewhere he speaks of God's gift of the spirit of power and love and a sound mind. These resources are the absolute antithesis of all that could be called neurotic, or psychopathic. These are the resources to which it is the Church's task to point, and in her fellowship to enjoy.

Psychotherapy, conducted in this way, stands in worthy succession both to the founders of the science on the human level, and to the Founder Physician, Christ Who commissioned and empowers His apostles for all time to engage in His Name, in the healing of the sick, and in the cure of souls.

February 1960   FRANK LAKE

PREFACE

THE people for whom this book is written are those who have little knowledge of psychotherapy, and for this reason it is written with as little psychological jargon as possible. It has in mind those people who, for one reason or another, have no awareness of the vast possibilities before the Church through the adoption of psychotherapeutic ministry in particular, and of a psychological viewpoint in general. This book should also be of interest to all who already appreciate the significance of psychology, and the part which it could play in our distraught age in dealing with the ever rising sum of emotional sickness. I trust that after reading this book many people, hitherto indifferent, will not rest until the Church is committed fully to a Christian psychotherapy as a major function of her life.

I have first to thank the many people whose sufferings have brought them to newness of life through this special ministry of the Church, and who have allowed me to understand something of their great torments, and in some very small way to share those torments with them. They have at times expressed a pious hope that their bitter experience may come to be a blessing to others who are walking in the valley of the shadows of this death, and that they may be used to bring help to them in their need. I only hope that this book will lead to a fulfilment of that desire. I wish to thank them for allowing me to use some of the material which they presented to me during their treatment; this has been disguised as far as possible to maintain anonymity.

Much in these chapters will be of a nature new to many of my readers. It may on that account put off the reader, and further, because these pastures may contain bitter herbs he may be inclined to close the book. If this is so, I trust he will be patient. Here and there I have ventured to express my own theological opinion, and should you at these points find yourself in considerable disagreement with me I hope you will not allow them to turn your mind away from the primary contention of the book.

In writing this book I have for the most part avoided any discussion of general psychological theory. To have done otherwise would, I feel, have necessitated my writing yet another text-book on psychotherapeutics, and that was never my intention, and in all probability, lies beyond my ability. I shall have succeeded to some extent if on reading this book some people are encouraged to pursue the matter further and they will find in the Bibliography at the end of the present volume an adequate guide to further study. This book has grown out of a living experience over the past nine years and my first intention in writing it is to challenge the Church to secure for her faithful, and for those who stand upon the fringe of Christian experience, an enlightened and scientific ministry, a veritable effective cure of souls. It is time that we understood that psychological growth and spiritual progress are integrally related, and that often the poverty of our Christian experience is a measure of our unconscious infantilism. But for those who are more familiar with our psychological jargon I have, with reference to the case histories appearing in the book, added some diagnostic notes. These are set down in brackets and may safely be ignored by the patient reader.

I wish to acknowledge my indebtedness to my wife for much help and encouragement; to Dr G. D. Yeoman for considerable help with the text; to my teacher The Reverend E. W. P. Ingham, whose knowledge on psychological matters ever arouses my deepest admiration, and to Dr Frank Lake whose critical minds have made many valuable suggestions and criticisms. I wish to thank very particularly Dr Lake for contributing so valuable a Foreword, and also the appendix on LSD. He has made an outstanding contribution which, I am sure, will win the gratitude of many people. Lastly, I wish to thank The Reverend Peter Etchells for undertaking the tiresome tasks of reading the proofs and making the Index.

1960

ACKNOWLEDGMENTS

Acknowledgment is made to the following publishers from whose books short quotations have been made: George Allen & Unwin *Adler's Place in Psychology* by Lewis Way; Hodder & Stoughton *Ways to Psychic Health* by A. Maeder; Methuen & Co *Psychology and Morals* by J. A. Hadfield; A. & C. Black *The Quest of the Historical Jesus* by Albert Schweitzer; The Bodley Head *Technique of Analytical Psychology* by W. Stekel.

CONTENTS

ONE

INTRODUCTION

WITHIN the church of St Margaret, Leicester, there is a board setting forth the social services performed by that church in bygone days. The church provided education for the boys and girls, work for the unemployed, its own workhouse and pensions for the aged. It laid sewers, paved, cleansed and lighted the streets. It organized casual work, and apprenticed boys and girls to trades. An almshouse gave shelter to the destitute. One by one such practical expressions of the Christian community have been taken away from the Church, until a new generation has arisen which sees the Church as having no relevance to their needs, and as nothing but a refuge for timid, tired folk. Now the civic youth centre caters for the young, and a multiplicity of secular organizations provide the social life for the rest; the doctor and the factory personnel officer give all the necessary counsel, and in general the Welfare State cares for them from the cradle to the grave.

The loss of ground has continued until there is no more ground to lose. We must ask whether there is a way of winning the respect and gratitude of people, so that once again they look to the Church for something which nowhere else can be so well obtained, and through which the full significance of the Church becomes known. We believe there is, and for that reason this book is being written.

It was at The Hayes, Swanwick, where a conference for clergy of the Leicester diocese was held, that the Reverend J. A. Sime addressed the assembly on the subject of the place of psychology in the Christian ministry of healing in particular, and in the pastoral ministry of the Church in general. He had been given a whole session for this purpose. As a result a group of clergy, who realized the possibilities of the practice of psychotherapy within the Church, decided to form a fellowship for the study of psychology at St Margaret's Vicarage,

Leicester, with the object of training clergy for case-work. The establishment of a 'clinic', called such for lack of a better word, was soon formulated, and after about two years' negotiation the Bishop gave his permission for it to be opened.

It is now nine years since the St Margaret's Clinic for Pastoral Psychology was founded. For a number of years four clergy and a social worker met, as a group, one evening a week to interview people suffering from emotional disturbances. We expected to find people unwilling to discuss their intimate problems in this open way, but they were in fact ready to unburden themselves within the group. Those who were not psychotic were given a place on the waiting list and the members of the team, as they were able, undertook the treatment in private at their homes. Unfortunately, the team broke up through the removal of all but the present writer, to other parts of the country, where individually they continue this special ministry. They could write their own stories of many people whose lives, and those of their families, have been transformed through the help they have received to the great gain of the Church. It is with a firm knowledge of broken lives restored, and a living faith discovered, through this ministry that it is possible to foresee a new era of service to the glory of God and the great benefit of His Church.

The belief that we were meeting a need of considerable magnitude was soon proved to be correct. A brief notice in the local Press brought at once a host of people to us, in spite of the fact that the newspaper mixed up our work with Spiritualism and poltergeists! No advertising was necessary, for people told their friends, and as the clergy came to know about the work they recommended their people to come to us.

Questions are asked as to what form this ministry takes. Is it just talking? or is something like hypnotism used? or is it mere suggestion? The answer to these and such like questions, will become apparent as we proceed, but even though we were able to overcome all the inherent difficulties of explanation there would still remain a mystery as to how the healing is accomplished. In the mind of the person seeking help, there is the idea that the therapist will perform some miracle by the waving of a magic wand, but nothing could be further from the case. The healing processes require of the person concerned a readiness to see the truth about himself, and often it is this realization which seems to set the sick soul free. Also, there is required the capacity to re-experience the long buried past, with its full emotional content, for which a good imagination is almost a prerequisite. When we have said this, there remains what must be described as an operation of the Holy Spirit. So often, in pursuing a Jungian approach, there is experienced by the person and the analyst alike, a situation so deeply charged with 'numinous' feeling that one is profoundly affected, and must say 'Surely God is in this place.'

It is a fact that only by living through an analysis can the process be understood. Psychological theory and technical terms are as a rule left out of the analytical session, and the problem is seen as a living one, far away from the text-book. Nevertheless, the difficult language of psychology must have been mastered by the therapist. His reading and learning never end. Further, not everyone who is able to undergo this discipline will make a good therapist, for he must be a person of insight, least interested in himself, and free from a desire to obtain power over people or 'lord it over them'. He must realize that censure, being commonly blind, is almost invariably calculated to drive the sick person into his shell, and has no place either in his speech or in his spirit. He must be altogether 'unshockable', have endless patience and willingness to listen beyond all normal requirements. Humility, sympathetic understanding, and an overwhelming love for all God's children will open doors which otherwise might for ever remain closed.

Here is a field which more than any other is the pastor's concern, for the work is most intimately involved with the souls of men, and desperately sick souls at that. Further, our Lord most solemnly charged His Church to exercise a healing ministry:

'And he ordained twelve, that they should be with him, and that he might send them forth to preach, and to have power to heal sickness, and to cast out devils . . .' ST MARK iii. 14, 15.

When the seventy were sent forth they were charged:

'And into whatsoever city ye enter, and they receive you, eat such things as are set before you: and heal the sick that are

therein, and say unto them, The kingdom of God is come nigh
unto you . . .'   ST LUKE X. 8, 9.

Has anyone the right to take this ministry from us? Are we
guiltless when we surrender so solemn a commission? Further,
the medical profession, by the sheer pressure of the number
of patients, is driven to use methods of healing which do not
give the detailed care which is here envisaged.

It is impossible to say how long an individual treatment may
take. Sometimes only one or two sessions are required; at other
times we may first see a person's problem to be simple, and
then, before we know where we are, it may develop into such
proportions that a major psychic operation is made necessary.
Wilhelm Stekel wrote:

'The analyst must not be misled by the first impressions. Cases
that appear very easy at the outset may later prove exceedingly
difficult. The first impression was false, the patient having
deceived us. Other neurotics, whom we began as regarding as
hard cases indeed, prove easy to deal with.'[1]

I regard two one-hour sessions each week as the minimum,
though in acute cases it may be necessary to see a person every
day over a short period. There are some people who, with all
the will in the world, seem unable to co-operate. Stekel advised
a trial week in which he tested the capacity of the patient to
co-operate. When this capacity had been ascertained he would
proceed with the analysis, knowing that it would continue for
a considerable time in certain types of illness. For example, he
regarded two years as a reasonable time for the treatment of an
obsessional neurosis, and I have had people who have come to
me for longer periods than this.

Doubtless it will appear strange that a person, distressed
beyond description, and who comes for treatment, wishes at
the same time to remain ill. This is by no means uncommon,
in fact it may be said that in every neurosis there is a fundamental desire to be ill, and that this is seen unconsciously by
the person as a definite gain. The gain through illness may
be based upon the principle of 'sin without guilt', where the
illness is regarded as a proof of irresponsibility and therefore

[1] *Technique of Analytical Psychology*, London, Lane, 1939.

provides freedom from guilt. It is as though the person says 'because I am ill I can enjoy my forbidden fantasies'. This device is, of course, unconscious. If one became well it would mean an end to such illicit pleasures, so why become well? It has been known that some people desire to be admitted to a mental hospital just for the reason that it absolves them from all responsibility, thereby placing themselves beyond censure. It may be, again, that the illness is less painful than the fears of independent responsible life, or than the terrors of some dreadful experience from which they escape. It may be that if they were well they could no longer enjoy their self-pity, or the delicious hate and resentment and sadism. Some people use their illness as a stick with which to thrash themselves, for their guilt requires them to make an expiation. So long as they are convinced, unconsciously, that they cannot face life, illness provides a splendid evasion of what otherwise would bring upon them an intolerable awareness of shame, scorn, self-rejection and such-like.

Recently a person was brought to me, in his early twenties, who had been blind for a number of years. The hospital had informed him that his condition was inoperable, owing to an infection at the back of his eyes which would not respond to treatment. It would have been easy to leave the matter there, but it was thought that St Margaret's Clinic might be able to do something for him. On taking his history the following troubles were reported: claustrophobia, a state of tension which would not allow him to express any emotion, a skin irritation, shaking fits, clammy hands, bilious attacks, rheumatic pains, headaches, nail-biting, bladder frequency under excitement. All this clearly showed a considerable emotional problem, and it gave encouragement to believe that the blindness was but one more symptom arising from the emotional disorder.

The father was a weak, unstable character, heavy handed with the children, a gambler, and in poor health. The mother, who likewise had headaches, was the dominant character. The father and mother led a 'dog and cat' kind of life. There was a young sister who was the apple of her father's eye. He was a 'horror child', and the mother once said 'if I had another like you, I'd drown it'. As a child he was left much alone, for his mother was employed in a factory, whilst his father was out of work. During this period he was placed in the care of the woman next door.

It was obvious at the beginning that here was a case of hysteria. Dream analysis was followed for a number of weeks, during which quite violent emotional storms blew up. During the session, at certain points, considerable pain was felt in the eyes. We were drawing nearer to some sexual experience of early childhood which seemed central to the disorder. The day came before long when he said he could vaguely see his hands, which was the cause of much excitement on his part. I noted when he came to the following session that he had donned dark glasses for the first time. He remarked upon entering my room, 'I thought you sat at a table over there, but I see you are sitting at the end of a settee. There is a bookcase behind you, and over there is a cupboard.' My wife brought in a cup of tea, and he said, 'You are wearing a grey skirt and a violet jumper,' which was the case. This proved to be the last session he attended. He went home and retired to bed. His eyes were being forcibly opened and he was determined not to see, this he had indicated by the wearing of the dark glasses. His total self preferred the blindness, and all the other symptoms, to the underlying dread and the responsibilities of life. For such a person nothing can be done. However, there may have been a deeper reason for the retreat from treatment, since often underneath hysteria there may be buried a psychotic element. In which case the person's intuition may have sensed the danger, and the retreat became an act of self-defence.

Another instance of a person unwilling to be transformed was that of a young man who came seeking to be rid of his homosexuality. He was a practising homosexual, and, as is not infrequent in such cases, his homosexuality was almost a religion to him. I suspected the last thing he really wanted was to become heterosexual, and that all he was seeking was to be freed from the aspects of his disorder which were distressing to him. I asked him if he would be willing to come for treatment, on the condition that, in the course of time, as the treatment proceeded, he would be willing to be freed from his homosexuality. His reply was that this was quite the most cruel question he had ever been asked. He began to sob as a little child, and left the room shattered, staggering like a drunken man. The sacrifice was too great for him ever to contemplate. I was reminded of the man in the Gospel who was unready to surrender completely to our Lord, and who on that account left Him, sorrowful. It is possible to do something for the practising homosexual, even if he is willing to be rid of his disorder; but, in view of the many people waiting for help who would respond, I felt this to be the only right course open to me.

Some measure of resistance to the analyst is expected, as he assumes, in the person's mind, the character of an oppressor the person knew as a child, that of the father who beat him up and made him afraid to express his individuality, or the rôle of the mother who seemed to have deserted him and, according to his infantile reckoning, would not understand him. Often the analyst is seen unconsciously as God, the stern Judge, Who sees the anger, the murderous hate, the self-pity in the person's soul, and because of His accusations He is regarded as hostile. Thus the analyst will be resisted as this 'God' is resisted. These situations have to be exposed, or else the healing work will not go forward.

The methods used in therapy are various. Dreams, not to be taken at their face meaning, are so valuable a guide to the unconscious, that every encouragement is given to dream and every known trick is used to set the dreams in motion. Drawings and paintings are, at times, just as helpful. Free-association, unplanned writing of the doodling variety, day dreams, in fact use is made of any method by which the buried past is recalled.

I believe that Freud, Jung and Adler have each something of real value to contribute. I allow myself to be taken wherever the unconscious leads me. It may happen that for several months the analytical material demands a Freudian treatment, and then for no apparent reason there is a flood of Jungian material, which is pursued in the way in which Jung has taught us. The analyst, I believe, should always follow the patient and not precede him.

A method I have developed uses the emotion experienced in a dream. This takes the person back to the occasion for which we are searching, and reveals the full impact of, and reaction to, the infantile scene. More will be said about this in a later chapter.

It is by no means pleasant for the analyst to witness the emotional recall, but this is nothing compared with what the person himself feels as he relives his utmost pain and distress. People undergoing this therapy have told me that it is more painful than having half a dozen babies. This could dispel any inclination to a notion that an analysis is something of a parlour game, or a basking in hot-house emotions towards the analyst. Using my particular method which I have called 'Abreactive Dream Analysis' I have enabled people to relive their difficult birth as they have felt their head to be crushed as by nut-crackers. They have kicked and yelled as babies, banged their heads just as babies do in their tantrums, thumped the chair, and gone into infantile rages hitting out right and left. They have grovelled on the floor and bitten the carpet. I have witnessed them enact murders upon imaginary people, when they have, with stealth, crept into the room, knife in hand, and attacked a cushion most violently, which was representing to them, perhaps the mother of the new baby sister of old. At other times strangling episodes are enacted upon the cushion, at the end of which I have seen the cushion raised and flung to the floor time after time, and finally disposed of by being kicked across the room. In passing, I must confess that at times this procedure makes it difficult not to show apprehension concerning the furniture, and the various objects of art, in the Vicarage drawing room! Most of the people seem to benefit from the peace and charm of this old room, and they protest against the use of my study. Such reactions as I have described must not be taken as the normal drill, since much depends upon the nature of the buried material, the disorder, and the person's capacity to abreact.

When people have the necessary courage to go deeply into the buried past, where the roots of the neurosis lie, their suffering is rewarded a hundredfold. How often we re-enact an individual's counterpart to Gethsemane, the Crucifixion, the Descent into Hell, and the glorious Resurrection and Ascension. In so shattering and awe-inspiring an experience, we can but draw near to Him Who went the self-same way for us men and our salvation. It is in a profound sense the experience of rebirth of which the Gospel speaks. This being so, no surprise need be expressed when I say that a good percentage of the people who come to be helped through this ministry take their religion more seriously than before, or experience it at a deeper level. The people who have had little contact with religion often undergo a spiritual transformation and, before the analysis is completed, they become attached to the Christian fellowship.

When the Clinic operated as a group of therapists a certain lady came to inquire whether we could do anything to relieve her asthma. One member of the group quickly perceived the cause of the trouble and, from that moment of insight, she was cured. The result of this was that her husband and her three sons became regular members of the Church, and one of the sons is now at a university preparing for his Ordination. In another case a young professional man had no use whatever for religion. His father, who was a scientist, had a scornful agnostic outlook upon religion, and this his son shared. The analysis, without any advocacy on my part, led him into a profound spiritual experience and active service within the Church. Later he brought his wife to church, who previously had lapsed from her religious duties. Another instance is that of a policeman and his wife who today go regularly to church, although before the treatment of the husband, they never entertained the idea. The change which had taken place by reason of the analysis led the wife to become Confirmed. Such are but a few instances of many people who today would be outside the Church had they not had the deep spiritual experience born of this ministry to the sick in mind.

There are other people whose religion is but a way of dealing with hidden guilt complexes. In such cases the therapy has a direct spiritual gain to offer, for a real spiritual experience replaces what was make-believe. A common complaint we hear is the unreality of prayer and sacrament, in spite of the utmost conscious effort to make their religion live. Rebuke, persuasion, and self-mortification are found to be of no avail in making them otherwise. These tormented souls carry an inexpressible burden of guilt without relief. The therapy reveals the cause of their spiritual deadness, and in due course their desert blossoms as a rose. All this makes the work doubly worth while.

There is no need to labour the incidence of emotional disorder in our day, or to stress the many factors which contribute to this sickness. The effects of the break down of home life and human relations, the threats of an atomic age, the lost state of modern man are well known enough. The stresses and strains of our high speed society, and the sense of not belonging to anything ultimate and enduring add their toll. I should like to mention the suggestion that the extensive use of drugs, such as penicillin and the sulphonamides, has driven people away from the physical outlets for their emotional disorders, and has caused them to be faced with the direct experience of their anxiety. In general there are many factors which combine to make a neurotic disorder, and like the many strands woven together to make a rope, they accumulate and reinforce one another to effect a stranglehold upon the person's life. No section of the community escapes, although some walks of life are more productive of neurosis than others. I am asked to help the high grade intellectual and the humble housewife, the professional and the artisan. It expresses the human predicament of our time, and it gives to the Church a new opportunity to set forth the power of Jesus Christ to save in that very situation where man cannot save himself.

I cannot refrain from closing this chapter with the well-known words at the close of Albert Schweitzer's *The Quest of the Historical Jesus*.[1]

'He comes close to us as One unknown, without a name, as of old by the lakeside, He came to those who knew Him not. He speaks to us the same word: "Follow thou me!" and sets us to the tasks which He has to fulfil for our time. He commands. And to those who obey Him, whether they be wise or simple, He will reveal Himself in the toils, the conflicts, the sufferings, which they shall pass through in His fellowship, and, as an ineffable mystery, they shall learn in their own experience Who He is.'

[1] *The Quest of the Historical Jesus*, London, Black, 1948.

TWO

THE AIM IN CHRISTIAN THERAPY

THERE is no question of the fact that our Lord commissioned His Church to heal the sick, and He demonstrated His words by His works of healing. These healings were a sign that the Kingdom of Heaven had been opened unto them, and also a sign of His Lordship over all life. This work was passed on to His Church to continue as His ever present physical body in the world. Our healing ministry is to be a sign that the Saviour has indeed come amongst us with power; it is to set forth His glory.

In our Lord's healing work we perceive a tension, which we also experience as we seek to fulfil our commission. He had compassion upon the people and He healed them, but the demands upon Him were too great to be met. He had to pass on, and declare the Good News of the Kingdom in other parts, both by word and by deed. This meant leaving behind in their distress many people whom He could have healed of their sickness. This is an ever present tension which all who exercise this therapy must feel, for more people seek help from us than we can possibly help. It is no easy thing to have to say 'No' to someone in a pathetic plight, perhaps with a family caught up in the distress, knowing full well that one might be able to bring them all, by God's grace, to newness of life. At times I have had a waiting list two years long. It is not to be wondered at that one always works at the maximum pressure, and that there are occasions when one simply cannot refuse a person, although the day is already full to overflowing.

There is also another reason why our Lord had to leave the people and move on to other parts. Although many people gave thanks to God for their deliverance there were always some, perhaps the majority, who, like the nine lepers, went on their way without so much as giving a thought to Him who had restored to them their lives. Obviously many people came to our Lord to be healed rather than to enter the new King-dom, and there was always present the danger that His primary mission would be harmed by healing overshadowing it. Faith Healing Missions may easily fall into the snare of healing for healing's sake, which although it is so good a thing to do, is less than what we are called to do. The significance of life is greater than health and a long earthly span. Thus Jesus had at times to leave the sick unhealed so that greater works might be done.

Sickness of the mind is something which comes between man and God. It distorts man's vision so that he cannot see Him, it perverts his feelings about God, and mars his acts of service. All too often it makes us do the right things for wholly wrong motives, which, by nature of the sickness, are unconscious.

A man with whom I spent many months of analysis was in a key position in his church, being an official of the Parochial Church Council, a Server and much else besides. In his religious observances he was scrupulous, not only on Sundays, but also on weekdays. In the bitterest weather he would be in his place in church early in the morning, having travelled a good dis-tance. Yet in his heart of hearts he hated God. He was to his way of thinking the tyrant of tyrants, the Egyptian Pharaoh who was demanding of his enslaved people bricks without straw. God was to him One Who watched every movement to see whether or not anything was done wrong to the smallest detail, and Who would be angry without measure should a child of His disobey any command or neglect any duty. His unconscious response was one of the intensest anger against God: he wanted, to use his words, 'to spit in His face', yet he dare not; he could not allow himself to think of such things for a single moment, nor feel the guilt of the blackest dye which stained his heart. The covering up of all this was repression, but it threw up the scrupulous demand for correct religious performances; and an overdoing of pious exercises. When his treatment concluded he did continue his pious acts, but they sprang from a heart overflowing with love towards God, and the many activities upon which he engaged within the church shone to the greater glory of God. I have noticed people on other occasions intensify their religious acts upon the stirring of their guilt complexes. Doubtless such activities save them from serious emotional outbreaks, but the greatest service to them is to rid them of this necessity by the cleansing of their inward parts. To this end a considerable knowledge of the mental process may be required and no small experience in its application. Nothing less than the truth shall set them free. As the Dean of St Paul's has said, consciously people may be converted, but unconsciously they may be far away from it.

Our ministry to the sick is therefore something which digs deep, it is that word of God which is:

'quick and powerful, and sharper than any two edged sword, piercing even to the dividing asunder of soul and spirit, and of the joints and marrow, and is a discerner of the thoughts and intents of the heart.'   HEBREWS iv. 12.

There is no doubt that psychological understanding revolutionizes the Christian ministry in its every aspect. It gives to preaching greater penetrating power, new relevance to human need, new awareness in depth of the power of the Scriptures to raise the fallen and to sustain life. The over-all gain is an increased ability to know people more intimately, and therefore more effectively to meet their need. The depth of personal relatedness is increased.

This leads us to an examination of our aim in ministering to the sick. It is possible that we have presented a poor picture to the world, a caricature, of what our Lord would have us do. It may be that we receive the response from people that we deserve because, in dealing with their sickness, we seem to have little or nothing relevant to say or do. The medical profession may visualize us as kindly souls taking flowers to the sick person, chatting about sweet nothings for a few minutes, perhaps having a word or two of prayer and then making a hasty retreat from a situation which is out of control. In the case of the mentally sick they may even think that, in a dim way, we are in part responsible for the emotional condition of the patient, and that we had better keep as far away as possible lest some worse thing may happen. There may be some justification for thinking of the Christian ministry in this way; this we may sadly admit, although there are always magnificent exceptions.

It is possible to be so heavenly minded that we are of no earthly use, and in our enthusiasm for those things which are

C

unseen and eternal we may do less than justice to the things seen and temporal. This attitude may be born, commendably, of an intense spirituality, or it may be the product of a despair which believes nothing can be done in the situation of human sickness. In the latter case there is a complete capitulation to the medical man of science, while in the former case, at the best, there is a watery hope that some kind of divine intervention may take place.

When the medical man has done his best, and the sick person is on his legs again, it is no proof that the clergyman was unnecessary. We must ask what is the aim in healing? The usual reply from the doctor and the patient alike would be: To be rid of the illness which incapacitates a man, and to remove the cause of the pain and the discomfort. This being done they will see the exercise to be completed. However, from the Christian point of view we cannot accept healing to be so materialistic in aim. Man is not a machine which has worn out in places, and which needs tightening up here, and the placing of a new part there, in order to put it on the road of life once more. The Christian should never regard a work of healing as complete if it leaves the once sick person essentially the same person as he was before he was ill. A person should leave the hospital ward or the sick room not only better in body, but also better in spirit. If this is true of the healing of the ills of the body, it is more profoundly true of the person who was sick in mind.

If the doctor's treatment of the sick body of his patient is often materialistic, the same is to be said of the treatment of the mentally sick person. Here the influence of the psychiatrist can be very considerable, and unless his spiritual values are in evidence there can be exerted much adverse influence. People have told me how their religion was ridiculed by the hospital psychiatrist, who seemed to think the destruction of religion to be a necessary part of the treatment. There is a considerable gain when the Church herself can take over the treatment from such a person, and conclude it with the person possessing a deeper faith and religious experience than before. There are, of course, some splendid Christians amongst the ranks of the psychiatrists, but one only wishes they were in the majority.

Apart from these considerations, in the approach to both physical and mental sickness there is at stake something of the deepest moment to the Christian. This applies in a very special way to the mentally ill. Our aim in our ministry to the sick must be the remaking of the sick soul, in the vast majority of cases, if not in all. We can use a long string of words to describe the experience for which we work in our ministry and they all mean the same thing in effect: rebirth, conversion, salvation, regeneration and such like. This is something altogether different from the aim of just putting a man on his legs again. The familiar shock therapy-E.C.T. (Electric Convulsion Therapy) where it is of service, still leaves the patient essentially the same person as he was before; if we may say so, he has the same soul. The man may be less depressed and appear happier, but that is beside the point. Drugs likewise have wonderful effects in certain cases, but when all is said the person is the same person after taking them as he was before. These mechanical methods are not substitutes for a deep and necessary reorientation of life, which in the case of the mentally ill in particular, must be the Christian's aim in therapy. It is one thing to push hatreds and resentments, burning anger and murderous rage, out of reach and harm's way, but it is something totally different to face these dangerous infections of the soul and take them away, replacing them with love and patience, understanding and forgiveness.

It is this which makes the Christian ministry to the sick so positive a thing, as it was in the Gospels. 'Son, thy sins be forgiven thee; arise, take up thy bed and walk.' That man's healing led to the glorification of God. In these days men give glorification to medical science. The total Gospel view of man simply does not enter into the picture, and that is why we have described it as materialistic—at its best it is humanistic. Our ministry of healing is to make the sick whole, and this cannot be done apart from bringing men to Christ. The methods by which this is done are manifold, yet their end is one and the same, a new, or renewed, living relationship with God. Thus the ministry to the sick is more than the preparing of the sick person for the last phase of this pilgrimage, or, if the prospects are still earth-bound, it is more than a restoration of the body and mind to their wonted vigour and function; it is a new impact of God upon the whole compass of our Being, and the drawing from us, by various means of grace, of a new response.

It is not man, but God Who heals through the ministry of His Church. From the beginning of the treatment the Christian therapist makes this known, and he sees that the person does not forget it. People often want to know what it is which effects so great a change within them, and the answer is that it is the Holy Spirit at work deep within the personality, and the person's total Self making a creative response. I tell them of how Fr Victor White described the work of the analyst as being like that of the midwife; we merely assist at a rebirth. This will remove the inclination to credit the therapist with the healing.

In order to play our important part in the rebirth of a soul we must know the person to whom we minister. The more we read, and the wider our experience becomes, the better able shall we be to assist people out of their sickness into newness of life. Our approach, with the advent of psychological understanding, has ceased to be solely to the conscious mind, which in the past has been well informed with good counsels, admonitions, and warnings, quite beyond our capacity to digest in a life time, and we now address ourselves to the far wider and less tractable sphere of the unconscious, with its mysteries and most powerful irrationalities. Should we have become expert in leading people to change their minds, we have lamentably failed to change their hearts, in fact this most important dimension of life has, if anything, become more insulated through intellectual exercise. It is to the neglected dimension of emotion that we are called to minister.

We would not suggest that in times past the Church has failed, in spite of much obvious ineffectiveness. The Church is always a glorious mixture of success and failure. There have been great Christian souls who have, through their native insight, penetrated deeply into the hidden springs of human action. They are the natural psychologists, and they can be read today with great profit. This wisdom is increased by the findings of recent psychological research.

Another great gain, through having psychological insight, is that we become aware of the harm done to the personality by spiritual misdirection on the part of responsible religious persons. Freud did not attack religion, and regard it as a neurosis, out of sheer malevolence; he had experience of the definite harm bad religion does. He went wrong in concluding that all religion was harmful, whereas, in fact, there is good and bad in religion as in all else. Like the prophets of old we must wage war against bad religion, and our new psychological insights will assist us in this, as they will also help us in our own self-examination lest we ourselves should be 'wolves in sheep's clothing'.

It is no kind of comfort to be told to 'pull yourself together', when one has been straining oneself to exhaustion point without avail. It does not increase a man's self-respect when he is given a dressing down on the theme of laziness, when he would give everything he has to be able to do a good day's work. It will hurt beyond measure to be told he is self-centred, when he is already driven to despair by his awareness of his self-love, and can do nothing about it. He is not helped by being told that he should have more faith, when faith is a sheer impossibility. The man will not be helped by increasing his sense of guilt, which already has brought him to the point of suicide. The person who despises himself for his sexual compulsions, and is distracted by them to what he feels to be the point of madness, will not be benefited by being told that he is a sexual maniac, and that he deserves to be skinned alive. What hurt we inflict by doing this God alone knows; what agonizing wounds are torn open by such ignorant handling must make the angels weep. When such judgments are passed upon the mentally ill in the name of Christ, we can hear once again the cry 'Father, forgive them for they know not what they do.' If nothing more is to be achieved than to prevent such devastating pronouncements, a study of psychology would be abundantly justified.

Through misunderstanding the heart of man, burdens too grievous to be borne are placed upon the soul. The chief source of such needless torment, inflicted in the name of religion, arises through the failure to distinguish between sin and moral sickness. Dr J. A. Hadfield has drawn this most important distinction in his book *Psychology and Morals*.[1]

'The difference between moral diseases and sins may be recognized, even apart from expert judgment, by the following characteristics: First, the moral disease has a *compulsive*

[1] pp. 56, 57.

character not characteristic of the sin, which is more deliberate. Secondly, sin is under the control of the will, whereas the victim of moral disease finds his will absolutely impotent to resist it. Thirdly, the sinner as such does not want to be cured, whereas the victim of moral disease, if he realizes that cure is possible, is anxious to obtain it. The psychotherapist as such rarely meets with "sinners", and this for two reasons: first, because the sinner does not want to be cured, and therefore does not seek a cure, and also because psychotherapy is not the appropriate form of treatment.

'It will be recognized that a very large number of disorders at present considered sin really come under the category of moral disease . . . if this is the case, our methods of treatment, whether on the religious and moral side, or on the legal,[1] need very radical revision.'

Thus we would think of sin as a wilful breaking of the commandments of God, when a man sees the light and prefers to live in the darkness. This traditional view of sin is all too often a correct estimate of the situation, and this needs to be brought home to the person. However, in our enthusiasm to do this we may appear to be priggish, and without grace, and the reason is likely to be that we are operating from an Old Testament standpoint with the threat of an angry Father God echoing from the mountain tops. Such a standpoint all too easily involves us in projections of the earthly threatening and punishing authorities of infancy and childhood on to the Heavenly Father. We shall stand on healthier ground if we think of sin as a wilful breaking of our relationship with God, and with a God Who has surrounded us with mercies and loving-kindnesses since our coming into this world, Who came in His Beloved Son to draw us closer to Himself, and Who died on the Cross to draw the Prodigal to his true home. The Cross is the price which love has to pay for wilful sinning; it reveals the cost to God today and tomorrow, and thereby overcomes the sinful attitudes by its appeal to better emotions within us.

The crucial word is 'wilful'. Before we discuss the bearing of psychology upon the accepted theological notion of the Will, we shall say something more about the difference

[1] Cf. *To Define True Madness*—Dr Henry Yellowlees.

between sin and moral sickness. Sin, as we have said, is always wilful, something for which we are directly responsible because it is avoidable. Moral sickness, although it carries all the recognizable marks of sin, is something for which we are not responsible. The practice of psychology compels us to recognize factors in human behaviour which are outside our control, which twist us into many distorted thoughts and actions. We have had many environmental influences which naturally have led to reactions of rage and hate, jealousy, self-pity and resentment. Accidental happenings, which so often are of a sexual nature, have made children afraid of themselves and of life. The 'best' parents all too often make the worst children out of mistaken zeal. A traumatic birth, followed by a chain of natural calamities to the baby, such as an illness in the mother, which prevents the proper feeding of the child, the death of the father bringing unavoidable grief and anxiety into the infant's surround, a serious illness of the baby himself, involving hospital treatment with its separation anxiety, and such like events, all conspire together to make a very sick person, one who is laden with feelings of guilt, and who manifests many 'sins'. A person greedy for money and possessions, the stealing of a child, gluttony and envy, may be but unconscious expressions of the person's unresolved hunger for love; a hunger that is unresolved because it was never satisfied when a baby. A pride which keeps one aloof from other people may be born of the need for self-protection; or out of the acute sense of injustice suffered in infancy, the lawless man may be born. A thirst for power and a ruthless drive for position may be the direct expression of a sense of inferiority, which is perfectly understandable in the infantile situation in which it took its origin. Sexual perversions, and uncontrollable outbreaks of licentiousness, may well have their deep roots in babyhood. In these, and similar cases, the person's responsibility may be nonexistent, or infinitesimally small.

There are times, however, when we could have taken the right way, and we have taken the sinister left, when we have not taken sufficient trouble to think and do right, when we have neglected to seek the guidance of God and His appointed means of grace, when we have been just downright self-centred and regardless of others, when we have believed that we know better than God, and have thought that what we do with our lives is our own business and no one else has the right to say a word. This is sin, and it is a healthy thing to be penitent about it, and to seek pardon from both God and man. Should anyone be tempted to think that psychology makes excuses for sin, and glosses over it, they would, on coming to an analysis, be amazed at their own dust-bins, and they would go away considerably humbled. What may give rise to this misunderstanding is that each 'sin' has to be judged according to its own history and motivation, and if it were analyzed in minutest detail we should only then be able to say whether it was sin or moral sickness. We might well find it to be a complex mixture of both. It is tempting for the Church, with a tidy mind, to systematize human behaviour, and to say that all such and such actions are sins, and to grade them according to their magnitude, and to fix to each an appropriate amount of penance. When we have an awareness of the unconscious factors in the moral situation it becomes grossly unjust to think upon these lines, and in fact it is a quite impossible task to weigh up every factor contributing to a specific act. God alone can apportion the degrees of sin and moral sickness; what is left for us to do is to exercise our charity, and offer the absolution of God to all who with due penitence seek it.

Things are made no easier by the fact that a trustworthy conscience is not easy to possess. Like sin, and moral sickness, the conscience may be true or it may be sick, and, more often than not, it is a mixture of the two. A true conscience is a very different thing from the sick conscience of the sick person. The Freudian Super Ego, made up as it is of the prohibitions, threatenings and thunderings of all the morbid and misguided authorities we have ever met, along with idealistic instruction, becomes our conscience. It can have a grave distorting power, and it may drive people into the worst of Hells for things they have never committed, nor would ever commit. Such a morbid conscience is negative and destructive of life, and itself has to be destroyed before its possessor can possibly be whole. On the other hand a true conscience presses us forward towards all things which we see to be good and true and beautiful: it brings peace of mind, a sense of well being and integration. A sin against this true conscience is to see the light, and to choose the darkness, 'to love the darkness rather than the light'. A repeated rejection of the light will gradually weaken our ability to see the light, and every time we choose the light it will quicken our moral perceptiveness and lead us to new refinements within the assessments of conscience.

It is not wise to regard conscience as inborn. It appears rather late upon the human scene, and it takes its life within the relationship of the inner- and outer-bodies.[1] In that outer-body are people whose standards and influences we have accepted, and incorporated as our moral and aesthetic system of measurements. In so far as the outer-body is concerned we may have been fortunate, for example, by being surrounded by the best Christian influences and examples, or unfortunate. In the inner-body there will be, perhaps, some measure of insight and originality, which will work upon the material supplied by the outer-body, and in rare cases there is brought forth a higher standard and clearer vision. In this we must not forget the third body with its spiritual dimension. Here are things both new and old: the products of new promptings of the Holy Spirit, and the great volume of spiritual experience and vision contained within the traditions of the Church. The conscience of the outer-body of society, and that of the spiritual body, often conflict; the voice of the people is not that of God: the prophets are stoned and the Son of God crucified. Thus a healthy and true conscience is our identification of ourselves with the best of our perceptions; once we have seen the best we cannot remain as we were, it is for better or for worse. This has relevance to our wholeness, for we cannot be whole if we are striving against the best within ourselves. Our guilt will not leave us in peace. In the case of moral sickness we shall most likely desire our best, and yet be unable to approach it, as by an inner compulsive prevention. Moreover, we shall not be able to attain wholeness until our good conscience rules in every aspect of our personality. A good conscience is productive of a good integration; the perfect conscience

[1] The concept of the three bodies is fully set forth in Chapter IV. The inner-body is all that is inside one's skin, and the outer-body is the total environment. The third or spiritual body is the spiritual dimension in which 'we live, and move, and have our being'.

will make for perfect integration. A conscience informed by Christ will supply the supreme motive of love to the total endeavour, without which our labour is but as lost.

The fear that one has committed the sin that cannot be forgiven is one which often torments the mentally ill; the Holy Ghost has only to be mentioned to send them into sheer panic. This problem, I suspect, has caused as much waste of clerical time as any other, for whatever is said makes no difference. The relevant passage is from St Mark's Gospel, and is as follows:

'Verily I say unto you All sins shall be forgiven unto the sons of men, and blasphemies wherewith so-ever they shall blaspheme: But he that shall blaspheme against the Holy Ghost hath never forgiveness, but is in danger of eternal damnation: Because they said, He hath an unclean spirit.'

iii. 28, 30.

We can, with good reason, point out to them that the fact they are concerned about their sin proves them to be anything but spiritually dead. We can with all emphasis state that the sin against the Holy Ghost is to be in a state where one can no longer make moral judgments, when we have for so long shut our eyes to the light that we have become incapable of perceiving the light. However, we do but waste our time, as they go away unconvinced. Whether anyone ever reaches the point when moral discernment ceases is debatable, and even if it is only a theoretical possibility, there is sufficient danger there for it to be a warning against not living according to the best we know. It will be found that even if the person who believes he has committed the unforgivable sin can accept the forgiveness of God, he will be left with the real problem with which he is concerned, namely his ability to forgive himself. He will require psychotherapy to unravel his guilt complex.

We must now return to the question of the Will, and see how its freedom is affected by the new psychological knowledge. The judgments of the Church and the community have been built upon the belief that a man is free to determine all his actions, and therefore he must be fully responsible for his deeds. The only exception is insanity. This is the rule of thumb upon which is based our system of law and its penalties. As a rule of thumb it is one thing, but it is altogether another matter when we take it upon ourselves to declare a man wholly responsible for everything, from the smallest peccadillo to a capital offence. We must grant that, things being what they are, it may be impossible to have any other calculus of sin and crime; obviously we can not wait for every prisoner to undergo an analysis before a judgment is pronounced, and even if the analysts agreed upon the general patterning of the offender's life, it would be impossible to state exactly the proportion of moral sickness and sin. Nevertheless, the established fact of the unconscious and the tremendous part it plays in our behaviour patterns, should make us far more alive to moral sickness, and therefore more cautious in passing judgment upon the criminal and sinner. If we can forgive the State for having its rule of thumb, it is less easy to forgive the Church, which should be the pattern of charity and understanding. Breakdowns in marriage, faithless partners, juvenile delinquency, the teddy boy, the homosexual, the prostitute, the confidence trickster, and the whole gamut of offensive behaviour should have a kindly judgment given by the Church, and the deeper our psychological understanding is the more so is this likely to be. This means that we shall rely less upon the old rule of thumb regarding the Will, and see that the responsibility for human failings must be shared by the whole outer-body, as well as by the inner-body, in varying measure.

In the fourth chapter we mention a number of people who were suffering from an Obsessional Neurosis. Although acute cases of this disorder are not extremely common, yet in a mild form there is more of it than meets the eye. Such people are indecisive and ever doubtful. They cannot 'continue in one stay', for as soon as they say 'Yes' they immediately follow it with a 'No', which continues ad infinitum. They are incapable of making a decision, although this does not prevent them from engaging each person they meet in a lengthy discussion as to what should be done; they appear to accept advice but never follow it. You will have met many people who in varying degrees are like this. It is absurd to treat them as though they had a Will of their own, since obviously the Will has not the measure of control which we like to think it has, and on this account it cannot carry responsibility. The Will is sick, and it requires specialist help to set it aright.

The Will, more often, is affected in a less immediate way, for we regard it as a function of the total personality. If part of the personality is disordered by sickness it must affect the operation of the Will. Jung helps us to understand the problem of the Will by his concept of the 'Autonomous Complex'. It is as though the main part of life is a continent from which an island has been split off. The mainland is now incomplete, and the island has many unpleasant ways by which it interferes with what goes on in the mainland. It is done secretly and most thoroughly. The life of the mainland wants to do the right thing, but these hostile influences prevent their performance. Thus the best endeavours of the Will are thwarted by what is unconscious and uncontrollable. This is obvious in the case of an advanced neurosis, but since all of us are more or less neurotic the principle of the condition must operate in all of us in some way.

These inner systems within the unconscious work as by law, and they are woven into the character structure. Within the larger system of the Self we see drawn together biophysical elements, the outer-body with its material conditions, the influences of family, class, nation and race, the 'collective unconscious', which contains the deposit of the experience of the ages, as well as our own personal unconscious. To all these is added the conscious life, and its adopted direction, and the spiritual influences of the third body. Our actions are the products of an amalgam of all this, and possibly much more beside.

The concept of the outer-body helps us to realize the part which our surround plays in every expression of the Will. It has entered deeply into our character structure. We live in our identifications of long ago. Besides this, the outer-body has elicited from us many deep emotional reactions, which have become repressed and which have formed complexes. These are manifested in our aggressions and compliances of today; in those outbursts of temper which the occasions do not warrant, and in our attempts to curry favour and recognition. The old patterns are being re-enacted on the present scene when we too readily take offence, or feel slighted and ignored, robbed or stifled. But when, from our psychological vantage ground, we take a second look at these primitive reactions to our outer-body, the infantile nature of our present behaviour is exposed for what it is; then the infantile misjudgments are rectified, the resentments and the angers melt away and good feelings replace the bad, and the infantile dependence gives place to the mature mutual dependence of the adult. The number of these powerful unconscious distortions is legion. But when, one by one, they are brought back into the light of day, new agreements with life can be made, new adventures undertaken, new personal commitments pledged; and we see a free expenditure of the Self and unfettered exercise of the Will. The Self is at last acting as something like a unity, and with a true measure of responsibility.

The Self should not be thought of as an amalgam of the many factors we have described in a state of rest, but rather as being made up of many factors which are in a state of flux or unbalance, unity and stability being sought. Our therapy rests upon fundamental and constant endeavour to reconcile the tensions and the play of opposite forces in the Self—the light and darkness, the good and the evil, the masculine and the feminine, dependence and independence, the individual and the community, the spiritual and the material. Our exercise of Will takes place amid a considerable number of opposite forces, and according to the measure of reconciliation between them will it be wholesome and stable. A perfect Will is the expression of a Self that is whole and entire.

A Will which is the expression of a divided house can not stand. What causes the division may be a part which has taken upon itself too great power or control at the expense of the rest. If consciousness exerts too much intellect, the unconscious emotional side, in a man, will effectively rebel, or if the moral side is repressed, and the instinctual assumes control, the kingdom will not stand. Any acting of one part without the consent of the whole, for example, any pride or compulsion in the one part, will be resisted by the rest of the personality. Thus an enforced goodness, or a 'goodness' for the wrong motives, will be unstable, whereas a goodness which is the free expression of the many parts all integrated by love will remain.

So far as the conscious part of life is concerned it will often have to 'suppress' impulses and desires which are alien to the aim of life; these are the many things we would like to do were it not for their being anti-social, or, if we are Christians we would not do them because our Lord Himself would not do such things. This suppression of bad thoughts and feelings could make us into hard, frustrated personalities, at war with ourselves, and given over to censure of the people who are doing what we should like to do, but cannot allow ourselves to do. In which case the energy involved in the desire has not been directed to noble use, or, as the Prayer Book says, 'hallowed and directed aright'.

The redirection of energy is what is called 'sublimation'; it is only a gradual process which takes place unconsciously as our consciousness dwells on well nourished ideals. From time to time there has to be suppression of bad thoughts and feelings, until we have grown into the ideal, which itself should be an ever changing and growing thing, and it has become part of our Being. Aggression, for example, may become the power behind our tackling of difficulties and our reforming zeal, or curiosity may be turned into scientific quest, or some sex may be expended in creative activity. This makes for integration, and a refined Will, for then, as was said of the fragments that remained after the feeding of the multitude, nothing will be lost (MATT. xiv. 20), and more of the personality goes into the Will. On the other hand, if the unruly parts are 'repressed' so much vital energy will be put out of conscious circulation, and will be out of reach for the service of our aim: in fact, it will work in powerful unconscious opposition to what we are seeking to achieve in life: it has thereby been placed beyond reconciliation. In the case of an 'inhibition' a good use of vital energy is thwarted by the unconscious, or partly unconscious, conflicting emotions, as for example, when shame, disgust or fear prevent a desired course of action. In such a case the Will is a poor maimed thing compared with what it should be.

So then the common belief, not far removed from our beloved Pelagius, is that the conscious man is the master of his life, the captain of the ship of his soul, which he can steer into his chosen port of Salvation. It is all so neat and simple to think of ourselves in this way, we know just what to do with the naughty and we are able to thank God that we are not as other men are! If the wicked are responsible for all their wickedness the righteous are responsible for their good works. Salvation man has willed, and by his worthiness he wears his own diadem.

Our psychological understanding completely destroys this pride, for if we cannot lay our 'sins' entirely at our own feet, neither can we credit ourselves with our achievements. Far too much of the outer and spiritual bodies are involved in our good works, so that, only allowing ourselves a modicum of the 'well done', the glory and the praise must go to God.

THREE

TECHNIQUE

I

WE have said something already in the Introduction about the technique of the psychotherapeutic ministry, but it is necessary to have a fuller discussion of so important a matter. Every therapist has his own individual approach and method, just as he has his own individuality and insights, so that we might say, with little exaggeration, that there are as many techniques as there are psychotherapists.

The people who come to us vary greatly, and so the approach made by the individual therapist must be flexible. Moreover, it sometimes happens that, for unaccountable reasons, one therapist will succeed where another fails. A person might ignore the counsel of the old Dutch farmer, that 'it is not best to swap horses while crossing the river', and leave one therapist, who has carried out much patient work with little apparent response, and go to another who, with the minimum of effort, gathers the fruits of the first therapist's labours. Of course, this matters but little if one's concern is simply that the person be made whole. Yet what a trial it is when it is spread around that the first therapist is no good and the second works wonders, which is true of neither of them. There is nothing easier than to malign a psychotherapist, and to regard him as responsible for the odd reactions, and the 'damage done' to the patient.

There will always be people who begin treatment and run away. They rationalize their action by saying that the therapist could not keep away from the subject of sex, or whatever else it was, and they had to leave him on that account. This may impress the ignorant and the all-too-ready critics, but those with shrewder perception will recall the words of Hamlet concerning the Player Queen, 'The lady doth protest too much, methinks.' There can be no analysis and recovery without the facing of one own's dark side, and the re-bearing of great mental pain. The people who demand nothing but pleasantries suffer a considerable shock, for in a real sense all analysis is shock treatment, which either they will accept with grace or go away in anger, complaining about the nasty therapist. Such is the risk that has to be taken, and it is part of the Cross-bearing of which our Lord warned His disciples. However, if the work is done in all humility and with manifest kindness, such dangers as these will be largely avoided.

Clergy are rather used to telling people what they should do, in a kindly way, of course, but when they come to exercise a psychotherapeutic ministry this propensity must be overcome; blame must be banished and the judging left to God. The question arises as to how much authority must be exercised in the analytic session, how much pressure of persuasion and direct teaching should be given, and therapists are divided upon the issue.

In the Directive method the analyst would press upon the person positive thinking; misjudgments and misinterpretations would be ironed out in a full-scale spring cleaning of the mind. Patterns of behaviour running back to infancy would be traced and clearly set forward from the first interview onwards. The religious issues would come into the forefront and be pressed, not in judgment but in understanding charity, and to the penitent full pardon would be offered as from Calvary. Positive suggestions would be made towards a future re-orientation. This method is much more than a direction to think right rather than to think the sinister left, although we would in no way decry this, for did not the Apostle bid us set our minds upon whatsoever things are lovely and true?

The non-Directive method leaves the person to do all the talking. In the case of a simple problem the person soon talks himself out of the difficulty, which is another way of saying he gains insight. The minimum of direction is given by the analyst, in fact he follows, picking up the crumbs, rather than directs the course of procedure. What is required is the not so simple art of listening, and a considerable knowledge of the subject, for the value of the analyst's work lies in a question put, which is just the right question at the right moment, which elicits new fields of insight. When such an insight has been obtained, the analyst will tidy things up by linking it with former discoveries, all the time seeing that the person does the work. The dreams and drawings brought to the session are treated in this way, the associations of the person always being the key to the understanding of the material; he deduces the facts and feelings relevant to the situation, and allows them to bring up from the unconscious, buried material which sheds much light upon the problem, and causes the necessary readjustments to be made in life. The person will see for himself where he made misjudgments in the past, where he took the wrong turning; he will become aware of the bad emotion he is carrying, of the volcano in his breast. People usually go away after the first interview feeling better because of an emotional release, and also because they have, by talking, externalized a little of their problem. The technique of this method is in line with the education principle which affirms the aim of teaching to be, 'not to insert but to elicit'. This seems to me to be very wise, for where a new way of life is imposed it is something second-hand, and must have less personal value than that which we have made our own by our vision and insight. This was our Lord's way of working,[1] for He did not come as a lawgiver saying 'this you must accept whether you like it or not', but He waited upon people's insight to recognize His significance; this, surely, is the rock upon which the Church must always be built. This principle was chosen by our Lord at the beginning of His ministry, when in the Temptations He rejected other direct and forceful ways of approach to men. His teaching by parable was another expression of this method, as is shown in the first and explanatory parable of the Sower (MARK iv, 1-25), which is a parable about parables and their interpretation. We come to believe, religiously and psychologically, not because we have been taught, but because we see now with our own eyes, which before were blind, and such a therapy is always a deep experience.

These two methods of analytical procedure are related to the Catholic and Protestant types of religious experience, which in Jung's psychology have a particular connotation.[2] For Jung, the Catholic, as a member of his church, is brought into rela-

[1] Cf. J. Oman—*Vision and Authority*, London, Hodder, 1928.
[2] H. Schaer—*Religion and the Cure of Souls in Jung's Psychology*. London, Routledge, 1951, p. 137 ff.

tionship with God through his experience of the rich and traditional symbolism of Catholic worship. The Church, as the great
Mother, will guide and protect her child through the manifold
dangers of the world, though in return she expects his complete surrender to her divine guidance and his implicit trust in
her Faith and teaching. For the Catholic the symbols of his
worship are vital symbols. They are living things and therefore
are able for him to be 'a means of grace'. For we must understand that a living symbol can do something for the soul of
man which is of greatest moment. In a way the symbol carries
us, for it gathers and unifies the untamed instinctual forces of
the psyche and through this transformation integrates them
with the life of the spirit. Admittedly, the Protestant, too, must
find his symbols and live by them, but his position is, nevertheless, different from that of the Catholic, since for him the
Church has not the same dogmatic authority and the traditional symbols of the Christian ages have been largely dissolved
in the acid of his more rational approach. He is thereby in
some ways much less sure of himself and in his search for God
may have to undergo in himself all the deep agony of 'a lost
soul'. Let us not think that the breakdown of the traditional
symbols of Christianity is of little moment. Undoubtedly, for
Jung there is a definite correlation between the disintegration
of these traditional symbols and the increased incidence of
neurosis in the Western world. Outside the Catholic Church
it is very lonely.

The 'Protestant' of Jung, however, is not to be identified
with any religious body and indeed may belong to no church.
He is a person with an individual religious standpoint. He
lives close to the contemporary world, interpretating Tradi-
tion anew and in the process becoming enriched by the encounter. If the Catholic is on the side of the Collective, the
Protestant stands for the Individual. These two, however, are
but part of the essential anthesis of life; the Opposites, without
which there could be no movement, no true progress. As
Authority is opposed to Freedom, as the Masculine stands over
against the Feminine, as Intellect is to Feeling, so the Catholic
and the Protestant are essential opposites, existing ever in a
state of tension and yet, nevertheless, enriching one another.[1]

[1] Jung—*Psychology and Religion: East and West*, Oxford University Press,
1958, p. 466.

For the Protestant, says Jung, the psychotherapeutic way is more difficult for he has not, like his Catholic brother, the ministrations of the Church to fall back upon.[1] Confession and Absolution, Penance and the rich symbolism of the Mass are not for him. He must find his way alone. He must stand before God naked and unprotected. In the same way he must encounter alone in himself the terrors of Hell. The agony of Gethsemane and the dereliction of Calvary are his utmost pain in his search after the true and living way. Out of this tribulation of the soul he comes, and is clothed with the white robes of salvation and the palms of victory are placed within his hands, but they are for him the reward of his individual and persevering search. Such is the 'Protestant's' path in the earthly pilgrimage, and not everyone is able to endure it. He may feel that the way is too dangerous for him and he needs therefore to be rehabilitated within the fold of the Catholic Church which need not necessarily be Roman. But Jung would maintain that those who are able to take the more dangerous way have in the end the greater reward.

For Jung, then, the great crisis arises when, for one reason or another, a man's symbols have ceased to live for him; when the Gods are dead. For then he becomes the victim of his own unconscious with all its primitive power, and either he must discover, out of himself, new and living symbols, or rediscover those he has lost, in order to integrate these forces of the unconscious. Catholic and Protestant alike may find himself confronted with this task but, even more so, modern man who has lost all contact with the Church.

These two paths of religious experience correspond to the two methods of analytic treatment. There is obviously a place for both, in fact they are essential, just as the Catholic and Protestant ways are essential to the varied life of man. The people who require analysis in depth will have to take the 'Protestant' way, the way of self-discovery. If, in the analytic session, the privacy of the person is invaded by the imparting of too much theory, we shall only find that it has not been assimilated, while it may even have increased the inner confusion. Much later in the analysis a day will come when the person will make his own discovery of what was said to him long before, and then the content of that knowledge will

[1] pp. 48 and 352.

become warm and alive, bringing forth the fruits of patience.

Between these two poles of procedure much latitude may be taken in practice, according to the requirements of the moment; we may well have to be eclectic not only in theory but also in practice. Every rule must have its exceptions, and just how far we go in clarification of the material a person has presented is a matter which must be left to the analyst's judgment. Intuition plays a very important part both in the analyst and the analysand, and experience repeatedly justifies the belief that in the analytic session there is a 'spirit moving upon the face of the waters' which itself baffles analysis: we see that which was 'without form and void' taking shape, and being filled with a content which we have not supplied. This is particularly so when the non-Directive form of analysis is followed, when the dream carries forward the whole healing process, so that we can but watch in wonder and awe, as did Elijah on Mount Carmel when he saw that which was sodden burst into flame. It must be this same force within the Self which, without any suggestion on our part, leads the person to face the profound spiritual issues of life, and which finally leads people to find their place within the Christian community. It is 'the light that lighteth every man that cometh into the world', which is the third spiritual body in which we live.

The need for neutrality in the analysis is important, and we should keep it in mind even when we are following the Directive path. The great value of the person making his own discoveries has already been mentioned, but in addition to this we may easily cause an analysis to break down if we try to enforce our own viewpoint on any matter which is unacceptable to the person. I heard of an analyst who happened to be impatient with a pacifist whose views he detested, and upon the development of an argument the person immediately ended the treatment. Unless the analyst can humble himself, and make himself poor so that others may become rich, he had better not consider doing this work; there must be no semblance of holding power over people, but rather we should re-enact the forgotten sacrament of washing the disciples' feet.

However much the analyst may seek to be detached, it is inevitable that he must be affected by the emotions of the analysand; something of his own personality will be involved in 'the transference situation'. It is inconceivable that anyone acting as 'a catalyst', as the analyst does, in the long and profound change of another person's personality should himself remain unchanged. The fact that the analytical task is exhausting, and in some cases leads to the analyst's own mental illness, only goes to prove that 'virtue has gone out of him', and that in a sense he has given his life for others. It is an ever present danger that the analyst may be caught up in the very problem he is trying to solve, because of the inevitable intrapersonal relationship involved, even though this may only be at an unconscious level. The emptying of the analyst should be met by the renewal of the Spirit.

Often the analyst provides the only support in this wide world to a soul unspeakably weak, and passing through its hours of greatest peril. The analyst's inner tranquility and spiritual security are the only peace and security which the analysand can perceive in his bewildering world; the analyst's own spiritual dimension may well be the only external contact which the person can make with the spiritual-body which he earnestly seeks. We need not be surprised that a deep bond with the analyst develops when his compassionate understanding is felt to be the only point of hope in the universe. Thus it is inevitable that any analyst who approaches the task with Christian feeling must be affected by the many, and almost violent, claims made upon him. Dr A. Maeder in his valuable book, *Ways to Psychic Heath*,[1] writes:

'He (the sick person) must be helped if he is to free himself from his burden. For this, more is required than explanations and the development of insights, namely a dynamic factor, something enlivening and confidence-restoring (despite all the dejection, despondency, despair and negation), a spur and an encouragement which help to call forth from the patient boldness, joy in struggle, and a new affirmation. This constructive effect of the physician upon the patient, this positive influence —the converse of contagion—takes place slowly, often laboriously and discontinuously. In contrast to the destructive influences it requires time, perseverence and devotion.'

There is a satisfaction in being able to put a

[1] A. Maeder, *Ways to Psychic Health*, London, Hodder, 1954.

diagnostic label upon the sick person, and to present a clear and rational outline of the mechanics of the disorder to the patient. If the patient is not seriously sick all may be well, but should the disorder be of a deep nature the diagnosis may have to be modified considerably, if not altogether changed, as the patient works out the various issues lying at different layers in his mind. In setting out the treatment of a particular case, however full the description may be, it must omit the most important factors in the work of healing. The living relationship between the patient and the analyst cannot be put into words. We must never allow ourselves to forget that the patient is living in a life-destroying isolation, both from essential parts of his inner self and of the outer world, which must be broken down if he is to live in any real sense of the word. The sick person is not himself, he is struggling to find his true identity, perhaps he is struggling to find at least some identity. The close relationship with the analyst is the one hope of life and finding himself. It is he who holds out a hand and holds firm whilst the well-nigh submerged soul clings to it in terrible desperation in the hope that he will be able to rise from the bog which is powerfully drawing him down into nonentity. It may be that the person has never known himself as a self, and to find himself is a matter of life and death which beggars description. Little will be thought of the Church if she cannot save such a soul from death.

What is known as 'The Transference Situation' was discovered by Freud; in it the repressed emotions, good or bad as the case may be, are transferred to the analyst, and by his aid they are now reassessed or assimilated. Past emotional blocks then no longer impede present-day life. I am suggesting here that the analyst is more than a kind of psychological peg on which the disturbed emotions are hung and given an airing, but rather, in addition to this, he is effecting a new experience of relatedness to every aspect of life. The analyst, without himself dying, is giving his own life to another. Therefore the richer the analyst's qualities are the better able is he to influence (in-flow-ence) the patient and to transfer his treasures of living to him. However, this should not be in the analyst's mind during any session, for, apart from other reasons, the patient must himself make the discoveries, so that the newly-found life is truly his own.

A neurosis is a disorder of the emotions, and therefore the healing work must be done upon the emotional life; as we have said, an approach to the head alone leaves the position unchanged, although the head is a pathway to the heart. I have developed a method by which the emotions are used as a key to the problems which are presented in dream analysis, and in the common emotional storms such as depressions and angers, anxiety attacks and the like. The person is encouraged to feel again the emotion experienced in the dream or elsewhere, then he is asked to let the rest of the dream fade away, then the isolated emotion is intensified by deep relaxation into it. The person will 'wake up' and say 'Yes, I can feel that strongly', and then he is asked to do it again, this time feeling it even more strongly; this is done until a concentrated emotion is felt. I speak of this process as 'making a culture' of the emotion. In order to obtain the emotion I sometimes suggest to the person that he is on a cotton wool cloud, and that he allows himself to rest lightly on the billowing cloud; then I tell him he is sinking into that cloud until it envelopes him and that the cloud is the emotion with which he is concerned. People vary greatly with regard to the intensity with which they can recapture the emotion of a dream, but when a person is imaginative and has the ability to re-experience the emotions involved, the treatment can be startlingly effective. But even when people are unimaginative, vivid dreams may occur with considerable emotional content.

The feeling of the strong emotion in itself results in a release of some repressed material which will never trouble the person again, and after such an exercise he usually feels somewhat better. However, there is more value in it than just that, for the realization of so much feeling is a kind of shock therapy in itself: the person has now become convinced of his own problem, and the intensity of the emotional pressure he is carrying, though apart from this exercise he would not have believed it. We then trace the emotion to the earliest occasions when it was felt, and its history is followed. This is a valuable exercise, and if nothing more than this were done the time would not have been wasted; however, my special interest in all this is that the emotional culture is of great value in the interpretation of the dream. It is often found while interpreting a dream that two equally sound interpretations of a particular part of the dream may be given, in which case the emotion felt in part of the dream tells us which interpretation to take. For example, if the person dreams of death, and he feels quite pleased in the dream, we should take it to refer to the death of the old self. We should expect such a feeling to occur towards the end of an analysis, and it would be a splendid thing, since it would indicate a rebirth taking place. But if the 'death' is surrounded with deep anxiety and guilt, the interpretation is a different one, and we should look for 'death wishes' still to be resolved. Thus the emotion is the key to the right interpretation of that part of the dream. In cases where the emotional content is absent, other methods of interpretation have to be used. However, in most dreams there is emotion, and I take this before any other approach to the dream is made and make the culture of it. Whilst the person is 'stewing' I form my own opinion as to the possible interpretation of the dream, relating it, of course, to the whole picture of the person's life experience with which one is dealing; or it may not be anything forgotten, but an experience of childhood which has been of crucial importance, the full emotional significance of which has not been realized. I have found that this preliminary emotional skirmish makes the whole dream fit together like a well made jig-saw puzzle, in that it reveals a sequence of events or pattern of life; we see clearly the rise of the tensions, the origins of the emotional pressures and the subsequent reactionary paths which have been taken, and successive dreams reveal a continuing process that moves on until the complete emotional tangle is unravelled. This approach to the dream makes it both impressive and illuminating to the dreamer. The same approach is made to the person's drawings and paintings, which can be used most effectively, although as a rule they are not so rich in emotional content as the dream. If any doubt had remained in the person's mind as to the significance of dreams and drawings, an experience such as that which abreactive analysis affords would make him wholly convinced.

The depth to which abreactive dream analysis can take a person has to be seen to be believed, and I gave some instances of its effectiveness in the opening chapter. Traumatic births are relived, as are the whole range of terrors which befall the infant. Dr Lake has pointed out to me that there is something in this method akin to what in the United States is called

'Dianetics',[1] and I have followed up this piece of information and found that it is so. However, there is one considerable difference, in that Dianetics has nothing whatever to do with dream interpretation, nor with psychotherapy, and is hostile to it; it is purely a method of abreaction in which explanations of the experience are abhorrent.

The procedure which I have outlined will not apply in cases where people find the recall of emotion for all practical purposes impossible, as in deeply schizoid personalities where, on account of the intensity of their mental pain, it is as though they have insulated themselves from ever feeling again any emotion. The defensive mechanism in some cases is so strongly maintained that a cure of the illness is impossible.[2] So far as the treatment of those who do really want to be better, but who are emotionally barren, is concerned, the straightforward analysis of dreams and drawings is the course to be taken, after the normal review of the past history has been made and the general course of life has been clarified. When people say they do not dream I insist that if no dream is forthcoming they make up a dream, any kind of nonsense which they might have dreamed. This serves the purpose of the dream and it is analysed, by the insistence upon some material of this kind usually sets the dreams in motion, for people find it far easier to recall a dream than to make one up. A person's drawings, which very often are seen to have a clear reference to the dream material, assist him in dream production. When a person produces neither dreams nor drawings the reason is investigated, for it is almost certainly due to resistance to the analyst.

Perhaps the most difficult personal problem of the analyst is to provide sympathetic silence, and this is especially difficult

[1] L. R. Hubbard—*Dianetics*. This is a method of emotional release effected by relaxation. The mere reactivation of unbearable emotions cleanses the mind of its store of bad feelings, thereby bringing health and well-being.
[2] Considerable strength of resistance to emotional release should make us aware of possible dangers ahead. Caution has to be exercised when the deep unconscious is activated, for in some cases the uprush of archaic material may be too great for consciousness to control. Jung has described the process of what he calls 'active imagination', when fantasies are encouraged and concentrated upon. When such activity can be used safely the reward is very great. However, he warns us to exercise care, for it can take the patient too far away from reality. A careful selection of patients for the use of this method is advised.
Cf. Jung, *The Archetypes and the Collective Unconscious*, London, Routledge, 1959, p. 49.

to people who are accustomed to doing much talking in their profession. We find ourselves saying too much, and this hinders the work. The analysand has a colossal amount of work to do in reassessing his values, in struggling with a welter of often conflicting emotions, of which he is afraid, and in wrestling with new thoughts and insights which come flooding in, all clamouring for attention at once; besides all this the unconscious conflicts and stresses, that are being lashed up by the analysis, withdraw much energy from the conscious. Under such circumstances the bewildered sufferer could not be expected to go at our pace and cope with complex explanations. He is like a circus juggler keeping in the air half-a-dozen balls, which is the maximum that he can control, and then having other balls added which would be too much for him. Thus it is important to avoid this undue strain and discouragement, and allow him to set the pace, and take us where he feels he needs most to go at the moment.

This is not intended to be a book on psychotherapeutic technique, and so the subject must be left after these brief remarks. It is hoped, however, to have given something of an impression of how we set about the work, and to have given information to those clergy who may feel that this is the kind of ministry which, with training, they could exercise.

II

I wish now to say something about the three great classical schools of analytical thought. Most analysts follow either Freud and his successors, or Jung, or Adler, and they often exhibit quite a religious zeal and partisanship for their master. I prefer to be eclectic. It is obvious that each of these great schools of analysis has considerable success to record by use of its particular method; were this not so it would not have survived. The keenness of its advocates bespeaks the value of the contribution each has to make. Moreover, these schools of psychological practice are empirical, their teachings have not arisen in the labyrinthine fantasies of the genius, but are the product of dealing directly with the problems of people, and in each case they have found a method of interpretation of the problem which led to its solution. I think it therefore wise to have in mind what each of the great masters of the art has to say about the deep emotional problems of the mind.

The use I make of Freud, Jung and Adler is very varied. The problems of some people, especially the cases of middle-age breakdown, will obviously be best treated from an Adlerian standpoint, others from a Jungian standpoint all the way through, and others from a Freudian point of view. However, it is not at all uncommon to begin with Freud and to end with Jung, not because of any decision on my part, but because the person himself has taken me from one to the other. This can be appreciated when we realize that our psychic problems are layered, rather like the various layers of an onion; sometimes the successive layers upon which we have to work are identical in the nature of the problem presented, so that at the new level the former problem has to be worked out all over again; at other times the new level may present a new problem, and a totally different kind of country has to be explored, which calls for a different kind of approach. No two problems are identical within the infinite variety of human experience, and therefore no two solutions are the same; this makes the work essentially personal and individual.

Of the three great psychological systems that of Adler is the least used, and, if I had to make a choice between one or the other of the remaining two, I should take Freud as my master, though it would be with utmost regret that I could not also have Jung. However, in my practice such an 'either —or' decision has not to be taken.

When I speak of Freud I refer to the neo-Freudian teachers, of whom Melanie Klein is, to my mind, outstanding. It is the Freudian who deals effectively with the first few years of life, and it is here that deep problems have their origin. It is in this period that the most amazing fantasies reside, fantasies which merely have been hidden, without the normal resolution which life should bring having taken place, and it is this resolution which the analysis effects. It may well be that an initial requirement in anyone setting out to study this field is credulity, and unless anyone is prepared to deal with the fantastic there is no place for him in the deeper reaches of psychotherapy. It may not be necessary to descend to these depths in every case, and in fact there is a vast host of sick people, to whom a most valuable ministry can be performed, who do not require this deep exploration.

It will assist the purposes of this book to show how the teaching of the three great masters can be of service to the therapist who is overtly doing the work in the name of Jesus Christ. The psychology of Adler besides being the easiest to understand, makes an immediate appeal on account of its commonsense subject matter. People who are interested in the philosophical approach to psychology, as well as in its therapeutic aspect, would do well to read Lewis Way's *Adler's Place in Psychology*. What strikes us first is that Adler is concerned with the *significance* of the person, the meaning of life and its value. This is ground which is familiar to the Christian, and we have very much to say about it which will be amplified by Adler's insights. It is because of the failure to be firmly rooted in significance, meaning and value that Adler sees neurotic illness come about, and for him the way back to health of mind lies in the rediscovery of the essential risk.

Adler turns our attention to the infant's feeling of utter helplessness in his relation to the adults about him, and to his complete dependence upon them. If there is plenty of assurance given to the infant, by way of responsiveness on the part of the surround, he will come to feel more and more at home in his surround, which is the outer-body; but should there be little or no response to him, grievous hurt can be sustained. This condition may obtain for a considerable period, in fact for the whole of his formative years, in which case we shall find what Adler calls "the neurotic style of life'. We need to understand how much encouragement the child needs, how he should build up his self-esteem so that he can feel that what he does is acceptable to the outside world, and that therefore he is of use and has a right to enjoy his life.

If we sought a single heading for Adler's approach to human need it would be the 'Need for Significance'; this is something we all require to feel for, whether we are children or adults, we must feel ourselves to be 'somebodies'. If this is not forthcoming from the surround we will do all in our power to gain the required significance, and it is commonly seen in a power drive in life which makes a 'good' man of business, but not a good man to live with, and in a thirst for power which may express itself in a lust for position or wealth as instruments of significance. A great number of compensations for a sense of insignificance will be devised, all of which will be exaggerated.

These in turn will be resented by the people with whom he comes into contact and they will endeavour to 'take him down a peg', an attitude which will only intensify his feeling of insignificance, and thus a vicious circle is set up. It is clear then that inferiority in the Adlerian view can lead to opposite attitudes in the neurotic individual. On the other hand there may be a demand for life in the outer-body which is felt to be denied, or conversely there may be a retreat from the outer-body lest commitments there would but demonstrate his inferiority, and thus he withdraws lest he should reveal himself to be the fool he fears he is.

These elements in Adler's system have been mentioned to show that a specific need, when unfulfilled, can be aided by a Christian approach within a psychological setting. The Christian faith when it reveals the Son of God 'coming down for us men and for our salvation', presents man as having supreme value. There is the fact of our Lord's life itself and, besides this, a multitude of statements to the same effect; for 'God so loved the world, that He gave His only begotten Son, that whosoever believeth in Him should not perish, but have everlasting life' (JOHN iii, 16); 'But God commendeth His love toward us, in that, while we were yet sinners, Christ died for us' (ROMANS v, 8); and 'Herein is love, not that we loved God, but that He loved us, and sent His Son to be the propitiation for our sins' (JOHN iv, 10). The Gospel is the greatest possible demonstration of the value which God sets upon us, and not on account of our spiritual and moral achievements, but out of His own mercy and goodness towards us; indeed, God does not spare Himself, even unto the death of His Beloved Son, to help us to take hold of His love. Human effort to achieve status pales into insignificance before what God has done, and continues to do, to bring us to where He has gone before, so that 'we may reign with Him in glory'. Surely this is the most potent way conceivable to deal with the sense of inferiority at the *conscious* level, and some of this awareness must percolate down into the unconscious with a measure of healing. Moreover, apart from this, prevention is better than cure, and this awareness of the value of man in God's sight must perform a prophylactic service. The child in us, who is still smarting from parental rebuffs and discouragements, will take deep comfort from Him Who set the child in the midst of his elders and said, 'Whosoever shall not receive the kingdom of God as a little child, he shall not enter therein' (MARK X, 15). The encouragement value of this incident to the child must be very considerable. Those people who feel themselves to be outcast will also achieve significance from Jesus Who was called 'the friend of publicans and sinners', and Who, repeatedly, was on their side as against those who were acclaimed to be 'somebodies'. Christ died on the Cross between criminals, and in His identification of Himself with them in their debasement, He was offering them a place in Paradise; thus those who had sunk to the lowest depths were offered the greatest significance.

Closely associated with the need for significance is the need to feel that life has a meaning, for a life without a meaning would be without significance, and it would produce an intolerable sense of inferiority. This loss of meaning is felt by the child who is overawed by the cleverness of his superiors, who is made to feel like a piece of thisledown carried senselessly by overwhelming powers hither and thither, and it is this loss of meaning that lies behind the present-day existential search. The hunger for an understanding of life is frequently revealed in the broadcast programmes in which celebrities are questioned concerning their way of life, their interests and values. The Teddy boy bitterly resents his loss of Being through not knowing the necessary framework of life; he feels detached, an outsider, and as though he had been deprived of the most important thing in life, which is his meaning. The Christian therapist, when meeting the loss of meaning in those who come to him, has an opportunity to present a way of life which is the richest in meaning, indeed there may be in this a hidden reason for the person coming to a Christian therapist, he is seeking his spiritual body.

Another ingredient in the significant life, as Adler would see it, is a sense of value which comes through being an accepted member of the community, which is revealed by a person's attitude to work and friendship. The sick soul may be angry and full of hatred towards other people whom he thinks have what he has not, demonstrating thereby his inferiority. Why should he in his position be expected to contribute to the welfare of other people? The community has robbed him of his birthright, or it has made things too difficult by demanding over much from him; therefore he has taken the law into his own hands and he has become a rebel and a gangster, he may refuse to work at all, and he thirsts for power by which to dominate the world which he believes has so badly treated him. He feels he is being treated as he is because people think he has no value and that there is no place for him in the scheme of things. Underneath this reaction is the claim he is staking in the outer-body. He may, on the other hand, fear that he can never demonstrate his value, and that any demonstrations to draw attention to himself are doomed to failure and will only bring upon him the condemnation of society. In which case he will retreat from the outer-body, with its expectation of work and good relations, and try to live in a fantasy world where he can give himself all the value he needs. The Church, which sets so great a value on her fellowship, can meet the loss of value which the neurotic feels, and offers him a place within her family life; moreover, she teaches the lessons of responsibility and sets him tasks to perform, and this because she stresses the unique services he has to give and her encouragement of those who do well. Thus the Church exercises a therapy through her fellowship.

We have mentioned the customary detachment of the analyst and the analysand, where the former keeps himself out of the picture as far as possible, even to the extent of not being seen. Adler will have none of this; on the contrary, the analyst must be in the picture, for he is the first real contact with the community which the person has had for many a day, and he has to play an essential part in the return of the person to the community. Lewis Way writes: 'A good indication of social feeling is the number and quality of a man's friendships. His nearness or distance from others is a better indication than the love he may profess for the whole of humanity.'[1] Friendship is a curative factor of considerable importance, and the door into the community where normal loving relationships are exercised may have first to be opened in the analytical session. The clergy are generally understood to be kindly and sympathetic souls, although some of them, I fear, tend to represent only the Church Militant, and most people will come to them knowing that they will receive gentle treatment. The 'transference situation', in which a

[1] Lewis Way—*Adler's Place in Psychology*, London, Allen & Unwin, p. 181.

welter of pent-up emotions are directed upon the analyst, cannot be avoided, and indeed it is regarded as an essential part of the therapy; this will be understood by the clerical therapist, who will not be altogether inexperienced in dealing with 'clerical collar' infatuations. In the framework of the analysis this situation may have to persist for some time, but the analysis can never be completed until the love is redirected into normal channels. The transference emotion may be negative, and then the analyst will be the object of aggression, though unless this is soon dealt with the analysis cannot continue for long.

Adler makes his appeal to the Christian therapist, with his combination of scientific detachment and understanding friendship, for he insists upon an intimate, and equal, relationship developing in which kindness and humour will be well mixed with benevolent roughness. He makes it imperative to discard all show of authority. In some cases the sick person seeks, in the therapist, the old paternal or maternal authority, upon which his weak will may lean, and then benevolent roughness will be the order of the day. On the other hand, the sick person may see the analyst as one having authority, and Adler insists that the analyst must demolish this faith in, or opposition to, authority by refusing to be authoritative himself. This particular reaction of the sick person may reveal itself in criticism of the therapist or his family, in which case subtle aspersions may fall like the dew, as when the analyst is asked whether he has ever healed anyone before, or when, in dreams, under cover of someone else, ridicule is poured upon him. Adler's insistence that the analyst must never set himself upon a pedestal, and must also avoid giving the irritating impression that he knows all the answers, reminds us of our Lord's words of instruction to the therapists He was training, 'The princes of the Gentiles exercise dominion over them, and they that are great exercise authority upon them. But it shall not be so amongst you: but whosoever shall be great among you, let him be your minister; and whosoever will be chief among you, let him be your servant' (MATTHEW XX, 25-27).

The neo-Freudian approach is less manifestly open to references of a Christian nature. The infantile life is deeply involved

E

in the unreal, and we have already spoken of the incredible fantasies of this period. Yet despite these facts, there is a Christian approach to the Freudian outlook.

Freud saw the life of the baby as a stream of energy of tremendous power; for his wants, which are few, are expressed with terrific force. The baby demands food and comfort but, as the neo-Freudian particularly sees, he wants more than the meeting of his physical needs. Of supreme moment to him is the sense that he is loved, that there is a place for him in the world now that he has been cast out of his mother's body. He needs to feel himself closely held and smiled upon, and to know that his cries will be responded to with loving care. There is no hurt so deep and protracted as that caused by the loss of love, and it makes no practical difference whether this loss is factual or fantasied. Lifelong damage may be done when, to the infant, love appears to be denied, when the appealing cry is ignored, the gulf of separation is too wide or absolute, and the punishments too severe. If the hurts are too intense to be borne, and dread and berserk rage are felt, then a serious contracting out of life begins with its consequent sense of emptiness and nothingness. The source of Being has been lost, and the infant enters the state of non-Being.

Such situations as these require analysis in depth, but the point will come when consciousness, serving the processes of reorientation, can take hold of a religious faith to its great benefit. The priest-therapist carries the news of the supreme care of God, such care as is shown in the parables of the lost coin, the lost sheep, and the lost son (s. LUKE xv), where that which is lost is sought until it is found, and as soon as they are required he can give many assurances that the love of God for every child of man is beyond human measurement. There is no love anywhere so great as that proclaimed in the Gospel, and there is in this great love, healing for the love-starved soul which can receive it. There is offered through the Church, the great Mother, that food which the child in us so sorely needs, and in the reassessment of life it is discovered that there has been love and care from the beginning, when at Baptism the Church received into her arms the infant life. The love of God is the background music of our therapeutic ministry, and, as the need arises, it is increased until the panic-stricken child is no longer afraid, and the chilled heart is melted by its consoling warmth. *The tragedy constantly before us is of people who know 'the good news' but, on account of their disorder, are altogether incapable of assimilating it; our ministry is to give such help as will enable them to enter into the joy of their Lord.*

The Freudian knows, as no other, the real extent of guilt and the frightful disciplines, and propitiatory tortures, which it leads people to impose upon themselves; it may require life itself to be surrendered in a final act of atonement. This devastating guilt may have had its origin in the raging destructiveness of infant jealousy and envy; or in a distorted and perverted sexuality, perhaps born of 'over-good' parents; or in the situation of utter dread, when the infant feels unloved, cold, and deserted, which may give rise to a terrible, murderous hate, and death-wishes upon those most loved and desired: all these, and other sources of guilt, are at the mercy of a morbid conscience which demands the atonements as only the worst of devils would. It is into this frightful scene that the Absolution of the Church comes with great relief, again, where it can be accepted; or where the Cross is set with its offer of absolute forgiveness and cleansing. The tragic fact is, as in other cases, that the good news cannot be heard more often than not, for the disorder of the emotional life prevents its assimilation and the good seed falls on the stony ground of the heart so that the seed of God will not sink in and bring forth its fruit; thus the ministry of the Church is rendered ineffective.

Another matter, of importance to the Christian therapist, which Freud emphasized is the conflict between what he called 'the Pleasure-Principle' and 'the Reality-Principle'. The Pleasure-Principle is the childishness within us which demands the immediate satisfaction of desires, and ignores the distant goals and values; whereas the Reality-Principle is the mature way of living in which we forego the immediate pleasure for a worthwhile end. The one is self-centred, antisocial, boundless and ruthless; the other loving and self-sacrificing. The baby is hungry, and extracts from the outer-body everything which will give him satisfaction, but he will soon find that he cannot have it all his own way; he may hate the mother for having a new baby, but the sooner he comes to accept the reality of the situation the better it is for all concerned. He cannot expect the wind to be tempered to him, even if he does feel the cold like the shorn lamb. There are hard lessons to be learnt in the school of experience, and these will demand a modification of the demands we make upon life to the end that a satisfactory compromise is reached between these two principles, which is that of 'live and let live'. This is not very far removed from the second great commandment, 'Thou shalt love thy neighbour as thyself' (MARK xii. 31), which holds together self-esteem and love for neighbour.

In all our scientific understanding of the Self we see there are 'laws which shall not be broken'. Modern man may think that he can do what he pleases with his life, and if he wants to live for his animal pleasures alone, he may imagine that there is no one to stop him. But Freud, as forcibly as any psychologist, insists that this is the way to disaster. There is a way in which we must walk, yet it is no easy path to follow, for it requires a working agreement with all parts of the personality. There is the natural instinctual side of the Self, wholly self-seeking, which Freud call the 'Id'; there is the 'Ego', the conscious part of the Self, which operates a compromise between the two principles mentioned above; there is the 'Ego Ideal' which contains all the good identifications we have made, which we emulate, and which may be pitched far too high; and there is the 'Super-Ego', the morbid conscience which we have already mentioned, which gathers together all the prohibitions and punishments of our authorities, along with our own inner self-accusations. This is no easy team to manage, and it is no wonder that its balance can be seriously upset. For example, if the Id is ignored the Self is seriously weakened, and it may easily break down. Jesus knew full well that elemental Id, and how understandingly he dealt with it; there was no Puritan in Him pretending that it did not exist and treating it as a factor to be expurgated from life, but rather it was to be accepted as part of the Father's creation, and to be baptized into a new level of experienced. But how shocked the pious were at His realism! In our analytic sessions we fully appreciate our Lord's gentle handling of the Woman taken in Adultery (JOHN viii. 3ff), there was no condoning, but there was an enormous release from unnatural guilt concerning a natural function. When we deal with the depths of sexual guilt, all so very infantile, we can ourselves feel the heavy burden being lifted, and God's fresh air bursting in, as we deliver people from the stifling of their God-given natural selves. It is a service to be rendered in the name of God Who made man, and 'was made man', and they will go away saying 'He hath done all things well.' It is just the frustration of the natural drives and hungers within us which Freud showed to be the cause of so much mutilation and destruction of life.

Freud regarded the healing of man's instinctual life as requiring nothing but release from its inner entanglements, and thus as merely a matter of readjustment. But life is not as easy as that; there are the other two bodies in which we live and have our being, and Freud scorned what we call the third spiritual body, the saving power and the sustenance which we draw from the unseen and eternal realm. The achievement of wholeness is more than the straightening out of existing material; it is an achievement, and one with which man needs help from God.

It has been said that Freud attacked religion, Adler ignored it, and Jung made use of it, which statement brings us to a brief consideration of the work of Jung. The massive use of religion by Jung makes a brief reference to his religious significance altogether inadequate. Jung sees 'religion' to be the basic need of every man, and Christianity he regards as essential to Western man. His treatment of religion is scientific and pragmatic, and he insists that he has no right to make any pronouncement upon the reality of the Object of religious thought and experience. He is a universalist in his religious outlook, and he cannot be regarded as a religious teacher in any sense, but he is an acute observer of the real gains which are to be had through the practice of religion.

Jung sees in man a great stream of life energy which is ever seeking to bring man to his fulfilment and wholeness. It at once reminds us of the life which our Lord came to make more abundant, and of the working of the Holy Spirit, mighty in operation and as mysterious as the wind, 'which bloweth where it listeth', such that one 'canst not tell whence it cometh and whither it goeth' (JOHN iii. 8). Not to be carried along upon this mysterious stream of life is to become ill, and Jung sees religion as aiding us to find the stream and to follow it in the direction it would have us go. The stream is seen to be deeply personal and caught up into the movement of life from the remotest past, and it is a stream of vast creative power such as we are accustomed to think of when we consider the dynamic of the Holy Spirit. In this we are far removed from the concept of life as a compulsion of quasi-mechanical forces with a blind goal, but are rather in the presence of a psychic energy which has infinite wisdom and adaptability in the work of transformation of the lower into the higher, and the making of all things to 'work together for good' in the interests of wholeness. This is so near to our accustomed way of thinking that we may easily assume that it is a Christian system of psychology, but in this we shall be mistaken for it is a scientific approach to experience, and the real content of religion always seems so near, and yet so far. However, this does not prevent us from using the valuable psychological tools which Jung has so carefully fashioned for us.

Jung sees the work before us in life as an immense task, a task both of creation and of deliverance. We have to be delivered from the earth, the bondage of the earth-mother, which has power over us like that of the great Leviathan, for to surrender to her and to retreat into her body, save to be reborn, is death. Life must follow the stream of the Spirit, and move into the future, or else the earth-bound lethal waters will overcome us and draw us down into a state of non-Being. We must be involved in the intensest struggle if we are to become free from the bondage of the earth-bound life, for the power of the containing mother works contrary to our fulfilment, and later there may be added the hostile power of a fearful father figure. The story of the Prodigal Son is a superb mythical expression of the work of deliverance from that which binds us to immaturity. H. G. Baynes, in his *Mythology of the Soul*, has made the Prodigal Son the hero of the parable; he was the rebel whom the Spirit drove to leave his father and his first home to discover his own unique fulfilment. People who have to fight for their liberation are usually found to over-do their demand for freedom and run into license, and thus the Prodigal found himself amongst the swine. But life had better things than this for him, and the Spirit would give him no peace until he found his true home in life. Moreover, as he set his course for home he was not the same as the son who left the home, for, in spite of his errors and his sin, he had won a major battle in life, as a result of which he had come to an expression of his true being and independent existence. But it was a life which could not be lived in the inner-body alone, so that there had to be a return into the outer-body of the community for that life to be maintained and further enriched. The fatted calf was killed and the best robe was put upon him, and a ring was set upon his finger. The psychological significance which Jung would see in the robe is that of the new man which all saw in the Prodigal; the ring would represent his own completeness; the fatted calf would be the new communion or relationship with his fellows. The elder brother represents the child who stays at home and is never independent of his parents; he lacks courage and therefore does not find life but is bound to the 'weak and beggarly elements' of which St Paul spoke.

The leaving of the parental home is symbolic of the quest which the soul must undertake, and we can feel in the parable the hurt involved in leaving home and the tremendous wrestling with opposite emotions—love and hate, the individual and the community, life and death, the spiritual and the material. The elder brother felt nothing of this tension of the opposites, which play so important a part in Jungian psychology, and on that account his soul was sick, for he was out of the battle of life and had contented himself with a parasitic existence, or one of drab conformity.

There needs must be intense conflict in spiritual growth, as the Apostle says:

'We wrestle not against flesh and blood, but against principalities, against powers, against the rulers of the darkness of this world, against spiritual wickedness in high places.'

EPHESIANS vi. 12.

and

'The flesh lusteth against the Spirit, and the Spirit against the flesh: and these are contrary the one to the other.'

GALATIANS v. 17.

This is not, according to the Jungian scheme of things, a conflict in which one is victor and the other vanquished, but it is a transforming situation in which the meeting of the opposites effects a new level of life. We have spoken of the cost of this in another chapter where we show Jung's use of the Christian symbols of the Cross and the Descent into Hell, and the Resurrection; it is involved in the Incarnation where the heavenly and the earthly meet, and the pain of this birth is the price which has to be paid for the new manhood.

An instance of the failure to reach the balance of heaven and earth was given to me by a professional man, who was taught as a child by a pious uncle of a rigid Puritan persuasion, who lost no opportunity to bring home to the little boy the horrors which befell the people of Sodom and Gomorrah. It must have been a very lurid presentation considering the impression it made upon his mind. The Sodom and Gomorrah story was linked in his mind with the story of the Garden of Eden where the villain of the piece was the woman, and in this we see again the influence of the uncle who himself was unmarried. It was the woman who made the alliance with the serpent, it was she who brought, through her sex, the downfall of poor Adam. The notion that sex is the worst of all evils, and that this evil comes to man by way of woman, was deeply embedded in his mind, and this produced within his personality a state of unbalance which was fundamental to his illness. He was set at war against a large portion of himself, which manifested itself in his feeling that all pleasure, and sex in particular, was wicked; the means of escape was into intellectual pursuits, and the typical Jungian picture of unbalance was given of the splitting apart of Intellect and Emotion. However, the Spirit, which is always on the side of healing, was making him feel ill in order that he might be driven to seek that which was needed to effect the making of a whole man.

There is a creative work to be done, besides the deliverance from the parental bondage and the onesidedness of personality. This involves the discovery of a strong sense of purpose, an awareness of a great work to be performed in which much raw material is fashioned into completeness, and if the task is not set in hand the soul will die. This may be thought of as like that of the alchemist, whose work was really psychological, though its true nature was hidden by his furnace and alembics. His work was the making of the pure gold of the soul from life's raw materials, for which many virtues were required including a readiness to pass through the furnace of affliction. The task, again, may be thought of as the Christian pilgrimage in which the story of our Lord's life is relived in our experience; or it may be presented as the mystic rose which draws its life both from the sun, the masculine and spiritual, and from the rich earth, feminine and instinctual; yet there is no flower until the thorns have grown and have been suffered, they form part of the crown of life. Behind all this symbolism is a great work which has to be performed, if true life is to be found, and we are reminded of some ancient words:

'I have set before you life and death, blessing and cursing: therefore choose life, that both thou and thy seed may live.'
DEUTERONOMY XXX. 19.

A necessary step in this creative work is to descend from the heights where infantile pride has placed us. The reduction of pride to a realization of helplessness is as essential to Jung as it is to the Christian, and the fate of Icarus, who tried by his own endeavour to reach the sun, the Divine source of light and creativity, is that of anyone who tries to put himself in the place of God. Our task has to be done on earth, and anyone who so elevates himself that he separates himself from the earth will have to suffer the hurt of earthliness if he is to be saved. The saving symbol, that of the Cross, reminds him of the inevitable nailing to that which is firmly set in the earth, and of the fact that the lowest depths must be known before the joy of the final triumph can be experienced. This earthliness takes us into what we have called the outer-body, the life of the community with its many demands and responsibilities. It was the community which crucified our Lord.

The creative work of finding fulfilment in life involves the use of the whole of our natural endowment. Much futile work is spent in the fruitless task of trying to destroy that which God has made for our use and well being, as was the case of the man I have just mentioned. We must come to terms with the darker side of ourselves, for example, our anger must be accepted and used positively rather than in negative destructiveness, as the Apostle admonished, 'Be ye angry, and sin not.' (EPHESIANS iv. 26). Thus we think of our Lord driving the money-changers out of the temple (LUKE xix. 25), and other instances of his righteous indignation. We need our hate, to 'hate the evil, love the good' (AMOS v. 15), in many aspects of our social life. It is in these ways that the thunder is stolen from guilt complexes that otherwise would be so destructive, and these emotions are then used in a fuller expression of our being. This method of approach is an aid in dealing with the difficult obsessional neurosis, which contains much angry and frustrated Will.

In our deep mind we hold images of both father and mother, and each is represented by both a good and bad image. In the healthy and adjusted person these opposite images are balanced, but this is not so in the case of the sick individual, where the negative image blots out the good and gives rise to bad emotional reactions. The required resolution is aided by the figure of the good mother which the Church carries, and the image of the good father in the Good Shepherd, although even here the need for balance is again seen, for within our own minds we must hold together the sterner and the kindlier aspects of the father and the mother, and these will lead us to know God as both Judge and Redeemer.

This rapid survey of Jungian psychology is manifestly fragmentary and must not be regarded as adequately representing the full teaching of the School of Analytical Psychology. Jung's many works require the most careful study to be fully appreciated and it would require much greater space than I can give in a book of this kind adequately to summarize and co-ordinate the Jungian doctrines. Nevertheless, I hope that I have been able to indicate not only in this chapter, but also in various other parts of this book, that in following him we are working in a realm rich in mystery and in the power to heal.

I shall conclude this chapter relating to the therapist's technique by mentioning the value of hymns when dealing with Christian people. They have grown so deeply into the lives of people that they reach to the depths which we are seeking in order to establish wholeness. These hymns are very rich in what Jung calls Archetypes, i.e. in themes which are universal in human history, or which have a long and significant history behind them; they are thus firmly embedded in the collective unconscious and when they are stimulated, although the person may well be quite unconscious of what is happening, a wealth of experience is released into the service of present living. We may have noticed at a meeting, when a certain theme is mentioned, that a rapt stillness descends, a stillness which can be felt; this is because an archetype has been used. When they appear in dreams and fantasies they bring with them a release of creative power, and a widening of consciousness, and it is a matter of profound wonder to see the effect they have in the work of healing. Hymns rich in archetypes readily come into our minds in the analytic session and they, with their long and deep personal associations, come to our aid. For example, the guilt-ridden person who has come to realize his utter nakedness, and from whom every evasion and defence has been stripped away, will derive help from Charles Wesley's hymn:

> Other refuge have I none;
> Hangs my helpless soul on thee:
> Leave, ah, leave me not alone,
> Still support and comfort me.
> All my trust on thee is stayed,
> All my help from thee I bring:
> Cover my defenceless head
> With the shadow of thy wing.
>
> Plenteous grace with thee is found,
> Grace to cleanse from every sin;
> Let the healing streams abound;
> Make and keep me pure within . . .

Or Toplady's hymn:

> Nothing in my hand I bring,
> Simply to thy Cross I cling;
> Naked, come to thee for dress;

Helpless, look to thee for grace,
Foul, I to thy fountain fly;
Wash me, Saviour, or I die.

The hymn I use most of all is by Charlotte Elliott which, at moments of considerable intensity, when the soul feels utterly lost and overborne by a sense of futility and weakness, brings an almost unfailing response. It might have been written specially for the analytic session.

Just as I am, without one plea
But that thy Blood was shed for me,
And that thou bidst me come to thee,
O Lamb of God, I come.

Just as I am, though tossed about
With many a conflict, many a doubt,
Fightings and fears within, without,
O Lamb of God, I come.

Just as I am, poor, wretched, blind;
Sight, riches, healing of the mind,
Yea all I need, in thee to find,
O Lamb of God, I come.

Just as I am, thou wilt receive,
Wilt welcome, pardon, cleanse, relieve;
Because thy promise I believe,
O Lamb of God, I come.

Just as I am (thy love unknown
Has broken every barrier down)
Now to be thine, yea, thine alone,
O Lamb of God, I come.

Just as I am, of that free love
The breadth, length, depth, and height to prove,
Here for a season, then above,
O Lamb of God, I come.

The last of the hymns I quote is by Mrs L. M. Willis and

it is most helpful on occasions where self-pity is uppermost,
and the feeling that 'life has been unjust to me':

> Father, hear the prayer we offer:
> Not for ease that prayer shall be,
> But for strength that we may for ever
> Live our lives courageously.
>
> Not for ever in green pastures
> Do we ask our way to be;
> But the steep and rugged pathway
> May we tread rejoicingly.
>
> Not for ever by still waters
> Would we idly rest and stay;
> But would strike the living fountains
> From the rocks along our way.
>
> Be our strength in hours of weakness,
> In our wanderings be our guide;
> Through endeavour, failure, danger,
> Father, be thou at our side.

These hymns are not imposed upon the person, but they
naturally rise out of the situation and meet it with the wealth
of the experience enshrined in them.

FOUR

THE INNER-BODY

In this chapter I shall begin a review of actual case histories of some of the people whom I have helped through the psychotherapeutic ministry. These histories will be given in the barest detail, with a view to showing the kind of problem these people were trying in vain to solve unaided, and the help I was able to give them. The long tangled stories do not concern us here, but occasionally a few details are given in order to reveal something of the path that had been taken so disastrously.

In order to aid our understanding some kind of framework is required for the survey, and I have accordingly presented our life as contained within three bodies, the inner-body, the outer-body, and the spiritual body. Between these three bodies a due proportion must be kept, and troubles descend upon us whenever we try to live in fewer than these three.

An ancient alchemist once remarked that there is as much of the soul outside the body as within it. This may sound strange, for we are accustomed to think of the soul as residing inside the body in spite of it occupying no space. On second thoughts, however, you will realize that much of our life, in a vital sense, is lived in our environment. We spread out into our surroundings, which carry us in the same way as do our bodies. Much of our life is projected into the outer world, and whatever we touch bears the stamp of our individuality. We see this extension of ourselves in the material with which we clothe ourselves. The colour, the arrangement and style of our clothes bear the stamp of our individuality. Likewise, something of ourselves goes into the manner in which we dress our hair, the peculiar way in which we use the materials about us, the type of work we choose to do, and how we treat our environment at the many points in which we meet it. The magical performances of primitive

people show an awareness of this fact in that in order to gain
power over a person they require some article which has
had contact with him in the exercise of their rites. Even the
name of the person could be used adversely.

Sir Charles Sherrington[1] in another context spoke of our
having two bodies, one inside our skin, and the other outside
it in our surround.[2] The body outside our skin affects us just
as does the body within our skin, and both of these bodies
are essential for effective living. Viewing these two bodies
in a physical regard we see in the case of the inner-body
that the total physical content affects our thinking and our
feeling, i.e. the body affects the mind. Thus a person's attitude to life may be deeply affected by the inadequate, or
excessive secretion of the ductless glands, so that the personality development is affected by purely physiological factors.
And the materials of the outer-body also have an important
bearing upon the Self, e.g. economic pressures, industrial
and commercial stress, climate, malnutrition and such like.
In a mental regard the personal aspects of the outer-body
are less obvious in their influence upon the total Self. Nevertheless, it is readily appreciated that lovelessness in the home,
the restlessness of people, the attitude of people towards sex,
the anxiety of folk, the intense competitiveness of people, all
have their adverse effect in the formative years of the child.
Worry in the parents is as infectious as measles. Such personal
factors in the outer-body are not limited in their effects to
infancy and childhood, for even a neurosis can be taken over
from one person to another when they live in the closest
relationship. Jung shows how the unsolved problems of
parents, who make up the most important part of the outer-
body in the early years of a child, are taken over by the child
who then has to wrestle with them. They are passed on again,
unless resolved, to 'the third and fourth generation'.

The third body in which we live is the spiritual-body,
which is the spiritual dimension of man where the Spirit
moves creatively upon the waters of the Soul. Here we have
passed beyond the physical, unless we hold with Lloyd

[1] *Man on His Nature*. Cambridge University Press, 1957.
[2] Sherrington uses this word rather than 'environment'. It is more intimate
and descriptive, and it serves well the concept of the bodies within which
we live.

Morgan[1] that this may be but a particular aspect or form of the Spirit. In a series of emergent forms the mind can most readily be perceived as the highest expression of the Spirit. St Paul regards the spirit as needing to be 'clothed' (II CORINTHIANS v), and thus there is what the Apostle describes as 'a spiritual body' in which our life finds its fulfilment. The physical, the mind and the Spirit are bound into a unity in the life of man, and their purpose is to move towards the fullest expression of the Spirit. Our first concern will be almost wholly with our life as it is contained within the first of these two bodies.

We have said that the Self must live in both the inner- and the outer-bodies. Whenever the two interdependent bodies are separated contrary to their nature serious trouble begins. For example if the outer-body appears to be too threatening or demanding, too frightful or painful, then the door may be closed on that outer-body and the person shuts himself up within the inner-body, which now becomes a fortress with lowered portcullis, raised drawbridge, and a full deep moat. The outer-body is interpreted as being hostile, and contact with it must be avoided at all costs, since such contact would result in a feeling of intense hurt or loss. But the inner-body, that has now become a fortress, can never sustain life fully, and the individual, deprived of the resources of the outer-body becomes poverty stricken. He lives to himself, and having no object to love or from which to receive affection, he loves this Self. But life within the inner-body is too limited to give satisfaction, and so such a person gives to himself in fantasy, in an exaggerated measure, what life seems to have denied him. This merely results in removing him further from reality, and strengthens him in his position. His songs become to him deliciously mournful, for they are of the great injustices he has suffered, the deprivations he has borne. Self-pity becomes his consolation. This terrible prison fortress has been created as the result of the most intense fears and pains, which seemed to be too great to bear. This is the result of the forsaking of the outer-body of the Self.

The Girl Who Ran Away

Cynthia was led to my front door by her vicar, for she

[1] *Emergent Evolution: Life, Mind and Spirit.*

was far too terrified to go anywhere alone. When she became less afraid, as the treatment proceeded, she would always run to my house, and after the session she would run back to her home, which symbolized her running away from life into the fortress of her inner-body. The following were included in the list of troubles she presented to me: she felt empty, hungry and haunted, she had obsessional thoughts about her ugliness (in fact she was uncommonly pretty), of death, insanity, stupidity and of making mistakes, she had lost her power of concentration, and she was full of doubts about everything. Moreover, because all things seemed unreal, her religion, which she carefully practised, meant nothing to her.

I suspect that in the earliest years there was an excess of attention given to her, until there arrived on the scene a sister and two brothers. The sister was a veritable Shirley Temple, who on many occasions took the first prize at baby shows. The father, who when he was good was very good, was violent in his drinking bouts, and the mother and the children would barricade themselves within a bedroom against his vicious attacks. On occasions the mother was knocked on to the floor, and Cynthia, protecting the younger children, would be hit herself. Such happenings were well known to the people in the district, and Cynthia's shame became unbearable. As long as she could remember she had felt herself unwanted and without a place in the world, and this belief seemed to be confirmed when the other children were born. Matters were made worse by her living with various relatives during her early years, which she interpreted as a proof that her parents did not want her because she had no value. It seemed to her that there was nothing she could do which would elicit love. It was no wonder that, believing her father and mother to have forsaken her, she ran away from life, and felt the outer-body to be no place for her. In addition to this there had been a terrifying infantile sexual experience which made her feel different from all other children and people. Homosexual complications followed upon this. The result of it all was a retreat into the inner-body in depth, and she became very seriously ill.

Besides Cynthia's retreat from reality, and her obsessional problem, there was a strong hysterical reaction which produced such symptoms as vomiting, stomach and chest pains,

F

and paralysis. She developed an overwhelming fear of the masculine, and of her father in particular, who was involved in her infantile sexual fantasies. At the same time she was inordinately jealous of the masculine, because of his freedom, and the fuss which always was shown to the baby boy and the latitude which he enjoyed as he grew up. She compared her feminine weakness most unfavourably with the man's strength. Jealousy may well be set in a class by itself, for almost no hostile emotion is so dangerous to the personality, so savagely destructive and difficult to eradicate.[1] Cynthia's paralysis was related to her jealousy, for in her jealous fantasies she spent herself in utmost sadistic rage, only equal to which in magnitude was her guilt, which demanded expiation of her crimes according to strict justice. Therefore she had to inflict upon herself her own sadistic rage, and this completely paralyzed her at times, for she must suffer the maximum privation. She was inflicting upon herself, unknowingly, what she had in fantasy inflicted upon her siblings, this hurt must needs be brought upon her yet unconceived child, and on this account, along with fantasied bodily defects, she became hysterical at the prospect of having a baby.

Under the circumstances it is no wonder that her treatment has lasted three years, yet during this time the obsessional feaures have disappeared, the hysteria has been reduced very considerably, and she is far less afraid of life. She had returned to her church, now with her husband who, as the result of the help his wife was receiving, was Confirmed. Although she has not altogether worked through her problems as yet she is a different person from the pathetic creature who was first brought to me.

(NOTE. Cynthia, aged twenty-five, was a case of severe hysterical splitting, under which was a 'borderline' position. She took pride in herself, in art and learning. As we should expect she was sexually inadequate. Her sexual traumatic experience, and the bad heterosexual pattern set by her parents made matters worse. A powerful Electra complex was further exacerbated by her father's attitude towards her in drink. An hysterical reaction, which was manifested in a thorough-going conversion hysteria, still further complicated

[1] Boris Sokoloff—*Jealousy, A Psychological Study.* London, Carrol, 1948.

the picture, while a homosexual deviation cut her off from self-committal to men and to her husband in particular.)

Elizabeth the Unwanted

Elizabeth was twenty-seven when she first came to see me. In the early sessions she would sit a whole hour and not speak a single word, but twist her glove unmercifully. Later she began to speak about the 'muddle' inside her which she could not understand. She told me of how she would sit and stare for long periods, of how she felt herself to be empty and without interest in anything. She was at other times restless and without feeling. Besides this, obsessional acts had to be performed: she had to keep counting numbers, sometimes to different tunes, or whenever anyone spoke to her she would have to twist the words round into different positions; then again, she would constantly see rows of bones passing before her mind. Suicidal thoughts added to her burden. It was at once obvious that her condition was very serious indeed, and every caution had to be exercised.

It is interesting to know, with the previous case in mind, that she was always aware that she was an unwanted child. Children have no need to be told such a thing for it is sensed at the earliest age. Some people would maintain that this feeling is passed on to the child before birth, and that an attempted abortion in particular has profound effects upon the unborn child.

Elizabeth had a brother and a sister for whom, at an early age, she was held responsible by her parents. Whenever they were up to mischief she had to take the blame and was punished. For example, the children were not expected to talk in bed, and their father would hide nearby and listen for sounds; when he thought he heard something he would dart into the room and thrash Elizabeth. Moreover, the relationship between the parents were most difficult for a child to understand, for her father often became moody and would not speak to his wife for weeks. At such times he communicated with his wife through Elizabeth, and when the speaking ban was lifted there would be frequent rows between the parents.

We can appreciate the sense of insecurity which the small child must have felt, for there is nothing so devastating as the sense of deprivation of love. Without love there can be no feeling of security or value, and it was the privation of this which led Elizabeth to withdraw from life. There was nothing firm or abiding in the outer-body. This was revealed in a dream in which she saw a girl walking alone in the country, and as she walked she became filled with great anxiety, for she felt that the girl might be pounced upon by a man hiding in the hedgerow. The sky became filled with clouds, making the whole scene sinister and dangerous. Then she saw people entering a boat, when again the anxiety came over her for she feared the boat would capsize.

This dream portrayed her outlook from the beginning of her life. Her world was sinister and the skies were threatening, and when, naturally, she turned to her father for strong protective care, she found him hostile, punishing, unjust, and waiting to pounce upon her. When she looked at the boat, which in her dream symbolism she identified with her mother, she again felt that she was let down and threatened with destruction. The boat, being a corporate thing, would also represent to her the family, that is, her outer-body. Her world, devoid of security, seemed to present to her but one course of action, viz. escape.

When her father died, Elizabeth interpreted his death as the result of her 'death-wish' upon him. Infants in a powerless state see themselves in fantasy as having almighty power, and in their dreams they fulfil their wishes. Such belief in magical power is given conscious expression in such stories as *Alf's Button* and *The Magic Carpet*. All primitive people believe in the great power of thought, so much so that merely to think a thing is to release power which cannot be controlled or permanently negated. Infants share in this primitive belief, and therefore if in their hates and rages they have wished death upon a parent or sibling, they feel thereafter unconsciously responsible for a pending death or a death which has taken place. The guilt derived from this unconscious thought reaches up to the heavens and casts them into the depths of Hell, and it will set in motion the desire for expiation which results in devastating self-punishment. This common psychological situation was fully experienced by Elizabeth at the time of her father's death.

Some of Elizabeth's resentment towards her father has unconsciously been transferred to her husband. Only with the greatest effort, and that not always successful, can she tolerate his presence in any room in which she happens to be, while at night she has to stay awake listening to his breathing which, when it becomes inaudible, drives her into a panic. Similarly, she must drive her mother from her. She recalls that, as a child, she wanted to murder her parents; so intense was the pain of isolation and rejectedness that, in fantasy and dream, she destroyed what she most wanted and hated those whose love she most desired.

One could not be expected to say that Elizabeth, who is still having treatment, is as flourishing as the proverbial bay tree, but she has improved so much that she is taking part in the social life of her church, and recently during a Mission in her parish she engaged in a house-to-house visitation.

The child's need to find the body that is outside his skin, and to find in it warm, secure, loving relationships, is very intense, for without it he will feel that he belongs to nowhere and to no one; unless he feels at home within it he will have no confidence. In his first experience of life he was one with his surround, his outer-body was one with his mother. If the physical and emotional separation effected at birth was not too frightening, and his newly-found aloneness was not felt to be absolute during subsequent months, his confidence will be built up and he will be able to accept his outer-body as part of his natural rhythm of life. If he finds in the outer-body the many and varied responses to his needs that he requires, and if there is sufficient stimulus to endeavour, then he will grow to feel that he is able to meet whatever the future may hold for him.

However, should the outer-body have seemed to be non-co-operative and threatening, he will face the new shocks which await him only with difficulty. Weaning may be a very serious thing for him. The arrival of another baby in the home will be another major event, especially when he sees the new baby being given all that was denied him. This event may lead him to believe that he was not good enough, and that his mother had to find someone else whom she could really love. Thus he believes himself to be despised and rejected, deserted and nobody's child. This may be built into his previous experience of birth, weaning and toilet training. I find the experi-

ence of such a child must be something like that which we
should feel were we sent off into outer space in a sputnik.
There would be the feeling of being utterly alone, with no
means of communication with mother earth, nothing but the
icy cold and dread silence. The sheer terror of being alone and
lost can be imagined easily. Hope would have died in the
finality of it all. A similar feeling would be that of being
dropped in the arctic, with the howling, icy wind, so merciless, against which our small, isolated cry would not be heard.
It is the terror of such feeling of abandonment which drives
the infant to reject the outer-body, which holds for him
nothing but dread. Elizabeth experienced all this when she
was separated from her mother on the pending arrival of a
new baby, for she was sent off to stay with an aunt in London
for a month. This separation from her mother, and her
jealousy of the new baby soon to appear, made her behave
aggressively towards this aunt, who was 'screening' her 'bad'
mother. The uncle put himself in the place of the 'bad' father
by locking Elizabeth in the cellar whenever she 'played up'.
We can imagine how this child, already bearing a sense of
abandonment, would react to this new hurt, and feel unbearable pain upon finding her mother nursing another child in
her place, and we can understand why, on her return, she
would have nothing to do with her mother. Elizabeth, again
resorting to her tantrums, was now locked by her mother in
her bedroom, and she recalls how other children would ridicule and taunt her when thus locked in.

There are obvious degrees in which all this is felt, just as
there are various kinds of reaction. The more courageous
infant may put up a fine fight to retain his place in the outer-
body for he realizes the importance of this wider dimension
to his very existence. We often see this in the case of the small
child who is naughty, for he is frequently a gallant fellow
ready to face punishments rather than sink into nothingness.
The anti-social adult is frequently produced because the child
feels that the outer-body is so hostile to his well-being that
he is opposed to it. In milder cases this may reveal itself in
nothing more than always being 'against the government',
but in extreme cases it may give rise to the criminal. On the
other hand, the child may feel that the giants around him
are too big and strong for him, and that a direct revolt will

never win for him the significance he needs. On this account he may become a good little boy, an example to all other children, and develop into the compliant person. He may even put himself upon a pedestal to be admired by all, and accordingly becomes an exhibitionist. Other similar courses of action may present themselves as a means by which admiration and approval may be gained. Someone once told me that to achieve this end he became the funny child; he was called 'the card', and he kept his elders constantly amused.

In less fortunate cases such attempts as these to gain the essential approval and security are shattered. The child finds he can obtain no purchase at all upon his surround, and the result is that he becomes locked up within his inner-body. He may unconsciously call for help in a hysterical way, as we shall see later, but if in a courageous frontal attack, in which his utmost will is engaged, he meets an overwhelming obstacle which drives back his will upon itself, there may well be created a deep-seated obsessional disorder most difficult to rectify. In speaking of an obsessional neurosis as a disorder of the will, I am fully aware that I am not in line with the usual account of its psychopathology, nevertheless I have found empirically that this approach to the problem is, at least in part, justified. The outer-body, essential for any normal degree of living, is prohibited; every movement towards it is met with such intolerable threats and frightful punishments and privations, that only stultified movements are possible, each movement being withdrawn before its fulfilment. We see these aborted actions as 'tics', and they are obsessional. Every obsessional neurotic has a secret[1] which he guards with every device at his disposal. The outcome of all this is that there is a restriction and a withdrawal, a contraction of life. In some cases the outer-body may be regained, but in other the regression has been made final. Fantastic will power is always operative in such disorders, which often is organized against the attempts to heal, and brings our labours to no effect. That these disorders are of the will may appear surprising, since such people as are possessed by them are often most pacific, judging by appearances.

(NOTE. Elizabeth, aged 27, was a compulsive obsessional with considerable schizoid stressing. In her ambivalence she hated

[1] W. Stekel, *Compulsion and Doubt*, Vol. II, London, Nevill, 1950.

the mother she loved, and destroyed the one she desired. Her rage of the first anal period was countered by the emotion of the later anal period in which she desired to heal and restore the mother whom she had hurt.[1] Her need for self-expression was neutralized by the fear of the consequences of such self-expression.[2] The schizoid barrier, being so firmly held, made the therapeutic task exceptionally difficult. Besides this, she showed the compulsively dominant aspect of the hysteric which drives away those upon whom she might be dependent.

Her father may well have passed on to her a bad psychic inheritance, for his behaviour towards Elizabeth was extraordinary, and his 'closed-in' moods, when he would not speak to his wife for weeks, encouraged such a view.

There was a latent homosexuality which showed itself by sexually inverted rôles in her fantasy life, both in her avoidance of masculine company and in her attitude towards her husband.)

There was no room for Jane

Amongst the things which led Jane to seek help were her strong suicidal tendencies, her constant need to escape, and her lack of interest in anything. She described herself as 'a complete introvert', she could not concentrate, there was claustrophobia, depression with palpitations and a burning in her head. At meal times she would have to rise from the table and run out of the room, she had to keep combing her hair to straighten it, she played the well-known obsessional game with paving stones, and whenever she came to a lamp-standard in the street or a tree by the road she had to jump.

The family to which Jane belonged was large, with two children younger than herself. Her father deified his work, and was far too busy to have much to do with the children who, as they grew up, were pressed into the service of the business which completely enslaved them. The father had little patience with the mother, and there were frequent scenes. The home had to be sacrificed to the advance of the business, with the result that everyone had to work at top pressure, year

[1] Cf. Melanie Klein, *The Psychoanalysis of Children*, London, Hogarth, 1949, p. 230 f.
[2] Cf. J. A. Hadfield, *Psychology and Mental Health*, London, Allen & Unwin, 1950, p. 260 ff.

in and out. In such a home this little girl grew up, needing, as all little children do, her father's love, but he was cold and as hard as granite. She loved him, and yet she hated him for all his indifference to the softer needs of her life, and for the way in which he treated her mother.

Suffering from a lack of love and living space, she reacted with explosive force, for she felt she would be destroyed if she did not blast her way out of her confines into a life of fuller significance. At all costs she must find her personal value. However, there were many odds against her, and in her struggle she felt her father to be too strong for her and that she would be destroyed by him. She remarked, 'I had to kill him (in fantasy) to free myself, but he got the better of me. I could scream to be saved.'

An early incident in her life made matters more difficult. There had been a sexual shock concerning which her mother's unfortunate reaction inhibited the little girl's sexuality. Her father, the first representative of the masculine and the object of her first heterosexual love, became inevitably involved in all this within her fantasy life. This made him appear to be all the more hostile and frightening. Because of her father's intractability, a surrogate father figure had to be found, and an erotic attachment with her brother was formed. Her deep guilt now put a barrier between her and all men, and since her own feminine position was intolerable she turned in upon herself and took up a pseudo masculine pose.

The outcome of the story is that as a result of the treatment the obsessional elements have entirely disappeared, and there are much happier relationships both with her parents and the younger children of whom she was jealous.[1] She became Confirmed and has married, and this very happy woman amazes all who knew her in the former days.

(NOTE. Jane, aged 29, was of a Napoleonic type, dominant, hard and aggressive. She was perfectionist in her defence against her repressed rage and desire. I viewed her, in the main, as an obsessional personality. She showed several stress syndromes—migraine, rheumatic pains, general pains and aches, and severe fatigue. Her anal aggression was revealed by frequency of micturition. However, the schizoid factor

[1] A much more feminine position has been taken up, and the hard strain has diminished.

beneath her obsession was apparent; and she was 'schizoid' towards men within a homosexual deviation.

There was also an 'Adlerian problem', for she had a strong Cinderella complex, for she had to slave away in the service of the family. She particularly resented the privileges of the male members of the family. This latter feeling, combined with a violent reaction to her oppressive father, led her to reject the masculine relation, and to take up a homosexual position in which she shut out men from her life. However, despite her envy of the masculine rôle, and her resentment towards her natural feminine submissive position, she adopted the masculine rôle in her homosexual relationships. She also hungered for the 'good time' of which, from her babyhood, she felt life had deprived her.)

Possessed by Fear

James is a middle-aged man who was brought to me by his vicar. It was not long before he revealed his most complex personality. Examples of the early material he presented are given in *A Modern Traveller's Tale* in chapter seven. The informed reader will draw his own conclusions from this material. At first, symptoms of a mildly compulsive nature were shown, but as the analysis proceeded the full extent of his obsessions were seen, which took the form of words and phrases which he was driven to repeat almost endlessly. These were held back because they were of a 'dirty' nature. He also revealed considerable hysteria. He was afraid of his work, of everyone he met, his wife, his small child, and even little children in the street; many places also made him afraid, particularly his office. He was to all appearances a very pious man, but his religion, like everything else, was unreal to him. He had lapses in his thinking, and at times he would go out and wander in a fugue-like state. A deep depression would come over him and on one occasion he attempted to commit suicide. The greatest of his fears was that he would be more successful the second time. He just wanted to run and go on running to nowhere for ever.

He began his life under great difficulties, and it proceeded in a minor key for almost fifty years. The initial shock of his traumatic birth was like a strident chord which reverberated through all that followed, and lingered on in overtones within the complex theme of his life. His main theme was one of complete rejectedness.

James was the child of his mother's later years, the home was poor, and his eldest brother, who had much to do with James's story, was many years his senior. His father was a dying man when James was born, and through the strain of the situation his mother could not feed him for long. Added to this the little fellow was sent away to an aunt for six months until the crisis of his father's last illness had passed. He was taken from his aunt, whom he must have come to regard as his mother, and returned to his mother, who naturally appeared as a stranger to him. His big brother took the place of his father.

When James went to school he was made to realize how physically small he was, and this smallness carried the whole weight of his intense sense of inferiority. When he came to choose his life's work he had no idea what he should do, but his big brother, without consultation, stepped in and made him take up a particular professional career which he, the brother, had himself always wished to pursue. This imposition was most bitterly resented and he hated his long years of arduous study. All his family impressed upon him the duty to be grateful to his brother, and that he must make a good return for the money his brother was spending on his behalf. Secretly he saw himself as but a pawn in the affairs of other people, and in schemes too big for him. Life was driving him to do things beyond his capacity.

After James had qualified in his profession he was given an opening in a very important firm, which offered him great prospects and which necessitated his leaving this country. His work was satisfactory, but after a few weeks of deepest misery he had to give up the post and return home. His family had no patience with him and blamed him unmercifully, which only added to his sense of failure and the feeling of being an outcast. The end of the story was that he could face life's demands no longer. The responsibilities of life in general, and of his work in particular, were too much for him, and there followed the attempted suicide and a subsequent inability to work.

Intense hysterical reactions marked his treatment, but underneath there lay the obsessional fear and the temptation to forsake the outer-body. He was engaged in a struggle with

Authority, all the aspects of which he drew together within his concept of God. Already his authorities had demanded from him the surrender of all pleasures in the interests of his studies. Other young people could play their games but not he, for he was told that such things would interfere with his work. An uncle came to live with the family when James was a young boy, and since he was very 'religious' he took in hand the welfare of the child's soul. Now James saw the heavens filled with threatenings and thunderings issuing from the throne of a terrible God, and there was a great Eye which could even penetrate his thoughts. Thus a spiritual terror was added to all his earthly fears, and a demand was made upon him which surpassed all others.

Under the frightening circumstances of his life it was quite natural that there took place an infantile sexual experience which terrified him, and which contributed much to his deep sense of inferiority and inability to face the world. This guilt was bad enough, in all truth, before the uncle came upon the scene, but now he was shattered by it. The knell of doom was sounded in church, particularly when he heard the words of the Litany, 'From fornication and all other *deadly* sin . . .' This deep sexual anxiety led him to reject nature as something evil and deadly: it was as though God had given him something highly desirable, and then had told him that if he had anything at all to do with it he would be destroyed. He sought to claim his birthright, but 'God' was too powerful for him, and He became the One in Chief Who laid upon him 'burdens grievous to be borne'.

This sad story is an illustration of how difficult life is for some people. We never know what burdens they carry; the people themselves only know that life feels too much for them, and although they strain themselves to the utmost it is in vain. Should they have the misfortune to meet authoritative people who condemn them for not being by nature other than God made them, their sad condition must seem to them to be beyond hope. We should, at least, withhold our censure, for we are not in a position to measure the blame, and in fact against all appearances they may be making a truly magnificent effort. We might not have done nearly so well under the same conditions. Who of us dare say how we would act were we bearing so great a degree of terror? At one of his sessions

James could barely speak a word by reason of the chattering of his teeth, and he begged the people about him not to frighten him. He cried repeatedly, 'Please do not frighten me,' and falteringly he promised to go on his hands and knees to everyone if only they would not make him so afraid.

He was afraid to do anything lest he would be punished, and he felt he must crave permission before attempting anything lest he should incur wrathful displeasure. It was found that one deep root of his fear was a frightening noise, with which he associated 'lamentation'. It seemed that this was his mother's crying, most probably when she had to send him away to his aunt, or it might have some connection with his father's pending death. In any case, his mother's intense grief and anxiety would be communicated to him. Lamentation had figured greatly in his young life; when staying with his aunt he must have cried for his mother at first, but this met with punishment from the aunt so that he became afraid to cry. In fact just to be afraid became a highly punishable thing, and he came to believe that God would punish him for being afraid. He said in his abreaction, 'I won't cry, but don't frighten me'. This inhibition of so natural and relieving a thing as crying contributed to the blocking of self-expression, and turned him back upon his inner-body. One was also a little suspicious that his crying was first used to gain pity and love, and its condemnation was interpreted as an absolute denial of love on the part of the outer-body.

At one point in the analysis he lost all power of speech for a number of days, and this was followed by a period of blindness. The analysis revealed the intense power of his hate towards the brother who held even his soul in captivity. On the death of the father, James's mother was completely dependent upon her eldest son, and this led her to look up to him and comply with him in all matters. This had the effect of leading James to believe that his brother had a monopoly of his mother's love, with the result that he identified himself with his brother in order to obtain the love which he was receiving. This union with his brother led to a latent homosexual situation with him, rich in sodomistic fantasies. In his utter weakness and sense of inferiority he drew into himself his brother's all-powerful strength, for by this alone could he live. And James observed that it was at the time that his brother was

taken ill that his own illness became manifest, that is at the time
that his supply of strength was threatened.

The analysis was a difficult one, not only on account of the
depth to which he had cut himself off from so terrifying an
outer-body, but also on account of the intense hysterical
element into which he so often took refuge. Today there is no
sign of his obsession and unnatural fear, he has put on weight,
and he is enjoying a quality of life hitherto unknown to him.
He has returned to his office, and he is tackling his work with
zest, for the day has gone when he faced his clients with
trepidation, and he now finds that people bring to him more
than his work, in that they are opening their hearts to him and
out of his own experience he is exercising a lay ministry to
them. He is no longer guilt-ridden, and at last he can enjoy the
good things of life. Above all his religion has been cleansed of
false, hidden motives which led him to do the best things for
the worst reasons. His feeling towards his mother and his two
brothers has been transformed into a warm, sympathetic relationship. Two factors have been on his side without which his
case would, in my opinion, have been hopeless; even in his
darkest hours he had courage, and secondly he had a capacity
to co-operate which never failed him. He is ceaselessly thank-
ful to God for restoring him 'the years that the locust hath
eaten'.[1]

(NOTE. James, aged 48, was, I believe, a borderline schizo-
phrenic. Mixed with his schizoid depression were hysterical
dissociations, and a homosexual deviation. At times he showed
the features of a severe depressive personality with its masochism and melancholia. Depressive hypochondriasis was
shown by palpitations and severe dyspepsia. There was a
danger that he might succumb to katatonic schizophrenia, and
there were phases when this was an all too real possibility.)

The Unconscious

We often find ridicule, hostility and impatience when

[1] His vicar wrote: 'May I say what I have been meaning to write and say
for a long time—how very grateful I am for all the help you have been to
"James". He is so wonderfully recovered and it is a great joy to us all. I
know he is more grateful than he can say—and so are we all. I bless the day
I rang you up about him.'
The latest news I have of James is that he, who once was afraid of even
little children, has canvassed for election to his parish council and proved
himself by being successful.

psychological matters are mentioned or discussed. At the root of this, if not a fear of the subject, is a misunderstanding of the extent of the mind. By persisting in thinking of the mind as being synonymous with conscious thought, people fail to appreciate the importance and magnitude of psychotherapy. The mind has often been likened to a tumbler of water, where the nearest film of the surface represents our conscious thought, and the remaining depths the unconscious part of the mind. It fell to Freud's genius to open up this field of the unconscious, and the revelation of its contents constitutes one of the major scientific achievements in the history of man. It would almost appear that we have many minds jostling one another, with now one, and now another coming up into the conscious life or making an influence felt. The unconscious part of the mind has its own thought-life in which are many themes, and upon them a vast number of variations are played. It is a realm with its own laws and patterns of behaviour, and it is by no means the formless chaos we might expect. In this hidden realm there is a reasoning, a vivid imagination, a fantastic memory in which nothing is really lost, a powerhouse of emotion of colossal magnitude, even its own sense of humour which, although usually crude, is a prominent feature of certain dreams.

This unconscious breaks through into consciousness in various ways, of which the dream is the most valuable revelation so far as our analysis is concerned. Day dreams are as useful as those of the night. The unconscious also leads us to make what appear to be senseless mistakes, strange remembering of long-forgotten incidents and forgetfulness of the immediate present. It produces strange mannerisms, and also the compulsions and the tics that we are considering in this chapter, when people are, by an inner compulsion, made to wash their hands many times a day according to a set drill, or to count numbers with a ritual formation, or to think swear words with no provocation whatsoever and which are beyond the conscious mind's control. In chapter VII a number of examples are given of the power of the mind to produce all manner of physical symptoms, and such is the reality and power of the unconscious that it is not at all uncommon for the whole range of the recognized symptoms of a known physical disorder to be reproduced without the person being physically ill at all. Needless to say this is quite factual, and the findings of psychotherapy are verified at every analytic session, so that one is left amazed at the sheer cleverness of the unconscious in the selection of the material it produces in dreams and drawings. People frequently draw or paint scenes without having the slightest conscious intention of presenting them in any particular way; unwittingly, however, they draw faces of people, and the forms of weird animals, all of which have an unconscious meaning. This kind of thing may often be seen in any imaginative painting. I happen to have before me a drawing, presented at the last session with one of my people, which portrays a labouring man with his spade. On his back is a little figure which was described as a manikin. Little did the man who painted the picture realize that the manikin has a considerable psychological significance in that it represents the dwarf god. This dwarf is one of the mythical Cabiri, of which mention is made in *Faust*, who work in the earth as artificers and smiths. They have a naughty, puckish character which bursts the fantasies of inflated pride, and bring down the mighty from their seats from whence they would rule the universe. Also they have the capacity to direct operations from the hidden places of the mind, as though they assist in the navigation of the dark, difficult passages through which the soul must pass. You will notice that this man's manikin was on his back where it could not be seen, it was operating from his unconscious.

The drawing obviously indicates that the man is 'coming down to earth', and he is dealing with the earthly side of his personality. He has removed much of the earth (mother), and his drawing reveals a blue bag which is marked 'gold'. Gold is the sun metal, the possession of which was the goal of the age-long striving of man, long before it was used as currency. Just as the alchemists strove to change the base metal (the instinctual) into gold ('divine humanity'), so the quest of early peoples was the discovery of gold. We are reminded of the streets of gold in the heavenly Jerusalem.

Moreover, on the man's raised spade is some earth, but he did not see that he had drawn the earth in such a manner that it depicted an evil head, which was in black. This symbolized that he was being rid of the devil which seemed to dominate his life, and as this was being done he was discovering his spiritual treasure, spiritual gold. The blueness of the bag which contained the gold represented the spiritual heavens, i.e. his treasure was in a bag which would not wax old. This was an emphasis upon the nature of the real treasures of life. The greenness of the grass on which he was standing represented the freshness of his new life, the freshness of the Spirit Who is the counsellor and guide of man. As in a cloud he represented a figure, very much like our Lord, carrying a Cross up a very steep hill, and he associated himself with that figure. The Cross, which had been drawn in blue, is the supreme reconciling symbol which brings together the horizontal and the vertical, the earthly and the heavenly. It is set in the blue sky, and at the same time is deeply embedded in the brown instinctual earth, which two aspects of the soul must be brought together, and their enmity reconciled. The person who made the picture had said farewell to religion in his youth, and you will easily realize what a joy it is to work out with him the spiritual implications of his material; he was, for the first time, finding his real treasure, on earth as well as in heaven.

Freud saw the unconscious as a great reservoir of repressed material. All that, for one reason or another, was unacceptable to the conscious self was relegated to the unconscious and, lying there, ceased to be under the control of the individual's will. By and large Freud regarded repression as something which takes place unconsciously, and is an automatic process. Jung, on the other hand, allows for an active repression by the conscious, a wilful act of turning away from and resistance against the contents of the conscious, with the result that they are expelled from consciousness.[1] In all such cases a person must accept some responsibility for the pattern of his life, and we can see how many big doors hang on small hinges. However, there are times when Freud is right and we cannot be blamed for repression. For example, a terrifying experience in infancy is too painful to be carried in consciousness, and therefore is repressed. It may be even that in adult life an experience may be so painful that it is repressed, and shell-shock can be an example of just such a phenomenon. These repressed experiences, and their emotions, do not lie quietly buried, but draw into themselves the vitality which should go

---

[1] Cf. *Contributions to Analytical Psychology* (1928), p. 362; *Two Essays on Analytical Psychology* (1953). The reader of these works will note the part which the subliminal plays in the mind.

G

into conscious living; they prevent the natural course of emotional growth so that the adult remains emotionally an infant, and this repressed material exercises a strong influence upon our daily affairs such as we have described above.

It is important to realize that repressions can only be maintained with a considerable expenditure of mental energy, and it is because there is this wasteful use of vital energy that the person is left in a weak and exhausted state, ill prepared to meet the challenges or, indeed, the everyday tasks of life.

Jung has extended the understanding of the unconscious by dividing it into two realms. The first is the Personal Unconscious, which contains all that we have described as belonging to the unconscious, and the second is what is called the Collective Unconscious, in which are stored the great experiences of the race, all those great themes which have exercised the life of man from the beginning. Indeed, we go back into the darkest depths where our life is one with that of the animal kingdom. In view of this it is little wonder that we are afraid of our unconscious. This concept of the Collective Unconscious may seem just too fantastic for words; however, in my small experience I have had themes presented to me on many occasions which take one back into classical times, and these have been brought by people who consciously are unaware of the literary significance of their work. One simple soul brought to me the clearest picture of Mithraic sacrifice, with the pit and the bath of blood from the sacrificed bull. Equally fascinating is the fact that the themes which exercised the minds of those most interesting people, the Alchemists, are very often reproduced in dreams and pictures, and they always have considerable therapeutic value.

This diversion will help towards a better understanding of the matters we are discussing.

A Hopeless Youth

A university student came to me troubled by the unreality of his life which he seemed powerless to change; he was a good Christian fellow in his way. He complained that he was completely self-centred, and was all the time modelling his life upon what other people expected of him. His outer-body presented itself to him as a dangerous bog, offering no security of any kind, and thus he was afraid to venture forth one single step, completely unable to make a gamble of any kind. He further described himself as weak willed, quite incapable of making up his mind on any matter, and equally incapable of living his life in the outer-body which he could call his own. He compensated for this loss of the outer world by giving himself, in fantasy, whatever he desired, and in this way he was able to see himself as a great hero. Various obsessional acts had to be performed: he had to see whether he had locked the door three times and only then would he be satisfied, and there were hand-washing rituals to be observed, together with others related to electric switches. There were also obsessional thoughts such as 'All will go wrong', 'All will be for nothing'; the sight of a church spire would make him say 'There is no God', and a question which constantly forced itself upon his mind was 'Do I believe the pure Christian Gospel?'

Things went badly with him as a baby, for his mother, becoming ill, was only able to feed him for a week or two, and the baby was placed in the care of another woman. The baby soon developed convulsions, of which there were thirty, and these made feeding almost impossible. The atmosphere of the home was another factor in the story, for it was dominated by his mother, who was possessive, whilst the father, not wielding so much emotional power, was dominating in a Victorian way. The child, feeling his life to be excessively controlled and oftentimes severely threatened, had a difficult passage to steer through these troubled seas. The little fellow soon realized that the outer-body was a very difficult place in which to live, and he retreated to the shelter of his inner-body, where the lack of living space was acute, for every attempt he made to express himself, and achieve some measure of independence, was stifled.

The young man, Kenneth by name, saw himself in a dream as a child of ten, dirty and huddled up, crouching on an altar in a church. In this static picture he felt himself to be incapable of making an offering, for he had nothing to give as, he said, 'his natural self had no content'. He felt that he had never possessed a single thing which he could call his own, and therefore he had nothing to give to God or man. His home background was socially good, and on that account he would not have seen himself as dirty and ill-clad save emotionally, where he placed himself with the poorest of the poor. The dirty figure on the altar revealed the dirty, guilt-ridden state of his soul, for there had been anger and bitter hate towards his father and mother for crushing his life and making him so ineffective. His black soul made him incapable of lifting up his head since by doing so he could only expect to see the face of an angry deity. He had nothing to offer because in his earliest experiences his proffered love seemed to be returned unwanted; thus today he has nothing to offer in life, because he would anticipate any offering that he could make being returned to him, with all the hurt that the return would involve him in.

His early experience taught him that he had little or no hope of coping with the outer-body; for him this body would be chiefly feminine, in the person of his strong, possessive mother, and since the feminine is naturally the down-to-earth part of the personality, he found it very difficult to adjust himself to reality. The feminine was his chief enemy; she was hostile, unresponsive, overwhelming and dominating, and thus he turned upon his inner masculine body, becoming detached from feminine company and a healthy, instinctual life, and devoting himself to the masculine and idealistic pursuits. A homosexual situation developed which, as we should expect, was well supported by self-love.

At the present the obsessional elements have almost disappeared, he is learning not to allow himself to be a 'doormat', his newly-found assertiveness and independence is giving him self-respect, no longer is he tormented by a moody petulance, and he has begun to have better relations with the opposite sex. The outer-body, at least at times, has become a wonderful thing in which to live.

(NOTE. Kenneth, aged 27, was a complex layered personality. On the one hand was a minor obsessional neurosis, and a compulsive compliant personality. On the other hand he showed the characteristic features of a paranoid personality—a strong projection of his repressed fear persecution on to the outside world; sensitive to hurts, always on the defensive and on the alert for insults, etc, unbending, quarrelsome, extremist, self-important. At times his placidity was broken by terrible hate and murderous feelings. Greed, which was virtually an expression of his hate, held an important place in his life. He re-enacted a pattern of love-giving, followed by a complete withdrawal of this love from the object, when the love was turned inwards to himself. Repeatedly he would begin to love, but suspicion, and his deep terror of hostility, prevailed. He longed to have his love accepted, but it ever seemed to be at the point of being thrown back at him unwanted and with hostility.

A further complication was his Oedipus complex, with its castration sequence, and this led him to take up a passive feminine position. He simply could not take up a place in the outer-body.)

The Man with 200 Obsessions

A professional man of no small standing recently sought my help and, although I did not like the look of his case sheet, I decided to see what could be done to help him. Everything depended, humanly speaking, upon his ability to co-operate, and he soon demonstrated this ability to an amazing degree. He informed me that he had '200 obsessions' and that he was a clear case of demon possession, which is a natural conclusion to draw when one is being driven, against every conscious effort to the contrary, to perform senseless rituals. He was not the master of his own house, for he was powerless to control both mind and body. He came along with the characteristic doubt of the obsessional, and debated at length whether or not to go forward with the analysis. For some time he remained critical of the procedure, but with the unmistakable improvement in his relationship with his wife and subordinates, and with a slight improvement in other ways, the analysis began to move forward, and before long it was proceeding at a most remarkable rate.

His mother was an exceptionally insecure person, and while her husband was away with the fighting forces, she and her small son lived with the grandmother. This amazing woman, within the space of thirty years, amassed from nothing a fortune which ran into six figures. Needless to say, she dominated the scene, and the child's mother was completely at her mercy. The anxiety of the mother, concerning her husband at the war, was so acute that she would ask her little boy whether his father would come back alive! She was in a constant state of panic, and we can imagine the effect of this upon the small child who, instead of being able to lean upon his mother in the absence of his father, had a mother who was leaning upon him. The child felt completely unprotected and unsupported. Moreover, whilst he lived with the grandmother the home life was far too busy to give him any living space; he was always in the way or doing something wrong, and as soon as he settled down with an interest he was told to do this or that, so that every aim was thwarted. After the war the family moved constantly from one place to another, which went to confirm the instability of all that belonged to the outer-body; for example, between the ages of five and sixteen he went to no less than fourteen schools. However, the real damage was done in the early years when he lived with his grandmother. The influence of the grandmother, both indirectly through her crushing effect upon the mother, and directly through her iron discipline, was a factor of great importance, while to it must be added the fact that the mother had been separated, by illness, from the young baby, and that there had been a breakdown in feeding. Such incidents as these latter ones are to be found at the roots of most of the serious emotional illnesses. There were occasions when the little boy would be crying upstairs for his mother, but when she wanted to go to him the grandmother intervened and forcibly stopped her, and said 'You must break his spirit.' The setting for the child's upbringing was completed by the father who, with his ability to fly into violent rages, came to be regarded by the son as a 'swine'.

The boy fortunately had inherited something of his grandmother's indomitable spirit, for he fought back with commendable gusto. He fluctuated between fighting and capitulation; on the latter occasions, when he found the world too much for him, he wanted to fade out into nothingness. At other times he became a very naughty boy, for which a great variety of punishments were meted out to him. The more he was punished the harder he hit back. But still he was hovering between an outer-body beyond possession, and one which might be possessed. This was often seen in his naughtiness, which his mother said 'was not ordinary naughtiness'. For example, he once walked through a lime pit, on another occasion he cut the sheet of his bed to bits with scissors, while on a third occasion he incurred the wrath of his father by pulling up hundreds of bedding plants which had only just been planted. Such actions as these, as his mother said, were 'not ordinary naughty actions', for there was no conscious intention at all to do them; in fact he was acting in an abstracted and withdrawn state and was never aware of what he was doing. His attention was being wholly absorbed by his inner-body, and was trying to solve a vast emotional complex.

The religious setting was puritanical, and everything enjoyable seemed forbidden. He was never allowed to speak to girls who, according to his mother, were a danger to him, while his father, being an impossible prude, added a generous quota to such instructions. He ended by running off with a barmaid! We can begin to appreciate how difficult life was for the boy, since far too much was expected of him.

Here was a child who, from the beginning of his life, was suffering deeply from feeling shut out from love and life, and it is a strange turn of misfortune that the favourite punishment meted out to him only accentuated the root cause of his sick mind. It is often remarkable how often parental punishments do the worst possible thing for the child. In this case the boy was locked in a cold bare room, which epitomized his unconscious emotional terror. In a less spirited person that treatment might well have had disastrous results in that it might have been the last straw to break his contact with his outer-body, establishing, had the genetic factors been present, the deep splitting which we associate with schizophrenia; it would have been the completion of the grandmother's work of breaking his spirit. However, in the present case the child fought back by shouting through the locked door that he would jump through the window to the ground below if they did not come and let him out. He would open the windows with great noise, and make most audible preparations, by way of moving furniture, for the act. Thus punishment produced in the boy the objectionable trait of the cunning deceiver, and this persisted; he was determined by fair means or foul to obtain that of which he had been deprived in life. School was Hell to him. He held the distinction of being the most caned boy of the school, which was the only distinction he ever gained at school.

The boy felt himself to have been robbed on every side

of life, but his mother taught him to be absolutely honest; in the conflict between these two opposite poles he chose to seek what he considered to be his rights, and he merrily stole on all possible occasions. It was a game to be played, and it gave him considerable satisfaction, though he did not want what he took, nor did he realize that what he was really trying to possess was love. His dreams were of things being stolen, and his sexual frustration led him to steal in this field of forbidden fruits. In all his nefarious activities he was proud of his deceptions, and his nasty ways gave him no twinges of bad conscience, for he had repressed his moral sense and his wickedness merely swelled his conceit. 'I hate people,' he said, and the reason he gave for this was that they always wanted to injure him. The outer-body for him contained fruits to be stolen, as well as a vast body of prohibition and privation. He rejected the standards and the responsibilities of that realm, and lived only for the pleasures of the inner-body. Indeed the only use he had for the outer-body was that it provided a hunting ground for his hungry instincts.

The analysis so far has corrected this repressed morality, and he now possesses a moral sense previously unknown to him. In addition there is a considerable improvement in his social life, so that, for example, he has undertaken work of greater responsibility and inconvenience without any return of financial gain. The obsessions have shown a most encouraging reduction both in number and intensity. His wife tells me that he is a different person in every way, the family relationship has been transformed, and these rapid changes show promise of an eventual liberation from all his obsessions.

(NOTE. The case of this man, aged forty-three, was complex by reason of various psychic layers. To begin with there was an 'organ inferiority' which dominated his life. Hate, envy and jealousy bore their fruits, and resulted at times in a strong 'paranoid position'. Apart from his obsessional neurosis, his life seemed mainly to run along the lines of a compulsive aggressive personality. His involvement with his mother, added to his 'organ inferiority', produced in him, at other times, a complaint attitude which was nevertheless equally an expression of his compulsive personality. Latent homosexuality was present in good measure.)

The Burden of the Obsessional

Godfrey is a man of thirty; he is married and has a small daughter. He begged me to help him because he was possessed by obsessions which were making his life well nigh intolerable and he could feel himself going to pieces. He is the only son of a worrying mother, and of a father who was kindly but who, during the years before he died, became quick tempered. A fact of considerable bearing upon his illness was that he slept in his parents' bedroom until he was six. When only thirteen months old he had an operation, which was repeated a few years later. Such events can easily be interpreted as punishments for infantile fantasies which abound in early years, and which mostly are of a sexual nature. These would be stimulated by sleeping in the parental bedroom. He recorded a nightmare which he had when he was about five years old, of a man riding a horse which dashed into a cupboard in his bedroom; he can feel today the terror of that dream. Here was something he had kept locked up in the deep emotional cupboard of his mind; besides the horse and rider he had a skeleton of his own hiding there which was really the cause of his deep fear. Whether the dream is interpreted along Freudian or Jungian lines the result is the same; sex has become a terrifying thing, full of danger and aggression.[1] In view of this it is interesting to note that one of his obsessions involves the storing of cigarettes in a cupboard in the shop where he works; he must not touch the back or the sides of the cupboard that holds them, and if such contact is made he must wipe his nails and put the cigarettes back once more in the cupboard but this time with them resting on the back of his hand.

Whenever he goes to a service in the cathedral of the town where he lives swear words crowd into his mind, and do what he will he cannot control them. Some light was shed upon this by a dream he reported in which a fair was being held in a town to which he wanted to go, but his mother said 'there is a service in the cathedral', and she asked him if he intended to be present. At this point in the dream he felt afraid, but he knew he had to go to the service. It is

---

[1] I am aware that the uninformed reader may be mystified somewhat by this paragraph, but on account of the sexual nature of the nightmare I thought it advisable, in a book of this kind, not to amplify its meaning.

clear that we have here a picture of the conflict between his natural desires to enjoy himself, and the authority of his mother whom he feels to be very much on the side of God. He wants to possess his outer-body and all the pleasure it brings, but this leads him into conflict with Him Who has power to cast him into Hell. He could do nothing but submit to so great a power, while all the time his repressed hate towards God and all his other enemies burns in his unconscious, for they are making unnatural and cruel demands upon him.

Another compulsive ritual is his counting up to sixteen, during which he says to himself that if he does not count this number something will happen to him, and if he does not count the number twice a dreadful thing will happen to his wife, while if he does not count it three times the dreaded thing will happen to his mother, and finally, to put himself in the clear without a doubt, he must round off the counting by a fourth time of performing, by which he has squared the four in the sixteen he has counted.

He also has to walk on the pavement lines, and frequently wash his hands, Pilate-like. All these rituals serve a secret purpose which is closely guarded by the unconscious. They are preventative of some unconscious wish, usually a death wish, we may assume, taking place. Any person with imagination will realize the torment which such rituals bring into life, and also the sheer waste of a life, which could otherwise be spent in energetic service to God and man.

The man is making progress with his obsessional problem, and also with the other aspects of his disorder. Both his wife and mother have, more than once, expressed their gratitude for the change which has taken place in him.

Another man I am helping has a tic which has been the plague of his life from his early childhood, besides which he has many rituals. He must test whether or not he has locked the doors of his house a certain number of times, he has to go through a performance with the sheets on his bed before he can get into it, a ritual has to be performed with the knife on the meal table, or with the book he is reading, when he drinks he must bite the edge of the tumbler, and he must return many times to see whether his bicycle has been left in top gear. I once met someone who took three hours every day to dress, and the same time to undress, so elaborate were his rituals—six hours a day for one's toilet!

These obsessions often take a religious twist, as with an undergraduate who was so obsessed with the thought of the Second Coming that he could not concentrate upon his work, but wandered around the streets incapable of giving his mind to his studies. Under the circumstances the ignorant may say that religion has turned his mind, and that he was 'too religious'. We can hear them saying 'a little religion, does not do anyone much harm, but too much of it is positively dangerous'! The fact is that the religious issue happened to be the most convenient peg on which to hang his obsession, and it could easily have been anything other than a religious concern. All these people have a serious diffi-culty with the outer-body in their everyday living, and when we look at the causation we find that a major frustration towards a natural life in the outer-body has taken place, a frustration so great in magnitude that it was shattering.

A very happy, though rare, occasion was a recovery, after only three sessions, from a compulsion to lie. It is the story of an attractive young married woman for whom life could have been very rosy, but who developed a compulsion to tell lies, and not little white lies but full grown black ones. Do what she could she had to tell them, without rhyme or reason, on all occasions. She, in common with all obsessional people, became deeply concerned lest she should be going mad for she no longer had control over her actions. Her worry became intense, so much so that it may have had something to do with her miscarriage which took place at the time of her emotional disturbance. Her relationship with her husband became seriously strained, and everything seemed to be set full steam ahead for the rocks. The turning point was the analysis of a dream brought to the third session in which she recalled a repressed incident. As a small child she had disobeyed her mother by playing with an older girl who lived nearby, and as a result of the disobedience there was an experience of a sexual nature which seemed to her to be so dreadful that it was repressed. Doubtless it was inter-preted as a consequential punishment. As soon as the incident was recalled she could not wait for any more of the session, and she went straight to her mother to tell her the whole story. From that moment she was a new person, the compulsion vanished, and now she is fully occupied with the tasks of motherhood.

In our search for definite origins of mental illness we may, in certain cases, look in vain. One or two items are cleared up, and we hope this is the end of the matter, yet the unsatisfactory living continues abated. In one of the above obsessional cases I found no single incident which was the final slamming of the door upon endeavour, but rather an over-all, almost indefinable, crushing by means of sentimentality and emotional pressure. The child had always the impression that if he asserted his will against his parents he would not be loved, and thereby he would lose every vestige of security. The pattern was: 'If you do that, I shall not love you . . . or God will not love you.' He commented that his efforts to break out from his smothering surroundings into the outer-body would be as ineffective as the passage of a bullet through cotton wool. In the cases where nothing outstanding is forthcoming I look for a general adverse atmosphere in infancy and early childhood, of which no particular instance may be seen. This method has wider application than the search for a particular cause of an obsessional disorder. I have in mind such general conditions as would be found in the home where love has died between the parents, or where little interest is shown in the children, and where people merely exist. I am coming to the opinion that such conditions as these are almost as important as the traumatic events which obviously cause deep hurt to the Self. The absence of real love between the parents may be the cause of a major withdrawal from the outer-body, and a state of deepest unease within the inner.

Harmful Effects of Parental Disharmony

A young woman of a definite schizoid type was born into a world which she sensed did not want her, and this fact laid the foundation of her unhappy condition. It would not have been nearly so devastating if the parental relationships had not deteriorated further into open hostility. She felt herself to be 'contained' by her parents until she was eight years old, at which time everything seemed to go wrong between her father and mother. By 'contained' she meant held by them in a relationship. She stated that during the next two years she began to want to be an independent self to some degree, but agoraphobic feelings at once intervened, and she felt hopelessly lost in the big world of her outer-body; however, when she retreated wholly into her inner-body terrifying questions presented themselves with obsessional insistence: 'Who am I?', 'Why am I living?', 'What is the *me* when I am alone?' These questions drove her back to her parents, from whom she felt she must have answers to her vital questions, which characteristically arise at that age, regarding birth, children, and sex in general. No answers were forthcoming from her mother, not soley because sex was a banned subject, which was bad enough in itself, but more important to her by far, because the unsatisfactory relationship between her parents itself presented, rather than answered, a problem. She could not put them together in love, therefore there arose the question: 'Whose child am I?', and 'What am I?' Because there was no togetherness in her parents, she could find no togetherness in herself; as she said 'I do not make a self.' She affirmed that the discovery of her own reality would only come through a new awareness of her parents as genuine parents.

The problem of the parents of another person was presented in a drawing which was divided into two parts. The man drew himself as bound hand and foot to the separate corners of a rectangle, fastened to which were two harnesses, the one on the right being attached to a bull, and that on the left to a horse, the animals facing in opposite directions. The lower half of the picture showed a strong masculine hand which held all the hair which it had torn from a now bald head. This person had a serious sexual problem. At an extraordinarily early age he was having sexual relations with little girls of his own age, in which, he said, he was trying to solve the fundamental relations between his father and his mother.

His mother had a biting tongue, which she did not spare upon her husband, who was a weak character. He well recalls his mother's words as she thrashed his father with her tongue, and he could still see the father in tears because life was too difficult for him, and he remembers how bewildered he was with it all. His father, a neurotic who could not hold his work, and who never arose early enough in the morning to find employment, caused much of this unpleasantness in the home. There were times when his mother said she was going to stand it no longer. On these occasions she informed the family that she was going to leave them, and on one vividly remembered occasion she actually packed her bag and began to walk out. It is easy to imagine the terror this would cause in the mind of the child. The father would add to this insecurity, for he would disappear from the home for long periods, so that the little boy never knew when his father would be at home. On coming home from school he would wonder whether his mother would be there, or whether there would be a great row proceeding between his parents. In the end his father left home for good, and the financial position of the home became very serious. However, the child's sexual problem was deeper than a hunger for the pleasures of life which had not come his way, and for lack of which he turned to his inner consolations; it was a deep desire and quest for a profound loving relationship. The outer-body presented an insoluble problem of disintegration, disunity and hostility, and there seemed to be no way in which he could come to terms with it. His drawing depicted the conflict not only between his parents, but also the pulling asunder of his own soul, which their conflict had created in him.

I also think of another young man, with schizoid components in his disorder, who had been divided at a deep sexual level by his father and mother; at least their one-sided relationships inflamed his already existing division. He was one of two brothers. The father gave all his affection and attention to him, whilst all that of his mother was given to his brother. The result was that neither of the boys possessed both parents, and a deep emotional fissure followed.

The last of these instances I shall give of the effect of parental disharmony upon the growing child was presented to me by way of a drawing. In the picture the young man had placed himself between both his parents, whom he was viewing through a pair of binoculars, the lenses of which were turned almost at right angles; he was focused upon his mother, but his vision was all wrong for the father. Both parents were riding horses and these were facing opposite directions. There is reference in this picture, so it was found, to the small child being present in the parental bedroom, and to his having witnessed more than he should. We have mentioned the fantasies which this arrangement helps to produce in the infant mind, and in this case they doubtless led to a deep confusion between the masculine and the feminine rôles; this made his later life receptive of the full impact of his parents' disharmony.

I think I shall do best by passing on to you some of the comments he made at the session when the picture was being discussed. He said he was trying to put his father and mother together, trying to see them together. They were to him separate entities, and this had given rise in early life to such fundamental questionings as: 'To whom do I belong?', and 'Where do I fit in?' It seemed to him that he had the choice of one or the other of his parents, which, in a deep emotional way, had caused him to split. He asked: 'If I do not belong to one of them how can I exist? Who am I? I can only solve the mystery of my existence by putting father and mother together.' He was struggling to find himself born of love. He said: 'Now I know why I cannot marry, it is because I know simply nothing of the relationship between man and wife.' He proceeded to ask himself the question: 'Why?', to which he answered: 'It is because I have never seen my father and mother together spiritually; my unity should spring from their unity.'

There should be a triangle in which father, mother, and child form the three sides. If one side is missing the unity and meaning is destroyed, so that father and mother together are incomplete without the child, just as the child is incomplete unless the father and mother are joined together spiritually.

All this explained why, as a child, he always insisted upon walking between his parents, and he would never walk beside only one of them. He had something of a compulsion to tie shoe laces together, which he now related to his unconscious need to tie together his parents. For many years he had been subject to an obsession of writing his name, which he now explained as an attempt to know himself and express himself as a Self, for he said: 'I don't know that I exist.' Also, he felt this was the reason for his always trying to prove himself to the outsider: 'I must put myself over to others,' he said.

He wisely observed that, when parents teach their children that sex is wrong, it divides the parents themselves from one another. He felt that his mother must have been as a nun to his father, which caused him to ask the bewildering question: 'How can I be the child of my parents?', and 'Whose child am I?' As no answer to these questions was forthcoming he felt deeply unrelated, and that he had no place in the outer-body.

In all such cases it is to be taken as certain that the lack of love between the parents was sensed long before it became apparent to the infant, and it would elicit a reaction both profound and enduring. The importance of the outer-body, of which the parents are the supreme representatives, is clearly exemplified by this material of which more examples could be given.

One of the persons I have just mentioned asked how she could put together her parents when they were still emotionally separated, to which I suggested in answer two things: first, the child would greatly exaggerate in his mind the whole content of the situation so that the good aspects would be swamped by the bad. Thus the actual situation would not be as bad as the deeply involved child would think. And second, through psychological insight the parents would be better understood. Their individual unconscious motivations, reaching far back into their own infancy, could be given due consideration and be seen to have played their parts in the later relationships of man and wife. An analysis gives such understanding, goes back and views the old scene, but now sees it far less emotionally, and the result is that *in his mind* he is able to put the parents together. I have often found the much-given advice to leave home, in order to be separated from the parents, has anything but the desired result, for the simple reason that the upsetting parental disunity is carried with them however far away from home they go. It is good for 'a man to leave his father and his mother', but only when there has been established a new understanding of the parents, and the old infantile reactions have been worked out.

The relationship with the parents is important because of the processes of identification, in which all children are involved. They impersonate other people, and their parents in particular; this is an essential process of growth, and it shows again the importance of the outer-body. Where the example and attitude of the parents is harsh and overbearing, this can only result in an exacting Super Ego, and so the child's standards and ideals inevitably carry the stigma.

There is an obverse side of this parental problem, which is observed when the parents are so wrapped up in themselves that the child feels there is no room for him; it is as though the parents themselves have devoured all the available love. It easily leads the child to see himself as an investment, and to feel that his purpose in living is to add all that he has to the parental coffers. A student has poured forth to me his bitterness towards his parents for such circumstances. In fact, he once told his mother that he hated her, and that he could take up the garden fork and stick it in his father. These parents were for ever playing upon the 'gratitude to parents' theme, and they were most possessive of their only son. In this case the outer-body was wholly extractive, and the response to its excessive demands was a withdrawal into the inner-body where he could call his soul his own.

Such then are the troubles of those who cannot live in their outer-body, and their story is as sad and as tragic as any one could meet. I hope I have succeeded in showing that these people can be helped, and some of them restored through an effective and patient ministry. The Church today, if she will train her priests, has the opportunity of bringing this tremendous service of love to a vast number of people who, in a profound sense, are lost to the world and to God. Unless we minister to them they will remain without hope in the world. We shall return to this subject in a later chapter.

We have so far been dealing with people who have had serious difficulty in dealing with the outer-body, and on that account have become basically introvertial, that is to say they face the total conflict as if what was important was to be faithful to their inner subjective demands. They do not really invest emotional energy in the outer-body, because of all the hurtful things that happened when, as children, they had attempted to do this. The outer-body at best appears unfriendly and unresponsive, and at its worst positively dangerous and hostile. The real introverts are, of course, the schizoid personalities, and a number of these are mentioned in this

H

chapter, and also in chapter VII where they are found beneath the hysteria. A number of the types mentioned have also obsessional characteristics and are a queer mixture of introversion and extroversion. I have described them as introvertial in this chapter on account of their inability to free themselves from their static position and enter the world about them with full commitment.

I will conclude this chapter with a story which concerns a rural dean, an archdeacon and a bishop. The rural dean, who is a very busy person, had given much time to a certain man in his parish who had a problem concerning 'Time'. After many abortive hours of discussion with the man, the rural dean referred him to the archdeacon, possibly a still busier man, who gave his most valuable time to the problem of 'Time', with the same fruitless result. All that remained now was to send the man to the bishop, who was a scholar of repute, although considerably busier even than the archdeacon and weighed down with the care of all the churches. The good bishop gave the man an hour-and-a-quarter of his most precious time, but the result was even worse than before, for the poor man was more befogged than ever! As a time saver psychology has much to commend it, for the man was another of our obsessionals, all of whom have a problem of 'Time'. Had he discussed his problem until doomsday with all the archangels in heaven, he would still have been unconvinced.

FIVE

THE OUTER-BODY

WE have seen the results of the disastrous retreat from the outer-body to the suffocating confines of the inner-body, and we shall now turn to consider what happens when the reverse takes place. This evasion of the inner area of life will prove to be as futile as the escape from the outer area, although for a time people may be able to mislead themselves into thinking that by such an evasion they can make life satisfactory and effective. The inner-body is far too vast and mysterious an entity to ignore, for the Spirit, who resides in these depths, will give us no peace until we have recognized its enormous significance and come to terms with it. Man must face his inner-body, both in order to live at peace with himself, and to find peace in his surround, and if he fails to do this no amount of external adjustment will make any difference to his unhappiness or inefficiency.

A variety of alternatives may be tried however. Thus rather than face his own inner uncertainties and weaknesses, a person may project them into an area of objectivity where they can be criticized, condemned, or laughed at with impunity. The case of the Woman taken in Adultery (JOHN viii. 3) was one where the Pharisees and Scribes projected on to the woman their own sexual desires, and their own guilt. It was so much easier to accuse her than to accuse themselves, but Our Lord, with profound psychological insight, dealt very effectively with the situation.

If we have failed to come to terms with our own innermost fears, then all attempts to ignore them or suppress them are bound to fail. The fears remain, intangible, ghost-like, unrecognized, lurking in the deep waters of the unconscious, and penetrating the realm of the outer-body in many disturbing ways. We are all afraid, to varying extent, of the deep levels of the inner-body, and this fear sometimes reveals itself as a fear of psychology: when people describe psychology as 'dangerous' they only reveal their fear of that within themselves which fills them with foreboding. Frequently the task of the analyst, during an analysis, is to help the sick person to interpret these vague and unnamed fears in order that he may see them for what they are, and face them rather than try to evade them. In order to achieve this end the analyst makes use of almost any material that the person can produce; thus drawings made by the person often contain forms and shapes, quite unknowingly, that the analyst is able to recognize, and which he can help the patient to interpret.

However, the attempt to project one's inner fears on to external objects, and the attempt to ignore them, are not the only means by which people try to evade the emotions of the inner-body. Occasionally one finds that a person moves into the outer world of idealism and abstraction, and of excessive intellectualism. In such cases the head is being used as an escape from the heart, because the heart is threatening life with unpredictable and explosive instinctual forces.

And as our last example we might consider the attempt to escape from the inner dangers through excessive activity in the outer-body, which activity, by its thoroughness, has the additional attraction of winning public commendation. The people who take this course may be numbered amongst those who are on every committee, who have a finger in every pie, and who cannot be seen for the dust they stir. The rush and bustle of present-day life suits their purpose admirably. These people cannot bear to be alone with themselves, or to sit quietly and listen to others speaking; they will have something to say on all occasions regardless of its relevance. The wireless set and the television, sporting attractions and the pools, and many other suchlike diversions, have value to those who wish to hide from their inner selves.

A common example of this evasion of the inner-body is that of middle-aged persons who suddenly collapse. There has been a pattern of success seeking, a ladder-climbing from one height to another in the world, which inevitably leads to dissatisfaction, for they have both neglected their inner being and put their trust in activity which cannot be sustained. The day comes when it dawns upon them that nothing more can be achieved, and they see themselves being surpassed by younger men. In one last supreme effort they force themselves to reach a higher step only to find themselves failing, whereupon they fall headlong into illness. Everyone offers appropriate comment: 'He has been working too hard,' which is true enough! or 'He is too conscientious,' or 'He must take a well deserved holiday'! A more discerning appraisal of the situation sees in it the consequence of the evasion of the inner-body, and that behind the driving activity lies an all-too-painful sense of weakness and inadequacy. It may be that in the inner-body they feel nothing but the shattering experience of being unloved, stemming from infantile privations; their only hope, therefore, appears to be in the outer-body, where by their excessive works they can win esteem and significance. By one means or another they are forced to realize that the outer-body cannot sustain them, and they are thrown back upon all the hopelessness of the neglected inner-body.

Manhood Regained

A man of thirty-five sought help as he had come to the end of his tether. One could hear his teeth chattering, his eyes were staring, perspiration was standing on his forehead and he looked generally emaciated. His work had become too difficult for him, he could not sleep, and he was spending more and more of his time in day dreams in which he was doing a better class of work than that in which he was engaged. Often he saw himself in charge of many workpeople, or he would be popular by winning much money, and in general being most acceptable to people. He felt himself to be emotionally 'bottled-up', passive and listless, and he was sexually impotent. Intellectually he was above the average, although he had been given meagre educational opportunities. However, he had used his intellect well since leaving school and with hard work established himself. For example when adding machines were to be installed in his office, he had asserted that he could work faster than the machines, and when a test was made he fulfilled his claim.

On the whole his parents seem to have been good to him, although as a child he was undoubtedly left too much by himself, and this apparent neglect aggravated his earlier hidden fears. He told of an occasion when he was alone in the house, and a fire broke out: the protective mother was not there, indeed no one who mattered was there and, as he told his story, one saw again all the evidence of his childhood panic. A further incident was recalled to mind and proved to be important for the understanding of his neurosis. It occurred at school, where the mother figure was taken over in its negative aspect by the teacher, a woman, who thrashed him unjustly before his fellow classmates. In the connection we may see a precipitating cause of his breakdown, though it is important to realize that these 'causes' in no sense account entirely for his illness. Later in life, he, ever expecting rises in his world of business, was demoted under a reorganization scheme, and the place he felt should have been his was given to another, a woman! Once again it was as if he was being thrashed by the woman; it was for him the last straw and he was thrown back upon his underlying sexual inadequacy. Here lay the kernel of this man's problem, and it was this sexual impotency which necessitated a therapy able to reach down to the deep levels of his mind. No wonder the electric convulsive therapy which he had received in hospital proved to be no real therapy at all, but left him, as he said, utterly unsure of himself or of his place in the world. These incidents, which are merely a selection chosen from many similar ones, geared all too well into the basic pattern of his life, and accentuated his anxiety and deep sense of inferiority. A few months after leaving hospital he felt worse than ever before, and loath to return there he came seeking what help he could from St Margaret's Clinic.

But the man had courage, and he tried to cope with his emotional deficiency mainly by relying solely upon his intellect. This was his compensation for the sense of inferiority which his loss of masculinity had produced. Within the inner-body his position was weak in the extreme for he had no real understanding of his secret self, and this lack of understanding of his 'within' led him desperately to cling on to anything or anyone who seemed to offer him a place in the outer-body. The maintenance of his contacts there, became for him the acid test of his worth. Hence all his day dreams were of great achievements in the world and of his easy acceptance there. But there, too, he was 'up against it' for his sense of masculine

inferiority made every woman a challenge to him, and a
challenge which he dare not take up, for always in his fevered
imagination the woman appeared as his superior. When the
teacher caned him unjustly, and the woman was given his
place at work, all his hidden fears regarding himself as not
being a man were unhappily confirmed. The outer-body
would not sustain him after all, in spite of all his efforts to
find a niche there, and thus he was thrown back again upon
himself and all the fears which he had buried deep within.

It would, I feel, be out of place in a book of this kind to
describe in detail the nature of those infantile sexual fantasies
which so profoundly distorted his life, and were the major
cause of his neurosis. But they were there deeply buried in
his unconscious, and were the source of an enormous amount
of 'unconscious' guilt. Little by little, through the analysis
of his dream material, they were brought to consciousness.
They were 'confessed' and fully acknowledged, and the
emotions of fear and anger were slowly drained away so that
the festering wound in his mind was cleansed of the 'foreign'
matter and allowed to heal. I do not say they have not left
a scar, but he has been released from the necessity of self-
punishment which had found its expression, hitherto, in his
sexual impotence.

Perhaps it will help some of my readers, unfamiliar with
the technique of dream analysis, if I record here a certain
dream which occurred fairly early in this man's treatment
and, as subsequent events showed, proved to be a turning
point in his long struggle for mental and emotional health.
This then was the dream:

*I was upstairs at work. An inspector brought up a lens,
which I had polished. He said it was not perfect, but that it
would pass. I then went down the stairs to see for myself,
but got into an argument with two men about apples and
potatoes. Then going down more stairs which were a tunnel,
I banged my head on an iron girder. I was absolutely in a
daze, and wondered whether I should be all right again. However, I got to the room at the bottom, which was brightly
lit; when I felt my forehead there was a lump. When I went
to have a look at it my hair lifted up away from my scalp
and there was a big cut underneath.*

'I woke with a terrific headache and felt rotten.'

The first point to notice in the dream is that the man was working *upstairs,* and the fact that the unconscious depicts him in this way is very important. In dream symbolism being 'upstairs' would indicate an excessive reliance upon the intellect, to the exclusion of the more 'down to earth' emotional factors, generally associated with the heart rather than the head. Thus the first sentence in the account of the dream tells us that the man, after several weeks of treatment, was still relying upon his intellect excessively. Nonetheless the treatment so far had done him some good, and had begun to make an impression. The unconscious in the dream is endeavouring to bring about this change in attitude.

An inspector brought up a lens which I had polished. He said it was not perfect, but that it would pass. Here his free associations revealed quite clearly that *one* meaning of this item in the dream had reference to myself as analyst. I was the inspector who brought him the lens in the dream, the lens being an aid to vision; but notice that the dream claims that he, the dreamer, had done the polishing. It is a charming little piece of criticism of myself, and of the whole business of the analysis. The instrument which I bring to the work, viz. analysis, is not quite good enough for our friend. He must make it intellectually 'brighter'.

The inspector said that it was not perfect, but that it would pass. He accepts my criticism of his over-intellectual attitude, and is prepared to pursue the analysis under my guidance; and further, as his free associations showed, by what is known as Reversal, that he still harboured some criticism of the instrument of analysis, for, as he said, 'it was not perfect'. But, and this is the important thing, he is ready to give it a trial, and, therefore, the prognosis is encouraging.

I then went down the stairs. The phrase indicates movement, and therefore a change of position. This is essential if healing is to be effected, and moreover the direction of the movement gives further encouragement in that it symbolizes a taking into account the deeper emotional factors that are excluded by being 'upstairs'. Despite the hours that the man had spent in my room prior to this dream, his unconscious had not, until the dream, really committed itself to the analysis, i.e. the man had been reluctant to move from 'upstairs', and had actually resisted any tendency to movement.

During the treatment of any neurosis the analyst constantly finds himself up against such resistances offered by the unconscious of the person being treated. These resistances have to be patiently overcome before the next stage of the analysis can proceed, and it is just this factor that makes the analyst's work so painstaking.

(I) got into an argument with two men about apples and potatoes. He does not get very far before he finds himself involved in conflict, and, as we learn from his associations, this conflict has to do with his father represented in the dream by the *two* men, i.e. two aspects of his father as he 'experienced' him. At this level there were problems of a homosexual nature, problems which were intensified for him by a certain incident which had occurred in adolescence. There was guilt here in considerable quantity, as we might expect from the dream reference to 'apples and potatoes' (Fr. *pommes de terre*) *the* forbidden fruit which lay buried in the 'dirty' earth of his soul.

Then going down more stairs, which were a tunnel, I banged my head on an iron girder. I was absolutely in a daze and wondered whether I should be all right again. His psychological journey becomes increasingly difficult, and he gets hurt. The shock of his emotional discoveries plays considerable havoc with him, and he begins to question his further usefulness. His erstwhile intellectual evasion of reality suffers a severe shock. Moreover, let us observe that in the dream his hurt is self-inflicted. It is a grievous self-punishment for all the mischief he has done down here in the tunnel. This punishment was indeed very real. It had maimed his life and had deprived him of his sense of manhood.

However, I got to the room at the bottom which was brightly lit; when I felt my forehead there was a lump. When I went to have a look at it, my hair lifted up away from my scalp and there was a big cut underneath. So here in the depth of his mind, 'the bottom room', he comes face to face with himself, and what he sees is the evidence of his sexual mutilation.[1] As so often is the case, at the centre of this man's problem lies the 'castration complex'.

Perhaps I ought to add that the analysis of the substance

[1] C. Berg, *The Unconscious Significance of Hair*, London, Allen & Unwin, 1951.

of this dream took many hours and used up many sessions. Only bit by bit did the truth come to the surface. The fantasies that he had experienced in his childhood had brought him into great conflict with his father, towards whom he had developed an unconscious 'death wish'. Consequently I was not surprised to learn that, immediately after his father's death, he had been taken quite seriously ill and had been confined to bed. Moreover his unconscious sexual fantasies had been associated with sadistic aggressiveness, and thus had been heavily guilt-laden. Such possible aggression, with all its associations could not be risked in real life, and thus the young man had taken what appeared to him to be the safest course under the circumstances, viz. to rule sex out of his life completely.

Under the conditions outlined, a normal and happy man and wife relationship is impossible. The young man in question is married with a family, but it was inevitable that his home life should be subjected to considerable strain, since the guilt that had become associated with sex was projected on to his wife and children. He would unconsciously want to isolate himself from this guilt, and this would result in an attempted isolation of himself from his family in every sexual regard. But behind his wife stood his unsatisfactory infantile relationship with his mother, a relationship that was underlined by the action of the teacher who thrashed him in school, and still later by the woman who achieved a position in work that might have been his.

Among the fantasy stories and pictures that he produced were two of a church (St Margaret's) in which he portrayed light and joyful music. Set free from his guilt fantasies the great mother figure appeared now under the guise of the Church. And this was understandable since he had come to feel that it was indeed through the ministry which the Church had freely extended to him that he found his way to the light and happiness which now was his. As he once said to me: 'However much the average person pretends God does not matter, He does help.' Before his analysis his religion meant but little to him, but under the influence of this therapeutic measure he had come to a new evaluation of it. This new evaluation was beautifully and spontaneously expressed in another drawing which he made towards the end of the

THE OUTER-BODY   123

analysis. It was the picture of the Cross inlaid with diamonds
and precious stones which flashed every colour of the rain-
bow. Thus he expressed what he had found through this
ministry; healing and richness of the personality, forgiveness
in the Name of Christ, and the reconciliation of the heavenly
and the earthly within himself, in the person of our Lord.

(NOTE. The splitting of the good and bad object was
very pronounced, and his repressed rage led him to take up
'The Depressive Position with Anxiety'. From this he
developed a compulsive compliant personality and anxiety
depression. Repressed libidinal fantasies led to a conversion
reaction. His castration complex contributed to a sexual
inversion.)

A Place in the Sun

Another man, whose confidence in life was shattered, found
both his work and family life too much for him. He was the
only child of a very poor home in the slums, whereas his
ancestors were of some importance and social standing. He
treasured as a relic of bygone days a miniature portrait of an
ancestor, and one day, when looking meditatively at it, the
head appeared to turn and look down upon him! Another
reminder of the past was the fine house in which some of
his forbears had lived, and from time to time he would make
a pilgrimage to the place. In his day dreams he pictured himself living in those days surrounded by spacious comfort and
elegance. His only education was that of an elementary
school, and this, with the 'pig-sty' conditions of his early
home life, was a constant grief and irritation to him. His
mother completely dominated his father and was a slattern.
As he grew up his father told him repeatedly that a son's
responsibility was to his parents, and he made him promise
that when he died he would look after his mother, a promise
which lay heavily upon him in later years.

Children never ask to be born, and the less they hear about
what they owe to their parents the better. More often than
not children owe an unpayable debt to their parents, and
obviously something has gone wrong when the old parents
are ignored; but the less the parents say about their children's
responsibility the more likely they are to be appreciated and
cared for in old age. The great debt which we have incurred

from the past must not be paid back into the past, but into the future, to our children. If it is put into the past it will die with the past, but if it is put into the future it will always be bringing considerable capital appreciation to mankind. All too often we find people whose parents regard them as investments in order to bring them credit, or to be a provision for later life, and it is no wonder that this has brought resentment and even bitter hate towards the parents. This hate may not be conscious, but it will be found buried in the mind as an unending bondage to the parents and as a source of guilt. The man whom we are now considering had been given such a burden of parental care.

Nature had been generous to this man by way of intellect, and, seeing himself as puny and insufficient, he used it to give himself place in the world. He told an interesting story of how he became highly skilled in a very technical occupation. After the war he held one of the highest positions in a branch factory of a firm of international fame. The trouble began when the head of the factory announced his intention to resign, and it was quite obvious that the door was opening to a possible further advance in his career, since he had gained for himself a singular reputation at the head office of the company. However, there was the possibility that another man might be given the post, whereupon there followed a most remarkable series of accidents, which took away from him his chance of promotion; it was as though he shied at the last hurdle, and retreated into a dream land where there could be nothing but success. He could say to himself and to others: 'But for those accidents I should have been a man of crowning achievements.' The outer-body gave him none of the guarantees in life which he sought, and the edifice he had so laboriously built, and which he trusted, fell to pieces. It looked to him as if all the king's horses and all the king's men could not put it together again, for now his capacity to work had forsaken him.

As a result of the treatment he went back to work, and by degrees his former capabilities returned; but before this took place there had to be a considerable revaluation of life, which made him a far better man.

There has already been mentioned the excessive use of the intellect as a ruse to obtain a firm foothold in the outer-body.

This is aided and abetted by our society which almost deifies the clever person, and gives him all the prizes no matter how emotionally impoverished he may be. One cannot help but feel that the present pressure which is put upon school-children to obtain scholarships is helping to make an unbalanced and sick nation. The bills will be sent in later unless this over-emphasis is rectified by corresponding emotional development. There must be many children who are led to believe that the only way by which to obtain value is to pass examinations, with the result that the source of personal value comes to reside almost wholly in the outer-body, since intellect is merely a means to an external end. The blame for this is not only to be put upon our system of life, but also on parents who value success in the outer-body as the only prize worth obtaining.

A similar pattern of life is often to be found in girls who have a very pretty sister upon whom are showered all the attentions of people. It would seem that the only way for them to gain a foothold in the outer-body is by specialist activity which usually takes them away from the natural order of life in the inner-body; femininity is forsaken for prowess in sport, or for scholastic or business achievements.

We might add to the above observation that another source of discouragement to the child and youth arises from their parents having reached considerable heights of achievement, and they feel they can never shine in the world amid so great parental light and glory. Under these circumstances they may retreat into the inner-body and become listless, dull and unenterprising. On the other hand, if they fight for a place in the outer-body it will be in a very different place from that in which their parents shone; indeed they are likely to take up a pursuit the very opposite to that of their parents, or, on principle, be nothing but rebels.

(NOTE. The problem of this man, aged thirty-eight, was in the main an Adlerian one, with the inferiority complex in great evidence. He evaded his intolerable position by recourse to sickness.)

The Escape through Intellect

I will give one more brief case history in which the intellect is shown as being used to obtain a place in the outer-body.

He is a young man, well endowed with intellectual ability, who had a most distinguished career at the university. He came along to be helped out of his deep frustration, which was marked by a claustrophobic feeling of confinement and a distressing inability to commit himself to his tasks. In spite of his Christian life he could work up little sense of purpose in his career. His home had been no easy place in which to live, for his father was an invalid and there were times when work was unobtainable. His mother was fussy and over cautious.

Life had been too hard and it had asked of him more than he could give. He had been subjected to toilet training at too early an age, and also religious and moral demands were made of him before he was capable of making a natural and adequate response. The result of all this was that his instinctual life was crushed by a great weight of demands and prohibitions. He had to be a very good little boy. This was made no easier by his mother's constant fussiness, and her undue counsels of caution. All this made his inner-body a difficult thing to manage, there being too many demands made upon it. An example of his mother's fussy ways was that, when at eight years of age he broke his leg, she persuaded him that he must no longer play rough and dangerous games. Thus once again life was presented to him as difficult and threatening. The complete absence of sex instruction made matters worse, and he had to struggle alone with forces within himself which he had come to believe should not be. It is no wonder that his vital contact with the inner- and outer-bodies was not a little withdrawn, and that at no point could he commit himself. His overall insecurity confirmed his attachment to his mother, which attachment, bound up with infantile fantasies, came between him and correct relations with the opposite sex. Finding no living space in the outer-body, all that remained for him to do was to drive himself by his intellect, the one thing of which he was sure, and with which he was so well endowed. But a life unadventurous and devoid of deep feeling became increasingly intolerable to him. This state of affairs has been remedied and his life is happier and more effective than he ever thought possible for him through the psychotherapeutic ministry of the Church.

(NOTE. Aged twenty-eight. A compulsive compliant

personality, with anxiety depression. Oedipus and castration complexes.)

Life was Too Difficult

The patterns of life are generally fluid; at one time a person may take refuge in his inner-body and then at another he may venture forth into his outer-body with a Box and Cox kind of movement; Mr X, a policeman, was such a kind of person. I suspected there was a hidden reason for his selecting this walk of life, and that by becoming a policeman he was both taking himself in charge, and gaining power and control in the outer-body. Early in his service he was given various opportunities for promotion which were in keeping with his expansive phases, but always before long, the retreating and withdrawing pattern was superimposed and the opportunities were lost.

His home life, which was unhappy, was dominated by his father who was excitable and aggressive. On one occasion he blacked his mother's eyes and smashed up the crockery, and such behaviour completely crushed the mother and the two older brothers. The mother, unconsciously compensating for the emotional poverty of her relationship with her husband, lavished her protective care and inordinate affection upon her little son. It may well have been that the elder sons resented this, like Joseph's brethren, for they seemed to regard this little fellow as having nothing but nuisance value. This hurt the small boy, who naturally would rather be with the big boys than hanging upon his mother's skirts. He well recalls one occasion when he wanted to go off with his brothers and they would not have him with them, so instead his mother found him a little girl to play with! His deepest desire was to be a man, like his biggest brother in particular, but he was thwarted in this and he had to retire into a passive feminine position. He became the exemplary good little boy in order to give himself place in the attentions of his elders. He was deeply discouraged from striking out in a masculine way by seeing his father thrash his elder brother unmercifully. He felt that if his brother's self-expression cost so much it was too great a price to pay, and thereby his passivity was confirmed. Another way in which he tried to gain some place in his outer-body was by being a 'smart Alec', and he was often called 'the nib'. But these artificialities were the poorest substitute for the real masculine thing, and they could not sustain his life.

His questions at this time were: 'Why do they hold me back, and not let me live my own life?' 'Why do they all sit on me?' To which questions there gradually formed in his mind the answer: 'It must be that there is something wrong with me.' This conclusion was unconsciously woven into his feeling of sexual inferiority.

He also had a problem which had arisen from his toilet training. Toilet training is a concern which mothers should approach with understanding, for if it is started too soon it puts a demand upon the infant beyond his capacity to fulfil. If the mother could realize that for the child his motions are his chief possessions and, as an expression of his creativity, are offered to her in love, her handling of the situation would surely become more enlightened. As symbols of the child's love, they must not be treated with angry looks and threats of punishment or else the love-life of the child may suffer almost irreparable damage. Love rejected engenders hate, and gives rise to anger, and so these symbols then change into murderous hate and destructiveness, with much consequent guilt. Further, if the former symbol of love is now charged with ideas of dirt, love will become a dirty thing. But that is not all, the organs of elimination have obviously the closest connection, if not identification, with sexuality. Thus when the infant is taught that the motions are dirty and shameful, sexuality may be grievously damaged by becoming regarded as dirty and shameful. This has a particular reference to masculine sexuality which is the outgiving attitude to life. To combat the destructiveness and shamefulness of the motions, and now of sexuality, the infant may hold himself in and become constipated. The constipated attitude in adult life may reveal itself in meanness, and a general unwillingness to give oneself in any respect.

Mr X was such a person in childhood. He well remembers how, as a child, he was always keeping back his motions and this with considerable tension and even pain. It made him distrustful of himself, for not only did no one want what he had to give but also he asked himself: 'What is the state of my inside as a result of retaining such dangerous and destructive substances?' Later he came to view his body as evil, and therefore his sexuality as well, so that he was at war with his natural self. His mother deeply seared into his mind the idea that urination was horribly dirty, and something which must be kept secret. We can imagine the mortification and self-accusation when, through holding himself back, he 'wet his pants'. This, happening, of course, at the most embarrassing moments, such as family gatherings or in a busy street, inevitably brought his mother's wrath and shame upon him. All this feeling regarding his natural functions made a normal sexual relationship difficult.

As if this were not enough, a serious complication had arisen when he was a very small child as the result of accidental self-stimulation. Terrified at what he had done to himself, he ran to his mother to ease his fear, but found her both terrified and angry, so that his terror was intensified and his sexuality distorted even further. It is no wonder that he became impotent as his sense of inferiority increased through parental mishandling. We can now understand the intensity of his need to appear well in the sight of men, and at the same time we can appreciate how natural it was for him, under the circumstances, to withdraw from situations which presented a challenge to his masculinity. He could not afford to be anything other than a 'yes-man'. When he went to work he was most scrupulous in order to find a place in the outer-body, though in fact he defeated his own ends by becoming unpopular in certain quarters through working at very considerable pressure. Through doing more than his stint, his mates thought him to be showing off or trying to make them appear to be going slow.

Ridicule is something which hurts the child very deeply and it makes the relations with the outer-body more difficult to establish. Adults can hardly appreciate the devastation caused to the child's feelings, particularly when he is ridiculed in public. Mr X had been laughed at so often in a scornful way, that when he looks back upon his early life it seems to him to be nothing but ceaseless ridicule. One occasion is of special interest because of its deeper psychological meaning. He was walking with his big brother down a path on which a large snake was lying. The sight terrified him, and he went as white as a sheet. On his arrival home, still ashen,

I

he declared to the family what he had seen, and the response was derisive laughter. He can still feel the petrifying effect it had, and the feeling that there was no way of coping with the situation. In that snake he was confronted with what was vital to his existence, viz. the symbol of masculinity, his libido, and knowing his profound distrust of his masculinity we can appreciate why the ridicule petrified him. That laughter was felt to be derision for his lost manhood, for which he held himself to blame.

Despite the presence of obsessional elements, which made analysis difficult, he made considerable improvement, so that his home life is much happier and his relations with men are stronger. He has himself experienced a renewed awareness of the spiritual aspects of life, the result of which is that he has become a churchgoer, and the latest news we have of him is that he has been appointed to an official position in his church. Through the improvement in the home relationships his wife was Confirmed.

(NOTE. Mr X, aged forty, was an obsessional personality, with anxiety depression. The treatment was Adlerian in the main. There was 'organ inferiority'. Libidinal fixation at the anal phase.)

Father's Footsteps

Our main consideration in this chapter so far has been with those people who have used their outer-body as an evasion of the demands which the inner-body makes. It now remains to say something about those people who put up a fight to possess both the inner- and the outer-bodies.

Help was sought by a professional man in his fifties. His condition was not serious but it was sufficiently unsound to cause him sleeplessness, a strong feeling of failure and an excessive drive to resist it, and a general claustrophobia. Neither his inner-body nor his outer-body was big enough. His story was one of a life frustrated from its earliest years. His father, who was of the same profession, spent many years away from his family so that the boy was given an overdose of his mother, was described as 'a dear', though she was evidently neurotic and took refuge in numerous illnesses. The father was an irascible gentleman of the sternest Victorian piety. Under such conditions we can easily picture the child feeling insecure, fearful of the distant father of terrifying dimensions, and so becoming excessively dependent upon his mother. From time to time the father came home and the boy's discipline was tightened, but even during the periods of absence stern letters, with considerable expectation of scholastic achievement, were written to him. No occasion was lost to stress the need to take every opportunity to ensure that he would be successful in life.

The boy longed to live a life which he could call his own, and to develop his own style of self-expression. The stern control of the father, along with the increasing demands for success and right living, were introjected into his own conscience and became to him the voice of God. Until the time of the analysis God was for him the terrifying figure of the Old Testament. In theory he knew the love of God in Jesus Christ, but in experience He was to him the dispenser of the wrath of God.

The feeling of inadequacy sprang from the narrowness of his inner confines, but over and above this was added the impossible standard of behaviour and achievement which he demanded of himself. No one could be more conscientious at his work than he, in fact every single minute of the day had to be accounted for, and should he be idle for a moment feelings of guilt would come upon him. He tried to carry on his own shoulders the responsibility of the whole world in which he lived, and he regarded everything to be dependent upon him and him alone. He held himself responsible when anything with which he was concerned failed or did not come up to the highest standard.

We should expect that under these slavish conditions this person would become more sensitive to what other people thought of him; this was the case, and he was sustained by the good opinion of other people which he laboured so hard to win. He was, on this account, enslaved to people everywhere. However, the severest bondage was to his father, whose approval he was ever seeking, and in another way to his mother. He was angry that his father should control and limit his life, and he also bitterly resented that he should be subtly bound to his mother. She had a power over him which made him fume and fret, and this was projected on to his wife, who inflamed his anger all the more because she had something of his father's efficiency and strong demand. She seemed to be able to do everything better than he, and with her intensive life she was taking up the room he should have in the world. This only led him to redouble his efforts towards his own efficiency and success.

When the subject of vocation was considered it was found that he did not really want to follow his father's footsteps, but he had felt this to be essential in order to gain his father's approval. He even followed his father's pattern to the extent of going abroad and doing there the same kind of work that his father did. We are not surprised that he broke down under the strain of unconscious rebellion, and that he had to return home.

Here is a man whose life had been plagued by endless frustration and by an enforced endeavour to be what he did not want to be. No wonder he felt his life to be claustrophobic. His final breakdown was a rebellion, born of the Spirit, against being confined both within the inner-body and the outer-body of his surround. He longed to know the fullness of life within both these bodies. He had a dream in which he saw an hotel on the front of a seaside resort, in the garden of which there was a concrete wall concealed with nasturtiums; this wall completely hid from view a glorious expanse of sea, and a very delightful bathing beach. He felt in the dream that the wall must be removed so that all might be fully enjoyed. The feminine flowers were a covering for the restricting barrier of the mother, as strong as concrete. Under the treatment the wall was demolished, and he was set free from the hotel which had an association with his old tutor, and who in some measure represented his father. Thus the root causes of what had kept him from the enjoyment of his life were removed. In vain he had tried to enjoy himself within his inner-body and to possess the happy world without; both of these are now his own possession as the result of a brief analysis.

(NOTE. Age fifty-six. A case of anxiety depression. There was some hypochondriasis (schizoid) with stress effect.)

Depression

More often than not we can assume that where there is depression there lies aggression beneath, and that both the inner- and the outer-bodies are involved in the state of depression. In the above case we can sense the man's depressive anger against himself, and the consequent guilt. This is a most common emotional complaint, the movement of which stems from anger at some infantile deprivation, and this is clearly a movement of attack towards the outer-body. However, this highly aggressive movement has to be withdrawn because of the intense guilt which it creates, or of other inhibitions, and the result is a retreat back to the inner-body, which now receives the full blast of the aggression; the state of depression is the direct consequence of this. A system of atoning self-punishment is often involved at this point. So long as the person is attacking the outer-body he is free from depression, but the depression returns the moment he begins to attack and hate himself. The outward and inward movement is very characteristic of many emotionally disturbed conditions. There is no simple one-way traffic. Nevertheless I have included the depressives amongst those who are trying to fight their way back into the outer-body. In the aggression there is an attempt to remove barriers which separate one from a full life, and, therapeutically, one feels there is much hope for these angry persons, in spite of their grim suicidal threats.

To be aware of the initial endeavour to work one's way back into the outer-body should help us to be less harsh with these aggressive persons. We cannot encourage people to be social nuisances, but when they are given an understanding treatment much of their aggressiveness may be reduced, and the misdirected energy is then free to be used in constructive ways. It is nothing but a gross misunderstanding of a person's inner life, and of the conditioning environment, which cries to the heavens for flogging and the gallows. The proverbial 'kick in the pants' will only increase the recipient's sense of injustice and deprivation, and therefore anger; but also it will increase his demand for living space which he will seek in unsocial ways. There is a vast task to be performed not only to remove the conditions which in the first place create a sense of deprivation and injustice, but also to reclaim those who are so affected. If this latter work involves a psychological approach the sooner we adopt it the better. This saving work should be a highlight of the Church, especially in those branches of her activity which deal with mothers—the Mothers' Union and the Young Wives' Fellowship. The door is wide open to the Church.

In the depressed state we have been discussing, where the aggression is turned from the outer-body towards the inner-body, we find the normal and healthy attack upon life has ceased, the needful energetic approach to tasks and the tackling of problems fades and dies away, with the consequent loss of all joy of achievement and adventure. A wet blanket covers life, there is insufficient energy to raise a smile or to bestir oneself out of the drab lethargy. This condition is often found in middle-age, and is known amongst moral theologeans as 'accidie'; frequently it is related to 'the sickness that destroyeth in the noon-day' of the Psalmist (PSALM XC. 6).

De-personalization

A lady in her middle thirties came to find help in dealing with her problem. She had been diagnosed by a hospital as a case of de-personalization. She had adopted a false identity through finding both her inner- and outer-bodies very difficult to bear. She felt she had not sufficient equipment with which to face the demands of life, and a false rôle was adopted as her real Self. In one way it was a running away from life, indeed there were aspects of her life which had beaten a serious retreat; but there were seen at other times attempts to do something about her intolerable situation and an endeavour to gain a sure place in her outer-body.

The history revealed a motley picture of psychic layers: there was some agitated depression, which is our concern in the present context, there were some obsessional characteristics, and various symptoms of an hysterical order. The main trouble with herself, as she saw it, was a deep sense of unreality, which we should expect from anyone acting contrary to her true nature.

The father was a professional man who was rarely seen in the home, and she felt herself at no time to be close to him. The same distance separated her from her mother who employed a nanny. She felt her mother to be irritable, strict, and one who brooded over her faults. There was a younger sister who could do nothing wrong in the eyes of her parents, and who had committed the unforgivable sin of being born pretty, whereas she herself, to quote her own words, was 'plain, plump and unsociable'. The only way open for her seemed to be in the intellectual world, and in this she well applied herself. We can understand her chagrin when she passed her examination with distinction whilst her sister failed hers, and the parents gave her no reward whereas they gave prizes to the sister as a consolation for her failure. Whatever she might do there was no recognition; her inner-body, she thought, must be all wrong for the outer-body to make no response to her.

The result of all this was that she adopted a masculine mask, and although she was married, and had a number of children, her function in life was abhorrent to her. She presented at one session a drawing of herself surrounded by the many tasks of a housewife and the mother of small children, all of which were making her very angry indeed. Much buried aggression was apparent, and this aggressiveness fitted her masculine pose. She felt she had been treated most unjustly in life, while the guilt arising from her bitterness and anger produced her depression, which was supported by the weight of her sense of unreality. There was also a deep sexual problem, in the narrower sense, regarding her femininity.

In order to obtain a place in the outer-body, an individual will sometimes in fantasy renounce his or her true sexual rôle and adopt that of the opposite sex. These fantasies are for the most part unconscious and need to be uncovered by analytical treatment, but it is easy to see how they can aggravate and intensify the problems of the sick mind. Such a reversal of the sex rôle can come about where the mother wanted a son and a girl is born, or where the treatment of the parents is unequal, so that the girls are given an easy time while the boys are made to grind away at their lessons and are expected to do the 'donkey-work', or maybe the daughter is restricted in her freedom whereas the boy is allowed a greater latitude. These conditions may not be sufficient in themselves to effect a 'fantasy exchange', but they can add considerable weight to other already existing factors tending in the same direction. Masturbation, for example, frequently gives rise to emotional experiences so terrifying to the child that they are repressed, and what remains in consciousness is a feeling that something dreadful is wrong with one, and that therefore the normal place in life cannot be taken. Thus the boy feels himself to be less than a boy, and the girl that she is less than a girl. The weakened natural rôle makes the way for an identification with the opposite sex. Strange infantile fantasies may arise through a desire to have a warm relationship with the parent of the same sex. For example, the girl, desiring her mother's love, sees her father holding a favoured position with her mother; this may lead the girl to identify herself with her father, so that, as it were, she puts herself inside her father's skin, and by this trick hopes to enjoy a special relationship with her mother. All this, of course, takes place in the fantasy life of the unconscious, and the result is a change of sexuality. This process obviously brings us into the realms of homosexuality, but underneath it all there is a deep desire for some sort of good relationships in the external world of the outer-body. Such cords as these, when woven together, can produce a strong rope from the bonds of which there is no conscious escape, and it is clear how the love life can be horribly twisted and unworkable under these conditions.

HELL
The tortured and divided self. Before treatment.

HEAVEN
The unified self—the reward of cure.

SIX

MENTAL PAIN

WHEN thinking about the problem of pain we are accustomed to have in mind only what is commonly called 'physical pain'. The extension of our knowledge into areas of our Being hitherto unknown has intensified the problem of human suffering, in fact it has given a new dimension. Moreover, this 'pain of the mind' not only affects the person immediately concerned, but also his family and all with whom he comes into contact. Further, when we accept Jung's contention that we have to wrestle with the unsolved problems of our parents, their pain is passed down to us and, unless it is resolved, to our children and our children's children. By far the greatest weight of pain is borne by the unconscious, nevertheless it is *our* pain, and all the activity of the conscious life is both related to and affected by it.

The weight of mental suffering baffles description, and only those who experience it really know its terrible intensity. The therapist who encourages abreactions gets a glimpse of the intensity of people's suffering, as they uncover their deepest dreads and agonies. I have already indicated something of this in my description of abreactive dream analysis, and it is seen by all psychotherapists who use the drug known as LSD-25.[1] It can be a terrible experience. But this apart, an indication of the unconscious pain which people carry is seen in the eyes of the great sufferers which, by their leaden and glazed stare, or darting movements of terror, betray untold depths of agony.

The picture facing page 136 is one of a number of equally unpleasant paintings presented to me during my treatment of a young man. It shows utmost agony of mind. Another picture he drew is of himself, naked, and chained hand and foot, whilst spears are approaching him from all directions. All he

[1] See Appendix page 216.

can hope to do is shield his eyes from the torture of these unending threats. The whole series of paintings can only be described as ghastly. However, the last of the paintings and drawings show the release from his pain, and his final drawing reveals the love which has overcome his hate and fear.

This young man was a charming youth, but he was giving much trouble to the youth organization of his church. He was violently aggressive at times, and naturally upset the activities and spoiled the fellowship. When he was wanted for some special purpose he would be found in a remote corner of the premises hiding in the dark. A display of intense rage would follow upon his discovery, and on occasions he damaged the property. The fellow members of the organization made matters worse by their attitude towards him. The curate was inclined to take a strong line with him, and thought he required a bit of sound common sense knocked into him by way of a thrashing. Most people, no doubt, would have agreed with him, being unable to recognize the intense suffering which lay hidden behind this behaviour pattern.

Driven to desperation, he eventually came to me for help. The analysis lasted about two years, and before it was completed he had to pass through many perils. His aggression was born of defence against the powers which he believed were set out to destroy him. His paranoid reactions told of a deep feeling of complete loss of love and care. He desired well-being and the sense that his world was sustaining him. He had known Paradise, but Paradise had been lost and turned into a Hell of hostility, and he sought to regain the Paradise. His in-turned aggression brought him perilously near to self-destruction. It is now seven years since his treatment was ended, and he is doing magnificently in every way. He had parted company with the Church, but the last time I saw him was at Holy Communion. He had found his way back to his spiritual body, and thereby to his completeness.

The degree of mental suffering can be so intolerable that the mind has evolved methods of dealing with it. By repression it is pushed out of consciousness, but even in the unconscious something has to be done with it, by substitution, conversion into a physical symptom, projection and the like. Our present knowledge is insufficient to tell us why repressed pain reveals itself in the particular way it does, as when, for example, a particular form of conversion hysteria is chosen rather than another in a specific case. The person may become what is known as a Hysterical Personality whose basic need is for self-expression, and, feeling intensely empty and afraid in his inner-body, clings desperately to the objects in the outer-body for safety and significance. His inner sense of emptiness makes him capricious, and he may vent his pent-up emotion in undirected and useless outbursts, of which the hysterical fit is an extreme example.

However, the chief hysterical outlets are two in number. The first is Anxiety Hysteria, which results in what are increasingly known as the Phobic States. A characteristic of this condition is that the anxiety is removed from the inner-body and projected on to an object, or objects, in the outer-body, as though the sufferer must put a 'distance' between himself and his problem. These objects are merely the pegs upon which the intense anxiety is hung. 'The affect is displaced,' as we say, and then projected. Such a situation reveals itself in the presence of certain phobias, e.g. claustro-phobia, cancerphobia, V.D.phobia, etc. The analyst readily sees that beneath the phobia lies the anxiety that has produced it, but at an even deeper level still lie feelings of insignificance and emptiness, with all the pain and the dread that they bring, and it is these feelings that cause the anxiety.

By far the commonest hysterical device, produced to deal with unconscious pain, is another displacement of feeling known as Conversion Hysteria. In this evasion of mental pain a physical symptom carries both an unconscious aim, such as 'illicit' pleasure or cunning, and also self-punishment for the same. Various psychological mechanisms may be involved in the process, and in the following chapter illus-trations will be given of these mechanisms. What I wish to emphasize concerning these cases is the testimony they bear to the intensity of the pain which is being evaded. People will go to hospital and submit to a physical operation being performed rather than be brought face to face with the mental suffering which the physical disorder conceals. It seems incredible to us that a person should be blind for the rest of his days rather than face the pain of his guilt, but this is by no means uncommon. The only conclusion to be drawn is that the physical pain and disability is less, or more easily endured, than the mental pain that it covers up.

Some people deal with their mental pain by projecting it on to other people. Guilt is one of the worst pains and, in order to evade it, it may be thrown unconsciously on to other persons, who are treated then as the guilty parties. A clergyman in the pulpit may denounce a particular sin. It may be that on this particular occasion he is merely revealing his own unconscious guilt with regard to this particular sin, and his method of dealing with it is first to project it on to the people in his congregation, and then to attack it. Projection of this sort occurs both in the neuroses and in the psychoses. In more serious psychotic cases this process may give rise to firmly held delusions of persecution.

At other times the guilt may be dealt with internally by means of unconsciously self-imposed sufferings and denials, even to the supreme denial of life itself. Thus, for example, a feeling of guilt with regard to relationships with the opposite sex is not uncommon, and it often has its origin in conditions that existed at a very early age. A person having such guilty feelings may unconsciously decide to have nothing to do with the opposite sex, rather than have to face up to the feelings of guilt which such a relationship would stir up; further, the denial is a stick with which to punish himself. The so-called 'confirmed bachelor' may be of this type, in which case he has to cope with the tension resulting from unconsciously self-inflicted abstinence from heterosexual friendships, coupled with an unconscious longing for just such a friendship in order that his life may be complete. Examples of this very common mechanism are given in the following chapter.

Another way of dealing with the greatest weight of suffering is to *isolate* that area from the rest of the personality, which division of the self is spoken of as 'splitting' or 'dissociation', and, in Jungian terminology, as the 'autonomous complex'[1] with its fragmented personality. This splitting is often a very serious mutilation of the Self, and it may carry with it a rejection of the capacity for feeling, for to feel means the possible return of the great dread. Thus the mutilation of life and the denial of its greatest pleasures are preferred

1 Jung, *The Structure and Dynamics of the Psyche*, London, Routledge, 1960.

to the agony of mental suffering. This is the method of dealing with pain by paralysis, whereas the other method represents the agitated response to pain.

Karen Horney[1] has pointed out that mental pain can make for personality distortion of a rigid kind. Thus the sufferer may become compliant towards those about him, rarely disagreeing with what is said and quite unable to take a firm stand in opposition to the prevailing climate of opinion. Alternatively he may compulsively resist those about him and angrily resist aid and sympathy, or he may detach himself from people and hide away to be a sick animal.

One of the most pathetic and tragic facts of life is that, whilst people recognize and sympathize with the hurt of the body, they shut their eyes to, and condemn, the suffering of the mind. This attitude towards the mentally ill adds a further burden of suffering to the already over-laden soul, for it deprives the sick person of the warm loving relationship and the sense of acceptance by the community which he needs most of all. It increases the agony of separation, drives the person more into himself, convinces him further that he has been sent to Coventry by mankind, and makes him exhausted and depressed by the futile efforts he makes to save himself and find a place in the community. When well-intentioned religious people tell him to have more faith in God, which is of course what he needs, but which is impossible because of his condition, he feels an even greater load of guilt which may finally drive him to suicide.

There are many people who regard pain, whether of body or mind, as an evil in itself. They cannot see that, more often than not, however unwelcome, pain is in a sense a friend to man, and that his existence to some extent depends on his ability to experience it. The annulment of pain may be of great disservice to life, for to remove pain without removing the cause of the pain cannot be described as 'healing' in anything approaching a full sense of the word. This applies to mental, as well as to physical, pain. The problem of pain should be formulated as the problem of the intensity of pain, and pain should be regarded as a warning, like toothache, that something is wrong. If the basic maladjustment, to which the pain is drawing attention, is then rectified

[1] *Our Inner Conflicts.* London, Routledge, 1946.

the pain has achieved its purpose and disappears. The difficulty lies in the fact that in some cases there is no pain, when pain would have been remedial, and in other cases the intensity of the pain is in excess of what is needed to call attention to the disorder.

Part of the problem may be dealt with by realizing that a personal factor has much to do with the way in which we feel pain. It is experienced in varying degrees of intensity from person to person, and given a certain attitude of mind, pain can be rendered negligible or even non-existent. Hypnotic treatment for the pains of childbirth, or the native woman's attitude towards childbirth in some parts of the world, show how much the emotions affect the sensation of pain. Helene Deutsch, observing herself during her confinements, concluded that fear is a large constituent factor in labour pains.[1] The masochist annuls his normal sensation of pain, in so far that his physical suffering assuages his greater guilt-pain. His self-inflicted expiation may also release him, in anticipation, from guilt-pain arising from his future perverse activities. I found an instance of this in a man whom I am helping, who would often stick long needles into himself without discomfort. The accident-prone person may act through a similar masochistic motivation, like the man I treated who, on more than one occasion, with full awareness, had to drive his car into a gatepost.

We should regard pain as a work of the vigilant Spirit within the soul. If mental pain is serving the same purpose as physical pain, that is, in pointing out that something is wrong, we should not be content merely to remove the pain by repressive drugs and manipulations, but rather we should always follow the moving of the Spirit and seek to heal the neurotic disorder to which the distress of mind is pointing.

The symptoms, as we come to read them aright, are a writing of the Spirit. Psychosomatic symptoms may tell us a great deal about the emotional conflicts of the neurotic person. The location of the pain in the head, and its nature, the nausea and vomiting, the hypertension and the palpitating heart, the eczema and urticaria, the hypothyroidism, fatigue and diabetes mellitus, muscular disorders, and a host of sexual disturbances, all tell us much about the path we must take

[1] Deutsch, *Psychology of Women*, London, Research Press, 1947.

to help the person to become whole. In the same way we
see the guiding of the healing Spirit in a multitude of unconscious mannerisms. When we pursue these indications we
are enabling the person to discover the healing power at
work within the spiritual body.

A neurosis, when analysed in depth, is invariably seen to
have been caused by factors that are a product of our surround. It brings to mind Jung's contention that the neurotic,
in his sufferings, is experiencing the problems of his age, and
in as much as we all draw our life in part from the great
depths of the collective past, these too contribute their share
of suffering. Thus, at least in part, the individual's suffering
is the suffering of all mankind. The fact that we, perhaps
through our greater insensitivity, or more fortunate circumstances, have not suffered to a very great degree, in no way
entitles us to stand aside. Indeed to Christians, committed
as they are to bearing one another's burdens, the situation is
one of compelling importance, and one in which they are
particularly fitted to take effective action, since that love
which is at the centre of their faith is the one factor that can
restore the neurotic person to a level of life that is complete
and full.

SEVEN

HYSTERIA

THE most interesting of all mentally ill persons are those suffering from various types of hysteria. They cause the therapist the most trouble, for they cling to their hysteria like limpets because it serves several most useful purposes, and it may cover trouble of a more serious kind. However, from the analysis point of view such persons are so interesting because of the psychosomatic symptoms associated with conversion hysteria and hypochondria. The therapist has to be on his guard in certain cases where the person's imagination is particularly vivid, for false charges of indiscretion could easily be brought against him, and they would be presented in a most convincing manner. Happily such cases are not often found, yet should one be involved in such a case the results might be very serious.

The hysteric is a person who has regressed to infancy and has recalled unconsciously that in those distant days illness had its uses. The child may have felt unloved and unwanted, and then by chance he happened to be ill. What rewards that illness brought! What magical power to bring the world to one's feet in humble and loving service! People cannot do enough for one now that illness has come, and there is given all the attention anyone could wish to have. If the child had secretly not been wanted by the mother, her guilt regarding her child would lead her to heap up upon him solicitude and tokens of affection. In later life he feels the same coldness and aloneness come upon him, he may repeat unconsciously the former illness. We see in our general hospitals patients returning repeatedly with one thing wrong or another. I remember seeing one particular young man appearing, without fail, over a considerable number of years. Having obtained permission to speak to him from a psychological angle, I learned a little of his story. He was an unwanted child. For five years he lived, emotionally speaking, in an icy cold world until he developed mastoiditis, and then his guilt-stricken parents lavished upon him excessive attention. In his teens his former coldness and loneliness descended upon him again, and he met it along the lines of his infantile experience, with severe pains in his ear. Year by year he turned up for hospital treatment with his pains, located at different places in his head from time to time. The hospital staff had not considered his case from a psychological standpoint, hence their bewilderment.

Such action on the part of the young man was an attempt to gain recognition in the outer-body; he was doing something to resolve his deep problem. In conversion hysteria, the phobic states, hypochondria, and anxiety hysteria, which are grouped generally as Hysteria, there is always a mute cry for help, a call which, it is hoped, will bring a response of notice and consolation. Hysterical symptoms, as the word implies, wander not only about the physical inner-body, but they are also found wandering about all the other forms of mental disorder.

Conversion Hysteria

I shall begin my selection of brief case histories, selected from people whom I have helped, by referring to Mrs B. She is a middle-aged person who had been blind for six years. She had been told repeatedly that nothing could be done for her condition, and that her dim sight would deteriorate until she reached total blindness. In spite of the verdict she visited, over the years, every optician in the city where she lived, in the hope that her sight might be restored, but everyone told her that the hospital findings were final and that nothing could be done for her. This insistence on her part, in the light of the end of the story, might well have indicated that she was dimly aware that she had not heard the last word on the matter.

At the first interview she presented various neurotic symptoms, which showed that, blindness or no blindness, she needed considerable help in straightening out her emotional life. She was an inveterate worrier, and suffered from migraine and blushing; she was scrupulous, and there was something of a 'locking-up' compulsion. The onset of

K

the blindness, which occurred just after her mother's death, was sufficient in itself to rouse one's suspicions, whilst in her dreams she was always seeing dead people, which roused feelings of deepest anxiety and guilt. Another frequent dream was of falling, usually into a bottomless pit, and if she could not smell the fire and the brimstone of that pit I could. Obviously she was carrying a severe guilt complex. However, her first dreams, in addition to revealing her guilt problem, introduced me to her father and his ways.

The father presented a strange combination of characters to his young child. His personal life left much to be desired, and he enjoyed the company of a number of lady friends, while the mother, as the result of the father's lack of loyalty, took to drink. Mrs B could remember that, when she was a child, there were frightful scenes in the house, such as when the father was enjoying the company of a lady friend, and her mother, who had been locked in a room by her father, would be banging on the door, shouting and making things as unpleasant as she could. Despite the grave moral lapses of the parents they nevertheless tried to impose considerable moral pressure upon their young child; there were to be no lapses so far as she was concerned. The father, who was a schoolmaster, had the reputation of being the strictest in the city. When the father died, the young child had to cope with her alcoholic mother, and she remembers how the police would come for her late at night and take her to the police station to fetch her drunk mother home.

The child grew up into a high spirited young woman, but all the time she carried within her the prohibitive moral pressures implanted by her parents. Nevertheless, underneath, she was determined to break out of her prison. The day came when this happened, and there was a baby on the way. The choice now before her was either to jump into the river Trent, or marry the man whom she did not love. She married the man. The episode was not closed thereby, but it was repressed, and the blindness was the symbol of this covering up of the guilt, as well as self-punishment and a cry for affectionate concern (which previously had thrown her into the arms of the man). As all this buried material was worked out, and she came to forgive herself, her sight came back. She now sees not only the outer world, but also her own inner world. Further, her frigid relationship with her husband was resolved as she ceased to project upon him her own 'sin'. Her optician informed me that her vision is now as good as could be expected of anyone her age, and she has put on considerable weight, which she regards as a doubtful blessing!

Another instance of a physical expression of an emotional disorder was that of a young boy who produced all the symptoms of poliomyelitis. His doctor called in a consultant physician, who knew something of the psychological history of the boy, and he regarded the symptoms as psychogenic. After a few days the boy was quite well. On another occasion the same boy was doubled up with appendicitis pains which persisted for an hour or so, after which time they passed off. Had the people around him not realized what was happening he would have been taken to hospital. Needless to say when such symptoms occur considerable caution needs to be exercised since the trouble could be organic.

One young woman whom I treated occasionally developed severe abdominal pains during the analytic sessions, and she would walk round the room doubled up with the pain. She shared with many other people emotionally-caused gastro-intestinal disturbances. In her case it was nervous vomiting which was most frequent, but there was a period of a month when she refused food (*anorexia nervosa*[1]) and in this period she lost two stone in weight and became too weak to walk. At other times she had severe chest pains, paralysis of the limbs and various head pains, the latter being frequently brought to every psychotherapist. On one occasion, whilst we were discussing a dream, she recalled a forgotten incident of her childhood. She was sliding on an icy road, and slipped, cutting her eyebrow on a curb stone. Whilst she was telling me this a deep red patch spread from her eyebrow down half her cheek, and within a few minutes it had disappeared. At another session she dealt with a dream in which she saw a large mushroom of the ornamental garden variety painted with red spots; by the time she reached home she was covered with spots which, again, soon cleared.

Rheumatoid arthritis is a condition which is being recog-

[1] F. Alexander—*Psychosomatic Medicine*. London, Allen & Unwin, 1952, p. 88.

nized in certain quarters as often having a psychological causation. The emotional factors which consistently present themselves in this respect are hostility and resentment in women, and rebellious hostility in men. They are usually of an active type which expends much energy in dominating and controlling persons and things.

A young man who had been treated for ankylosing spondylitis (which may be described as rheumatoid arthritis of the spine, and which causes a rigid or 'poker' back) sought my aid. On looking at his story it was clear that, whether it had anything to do with his disorder or not, he had enough bad emotion about him to cause anything. He was bursting with anger, resentment and hostility. I set to work to deal with his anger, believing the disorder of his spine would look after itself.

His father was a kindly soul, whereas his mother was aloof to him, dominant and of an hysterical type. She was uncommonly severe with her son, and frequently administered corporal punishment, though the father would never punish in this way. There was a younger sister, and his mother went out of her way to favour her daughter on every possible occasion and to degrade her son. He could do nothing right in her sight, whereas the sister could do nothing wrong. At mealtimes the mother would give her daughter an extra helping, but not her son; the daughter had two shillings a week for pocket money, he only one. So it went on down the years. No wonder he carried a scalding resentment and bitterness towards his mother in particular, and in a less degree towards his sister and all women in general. His mother had most successfully instilled into him her own sex warfare.

The young man was phenomenally strong and anyone who attempted to cross him would never do so twice. Whilst in hospital, without any conscious intention to hurt, he would grasp a nurse's wrist so tightly that it would be bruised. I gave him a simple treatment in the main, in which I encouraged him to let off his rage and bitterness, always showing him why he was so angry, and that he was all the time living in the past world of hatred and hostility towards his mother. There were, of course, other matters to be attended to by the way. The result of it all was that his pains and stiffness vanished, and finally he fell in love with a very charming nurse and married her.

George was seriously ill when he came to be helped: he was pasty-faced, painfully thin, and presented a picture of abject misery. He complained of pressure in the head, constant worry, trembling, cold feet and sweating: there was a lack of concentration and an inability to enjoy anything, he felt empty and unreal. He had a cancer phobia, and also had a shoe fetish. His drawings confirmed my opinion that he was very seriously ill. He had been recommended by a psychiatrist to have residential treatment in hospital, which confirmed my opinion of him, but he insisted, probably owing to the stigma upon hospital treatment, that he should be allowed to come to St Margaret's Clinic.

His analysis revealed a super-abundance of infantile fantasies such as would rejoice the heart of the Freudian psychoanalyst. The most interesting part of his treatment, although *most* unpleasant to deal with, was the development of a body odour of quite staggering potency. It was produced only on Tuesday and Friday mornings, when a certain girl came into his office in pursuance of her work, and when in the evenings of those same days he came to his session with me. His body odour was so strong and unbearable that the people in his office could not stand being near to him, and in the end he was given a room in which he could work by himself with the windows open. This state of affairs could not continue indefinitely, and his firm gave him a month's leave of absence in which to be rid of the smell, but since it still persisted on his return, he was dismissed from the firm. He soon obtained other employment, and by this time, having made a good response to the treatment, the odour was considerably reduced and it went unnoticed until it finally ceased.

Besides the odour there were other physical symptoms such as shooting pains in many parts of the body, blinding pains in the eyes, pains in his teeth (false) and ears, in the front and back of the head, in the middle of his back, stomach and neck, and he had difficulties in swallowing (*globus hystericus*), and feeding in general. All these symptoms would come and go during the sessions. By degrees the cancer phobia and the stomach pains subsided, weight was put on and there was an all-round improvement. A change was effected in his religious life, and the religious symbols which dominated most of his drawings played an important, if not crucial, part in his treatment; of these symbols the Cross and the guiding star were the most frequently used, also alchemical symbols abounded. He was an able fellow, and yet, but for the help he received his life seemed to promise nothing but misery and waste.

Bronchial Asthma

If asthma is a distressing thing to see, it is a far more distressing thing to suffer, and the tragedy is that so often the psychological aspect of the case is not considered. The doctor may be fully aware of the psychogenic nature of the disorder in a particular case, but even so, where can he send his patient for analytic treatment? The cases I have treated psychologically have had medical treatment for years without any prospect of a cure. I may have been fortunate in the cases that have come to me, but in every case the asthma has responded to treatment, and a cure been effected.

My immediate quest in a case of asthma is an understanding of the person's relation to the mother. The choking sob of the spasm is the infant's cry for the protective mother from whom he has been separated, a separation which he may have interpreted as rejection by her, with all its intolerable hurt and panic. Thus in later life, any separation from a familiar and secure situation throws him back into infancy, and an attack follows.

In the early days of the St Margaret's Clinic, when it worked as a group, a person who had been suffering for six years with asthma was cured at the preliminary interview. A boy of sixteen, who for years had known scarcely a day when he was free from his attacks, had one session with me; three months later he informed me that he had suffered only one attack during the whole three month period. I remember, again in the early days of the Clinic, a middle-aged man who had been tortured with asthma for a considerable number of years; indeed it was so long established that we feared that real physical damage had been caused. At the man's insistence a course of hypnotic treatment was given. After eight sessions he was so much improved that he declared that he could run up and down the road, and was so satisfied that he broke off the treatment. We knew full well that in his particular case this was not a fundamental cure, and we were not surprised when a little later he produced other psycho-somatic symptoms. He came out in mysterious 'boils' which perplexed the hospital staff, especially since they would not respond to treatment.[1] Obviously this symbolic physical dis-order was not due to an infection, which would be the case with an ordinary boil. It provided, however, a most interesting example of the way in which the person's emotional system, through the hypnosis, had changed its tactics in the form of hysterical expression.

Mrs Brown is a middle-aged woman who, apart from her respiratory affliction, had a psychological 'lump' in the pit of her stomach, and another in her throat; she suffered from loss of appetite, and she had palpitations, neckaches, sweating, and tingling sensations. Although as a child she thought of herself as her father's pet, she was nevertheless afraid of him, and she remembered that he drank and was very strict. The mother was possessive, and because the was often ill she had little time to give to her daughter. Mrs Brown felt herself to be the 'odd one out', a feeling which was characteristic of her childhood in general, and her reaction to the situation was one of self-pity.

An event which had considerable bearing upon the asthma took place when she was six: it was after this occurrence that the asthma made its appearance. There was a well in the garden of the house in which she lived, and naturally the children had been warned against going near it. One day she fell into it, and had not a man jumped down the well she would have been drowned. She had abreacted to this experience in a number of sessions, and tasted again the horrid water in her mouth, she has seen vividly the darkness with the circular light at the top of the well, she has smelt the nauseating dankness, and she has clawed in vain to gain some purchase on the slimy wall of the well. After she was brought out of the well she was taken to her mother. You may picture the mother hugging the terrified little girl and comforting her; but you are wrong, for the mother set about

[1] Often a very angry person may almost choke with rage, and such choking rage may be a prominent feature of the asthmatic attack. We speak of 'boiling with rage'.

the child telling her it was all her fault, for she had been warned repeatedly never to go near the well, and that the next time she would really drown.

This was a traumatic experience, and the mother should have done what she could to have healed the hurt. In actual fact she acted in a heartless way, and it increased the subsequent asthmatic rage. However, although the mother acted unsympathetically in a crisis, she was following out an agelong principle in dealing with the young; her scolding of the child was the taking of an opportunity to rub in the lesson to be drawn from the experience. The young of all animals have to be taught the lesson that life has many dangers; that is why the mother animal appears to play cruelly at times with her young, giving them cuffs and nips. They must not be allowed to think that mother nature will always provide them with tit-bits, and will be there to protect them; the function of the mother on these occasions is to inculcate an essential fear, without which the young could not survive. 'The fear of the Lord is the beginning of wisdom' (PSALM cxi. 10) is the religious application of this principle. In the case we are following, the mother should have made an exception at an exceptional time, nevertheless, she was following a natural course of action with regard to her child, who, despite warning, had been so careless as to walk into grave danger, and by making the child deeply afraid she was ensuring that the incident would never be repeated.

I remember once seeing two young mothers talking together in a busy street, as mothers will: one of them had a small child who, whilst the mother was deeply engrossed in conversation, wandered on to the dangerous street, whereupon the mother, seeing the child, picked her up and gave her a good spanking. I suspect many people would say that it was the mother who deserved the spanking, but although she was not without blame, her action in principle was a necessary one, and it is upon this principle that the reasonableness of human disciplines depends. The wider psychological application of this has been worked out most interestingly by Dr C. E. H. Turner.[1]

To return to our little girl, she did not understand that

[1] C. E. H. Turner—'The Psychosomatic Sexual Life of the Family'. *J. Ment. Sc.* 93/522 & 94/397.

there was, in part, a wisdom in her mother's treatment of her, and all she could feel was her mother's cruel coldness, which she bitterly resented. This incident crystallized all her previous feeling about her mother, and it became expressed in the choking sob of asthma. The realization that there was some reason on the mother's side helped Mrs Brown to re-adjust her emotional attitude towards her mother, though the experience of the well was too intense for this alone to overcome it.

This incident had seared itself upon the memory of the child because of its deep psychological significance. The baby life at first is one with that of the mother, she is the one and only source of Being, and since this is so, we can understand something of the abject terror and loss to the child who feels separated from the mother; it is in fact to fall into a state of non-Being. Now the fall into the well, with its complete separation from the mother, was as near as could be to falling into non-Being.

One wonders why the child walked into the well, and whether already she felt herself unsupported and alone, so much so that in her fantasies she was seeking the intimate security and protection of her mother's body, which the well (in mother earth) would symbolize to her. If this were so she discovered the desired mother to be indeed a terrible mother who seeks to destroy her child. In which case her mother's punishment would be punishment for her regression from life, the retreat from and betrayal of life's trust; on the other hand she would use her mother's treatment of her on this occasion as a justification of all her negative feelings regarding her mother who 'never' protected and consoled her.

There was also a strong sexual element, as we should expect in the hysteric. In this the father was involved. He had petted her, but he had also been stern with her to such an extent that she had become afraid of him. There were deep waters here, and they affected her marriage, which itself began with an unfortunate incident that may well have been psychological in causation. A few days after her wedding she had a haemorrhage which her mother disregarded. Her husband, naturally mystified in regard to sexuality in women and taking his lead from his mother-in-law, left his new wife at home in bed and went off to another wedding in the family. On the return of the husband and mother, after many hours, the wife was found to be in a serious condition. Once again the pattern of childhood had been repeated in her mind, for those to whom she looked for love had deserted her in her hour of need. This incident, with its sexual component, put her relationship with her husband out of gear until the time of the analysis. She demanded of her husband more than he could possibly give, and because he did not give it she was angry with him, and she withdrew from him. The asthma persisted for, according to her reckoning, life did not give her sufficient air to breathe, her living space, like the well, was too confined, because there was insufficient love. Although in fact she was offered love, she would not have anything to do with it. When her husband went off to the war and there came along a dashing man who made much of her, her love-starved hungry self seized the love he offered her and which she had been demanding of life since her infancy. In this period her asthma completely disappeared; it only returned when her husband came back from the war.

A dream revealed the situation clearly which ran: '*It was before I was married, and I was in a great room with no furniture in it. It was barn-like and very frightening. There was a small fireplace, but it did not warm the room. My father and mother were there. A strange man came in, well dressed, and a perfect gentleman.*'

It was before I was married ... The beginning of the dream shows that her problem with her husband is one older than her marriage.

I was in a great room with no furniture in it. This indicates the real nature of the problem, in that her Self, the room, was felt to be an empty self; there was no cosy warmth, no experience of comfort or pleasure, no welcoming relaxation. She reveals the root cause of her disorder, the barrenness of soul which the deprivation of love brings; she felt outcast and separated from the source of Being. The empty room could also represent her mother, whom she was seeing as *barn-like, and very frightening.*

There was a small fireplace, but it did not warm the room. The fire of sexual warmth burnt very low, but, as we have seen, it was only waiting to burst into flame. Her *father and mother were there*, whose relationship, as man and wife, was chill and empty, and, also, whose prohibitive influence had done much to stifle her sexuality. Further, we may see here 'the eternal triangle' and all that goes into the infantile rivalry with the mother for the possession of the father.

A strange man came in, well dressed, and a perfect gentle-man. This man was associated with the man with whom she had become friendly during the absence of her husband. He came into a life which, she felt, contained little warmth. He was seen unconsciously to be the one who could furnish her emptiness and make it glow with the fire of love; he was in fact the 'Saviour archetype', and that is why she fell in love with him. Her real love for her husband was 'screened' by the negative 'father image'. Her husband did not appear in the dream, that is she could not see him, which in actual experience was the case, for she felt she had no love for him. She complained that he gave her no 'sweet nothings', and not a shred of encouragement; he would not move from behind his newspaper and take her out. This was found to be an exaggeration, e.g. at Christmas he put beside her bed a card on which he had written 'my darling', which she tore up: he also gave her a ring she had longed for, but she would not wear it. She was playing the game of the spoiled child.[1]

The spoiled child, it should be remembered, is not neces-sarily the child who has been fussed over, and given into without any exercise of discipline. There is in addition the genuinely deprived child who, as the above case shows, behaves in a somewhat similar way to the pampered child, though the root cause of the trouble is very different. The pampered child who has been fussed over and has never experienced any real discipline, comes to regard the world as being organized for his convenience and enjoyment. The genuinely deprived child, however, though showing much the same pattern of behaviour, may result from circumstances where the mother was cold, or too busy, to satisfy the emotional hungers, and the father was stern and unapproach-able. The pampered child is given an expectation of life which life cannot fulfil, and when life fails to meet this impossible expectation, the person feels that he has been wronged and calls out to high heaven for justice to be done. The deprived child, because of his deprivation, and whatever the source of

[1] Cf. E. Graham Howe—*Mysterious Marriage*. London, Faber, 1949.

it, grows up into a demanding adult and exhibits an extractive attitude to life. It is essential, if a balanced attitude to life is to be produced, that the young child should be conscious of the love and care that surrounds him, and at the same time should be taught that life is not all milk and honey, and that disappointments and privations are to be expected and used as stimuli to new endeavours.

Mrs Brown experienced a truly Christian regeneration. Her asthmatic condition had for long prevented her using her fine voice in her church choir, but now, with the removal of this complaint, she 'sings the praises of her Lord' from the bottom of her heart. She was born again. She had to confess and receive forgiveness for her infidelity, and she had to forgive herself. A turning point in the treatment of her marriage relationship was an understanding of her infantile fantasies of an incestrous relationship with her father, which her husband was screening. Her love life was blocked by these fantasies, and, of course, her husband was there to carry all the blame! A factor which protracted the treatment was her pride; she could not admit her 'affair' which clashed with her Christian upbringing: 'That this should happen to me!' She now goes to business, which was previously prevented by her asthma; a new joy has come into her everyday life, since the removal of her inhibitions, and not least, she cannot understand what has happened to her husband since he has suddenly blossomed into a most delightful man!

Another asthma sufferer we shall call Brenda, who was the elder daughter and whose sister had been delicate all her life. The birth of the new baby is normally very hard for the older child to bear, since the new-born child is seen as the supplanter, but when the new baby is delicate and receives excessive attention it is far worse for the older child. His destructive fantasies grow from his rage as he hears the baby so often spoken about and treated with so great attention. Feelings of guilt will choke the expression of this rage, which now is but partially expressed in the choking asthmatic spasm. Moreover, in view of the special care given to the sick child, it is not surprising that the unconscious puts a premium upon sickness. Thus Brenda's asthma was a cry of distress by which she hoped to bring a comforting mother to her side.

Her father was on the strict side, while the mother was

kindly but efficient and strong-minded; it was well that she was for, before long, her husband died and left her with the care of the two children. The father and mother were a devoted pair, and after the father's death the three women-folk were most closely knit together: indeed they were so close together that it suggested too much of a good thing.

During the war a delightful service man appeared on the scene from overseas, and the happy issue of the acquaintance was marriage for Brenda. The married couple left this country for the other side of the world when the war ended, and it was then that the asthma began. The early pattern of child-hood was put into operation, and sickness was used, uncon-sciously, to bring her mother to her side, and asthma developed. The disorder became so serious that the husband gave up his professional career and they returned to this country. The asthma persisted and help was sought from the St Margaret's Clinic. The psychotherapy was not difficult and the asthma soon disappeared.

The last case of asthma I will mention is that of John, a policeman, who was a fine specimen of manhood save for this affliction. He was hoping to be promoted at work, but his asthma caused him so much loss of time that, not only did he miss his opportunities for promotion, but also his further employment was beginning to look uncertain. He was hoping to marry, and this prospect was endangered by the asthma. However, there was more than the economic factor in the matrimonial prospect; he kept falling out with his young lady, and things, somehow or other, just would not go straight.

His breathing had been bad all his life, from time to time he suffered from plagues of boils, and he was claustrophobic. He had never been allowed to forget that he was 'the baby' of the family, and being treated as a child was a cause of considerable irritation and resentment. His father was domineering and his mother most possessive; she was not averse to threatening the little boy with the police whenever he was naughty, which may have had something to do with his becoming a policeman himself. His eldest brother was also very domineering, and when his father died the brother naturally took his place.

Here was a young man who had never been allowed to

breathe for himself, frustration met him at every turn, even as a man he was being treated as a child. He had become very angry at all this frustration, he was choking with rage, and this along with items in his story built up into a considerable weight of guilt in his unconscious. As he worked off his anger and felt himself free to live his own life, and as his guilt was dissolved thereby, the boils vanished along with the asthma. The disappearance of the boils may have been but coincidence, but it is worth noting. He married, and today he is possessed by a surprising degree of initiative and spirit of adventure; he is a very happy and fit man.

We do not wish to imply from these cases that every case of asthma can be regarded as 'purely psychological'. Allergy enters into the picture, but it *may* be this also has a psychological basis. Be that as it may, what I do stress is the importance of giving due weight to the *possibility* of any case of asthma being psychosomatic, and that it should be investigated along these lines. A preliminary investigation of the patient's emotional background might save much suffering, time, and expense.

Phobic States

I end this chapter with a brief description of two cases in which phobic states had occurred. The first is that of Mrs T, who is suffering from disseminated sclerosis, a disease of the nervous system, of unknown causation, which produces scattered areas of degeneration in the brain and spinal cord. Beside this physiological aspect there was much disorder of an emotional nature. Although the analysis has yet much work before it, this person is so interesting that I feel justified in mentioning her. In such a case as this, where there is a strong hysterical element as well as a physiological one, it is difficult to sort out the one from the other: the hysteria is likely to use the genuine symptoms for its own purposes. One has to work in the dark without the light which pure hysterical symptoms shed. I have every reason to believe that so far the emotional change has affected some of the D.S. symptoms.

Mrs T's father died when she was nine, and she was left with a mother of a managing kind, who was also a considerable worrier. There was a younger sister upon whom nature had bestowed much by the way of good looks, whereas Mrs T had a physical deformity. Apart from this, life opened with difficulties in feeding. When the sister was born she was fussed because of her jaundice, a factor which contributed to Mrs T's jaundiced view of life. She recalls how bad tempered she was when her sister was born, she would not go near her mother, and she wanted to be with the father as he worked in the fields. When she went to school dizzy spells came on and she would have to lie down. When she was eight she had peritonitis, due to her mother's delay in calling the doctor, and the serious illness lasted six months. She well remembers the great welcome she received on returning home, and the fuss which was made of her. The pattern was thereby set for the hysterical use of sickness. Her deformity was of such a nature that other children ridiculed her. She had pains at puberty, and she was frightened at what was happening to her body.

The troubles she reported at the first interview, apart from those appertaining to her physical illness, were poor sleeping, worries of various kinds, claustrophobia and various other phobias including fear of heights, of pipes, and a hypo-chondriachal phobia of V.D. This latter phobia seemed to rule her life, and no amount of assurance could shift her from the conviction that she was infected, although every doctor she consulted on the matter laughed at the notion. Amongst other things she was a blood donor, and yet she believed she had the disease; hospital tests were not believed. Until D.S. appeared she had migraine—the one taking the place of the other. As a child she sleep-walked. Whilst in the Forces hypo-chondriasis developed.

At one analytical session Mrs T reported the following list of symptoms: a rash, a burning sensation in the neck, a stiff neck, toothache, jawache, legs and toes tingled, a solid feeling inside and in the left arm and hand, and a loss of control of the legs in particular (her deformity was in her legs). There was a long history of bladder frequency, diarrhoea and con-stipation, and, strangely enough, double vision. As long as she remembers, her mother had jerky knee movements at times, and these characteristic symptoms of D.S. are produced at every analytic session by touching upon her emotional com-plex. During the above mentioned session she remembered saying as a child to her mother: 'I have earache and headache, and I shall have toothache in the morning!'

Her physical deformity, one particularly trying to a girl, was interpreted as saying to the world that she had no value and that she would never marry. This deep frustration led naturally to an exaggerated desire, which she regarded as criminal, and it was repressed. There were difficulties of an inverted sexuality, for she saw herself as feminine with no hope in the world, and she developed the masculine side of her personality, which brought her into difficulty when marriage appeared on the horizon, and significantly it was just at that time when the D.S. appeared. Indeed, we can see what useful purpose the V.D. phobia served when it was used to protect herself from sexual commitment, due to her deep fears regarding her femininity. She became a prim, efficient and intellectually bright person, going out to business in rather a big way for such a person. She invested much in the outer-body. Her illness served as self-punishment. It is obvious that her body would carry excessive values both on account of her defect and her sister's 'perfection', and although this value was of a negative kind, it served the purpose of calling attention to herself, by means of illness. There is everything to suggest that she is using her body as a means to satisfy her emotional needs, and as a rod for other people's backs.

My last person to mention in the connection is Mrs G who appeared on the analytic scene as the epitome of misery, frightfully thin and haggard; her heart palpitated, she was a poor sleeper, but the chief item on her agenda was her phobia of cancer. This affected only one side of her body where intense pains were felt everywhere from head to foot. She had spent many weeks in hospital with endless examinations, all to no effect. In the end she was told she was imagining it all, yet she looked so thoroughly ill, which always raised a doubt in her doctors' minds.

A glance at her early life was sufficient to reveal every promise of a neurosis. Her home life presented an all too familiar scene of a drunken father, who when drunk was irascible, and on occasions she remembers how her mother was hit by him. She felt her mother to be cold and distant towards her, and she well recalled how she wanted more love from her than she was ever shown. It was the sad story of an unwanted child. Punishments took the form of threats on most occasions, threats which cut at the roots of her security; a favourite one was that the coal man would come and they would ask him to take her away in his bag. Whenever she saw a coal man in the street she would run to some shelter in panic. Her mother died of carcinoma in later life, but prior to the development of the cancer phobia.

The usual sexual element was there which was shown in a phobia of being touched. Cancer was believed to be God's punishment, which clearly was regarded by her as following a death-wish upon her mother. As the analysis proceeded she put on weight, the haggard look changed into one of happiness, the pains disappeared, the cancer fears were completely forgotten, and she felt reconciled to her parents.

The kind of symptomatic changes we have discussed in this chapter might well be considered when the subject of Faith Healing arises. It is doubtless that remarkable physical effects are produced at faith-healing services, and it might be that in some cases the deep roots of the illness in the soul have been influenced, and the person has been healed. Since a deprivation of love lies at the root of neurotic disorder we might expect that the new awareness of the infinite seeking and forgiving love of God could deeply affect a change. But the problem with so many people is simply the fact that their illness prevents the love of God breaking through into their lives, in fact they feel incapable of feeling love, human or Divine, and this is where the long and patient work is required of the kind we offer in this ministry. In some of the cases where, through faith-healing, a person appears to be cured, there may be only the removal of a symptom which, at a later date, will be exchanged for another.

Here, of course, we are viewing the whole healing action as working along psychosomatic paths, well known to our particular science. Whether God intervenes upon the scene of sickness, from outside the laws of nature, is a much bigger question, which takes the discussion into the realm of miracle. My personal opinion, for what it is worth, is that 'miracle' is something beyond definition, for if we regard it as a Divine disregard of natural law in favour of direct action, the definition will not stand in any specific instance, for in this very instance it may be only our ignorance of natural law which leads us to ascribe a miracle. We should first have to know *all* natural law, before we could say here is an event which falls outside it, and this knowledge is for ever beyond our grasp.[1] Be it as it may, it is difficult to be definite as to the cause of any healing, for most often one feels it to be a mixed activity involving bio-chemistry, psychotherapy of some sort or another, the person's quality of spirit, which is an area where we can most readily understand the operation of the Holy Spirit taking place—and may be much more beside.

We would very humbly suggest that the medical profession might save itself considerable trouble if more notice were taken of the hysterical elements in the histories of patients; and that the Church should have adequate services available to help people through the problems of their emotional life. In fairness, however, I am fully aware of the difficulty which confronts the medical practitioner who is unable to pass his patients on to places where they can obtain help, for generally speaking, such places simply do not exist, and until such help is available the position must remain much the same as it is. But what an opportunity for the Church!

[1] F. R. Tennant—*Miracle, and its Philosophical Presuppositions.* Cambridge University Press, 1924.

EIGHT

DREAMS AND FANTASIES

I NOW propose to present some of the material which people bring with them to the analytic session and to illustrate its value both for the analyst and for the sick person. I realize that this is not a wholly satisfactory procedure since in a very real sense we can never separate the material of one session from what has gone before or from our general assessment of the person and his problem, but it is the only way in which I can demonstrate to the general reader the kind of material that is of value when one is seeking to implement the recovery of mental and emotional health.

The material presented is varied. I have already said enough about the abreactive technique which I use in dream analysis, and of the reactivation of the emotions in general. In addition, or in place of this, a person is encouraged to relax and allow some picture to come to mind which, more often than not, may develop into a story. This story upon analysis, is frequently found to screen some incident of his early life, which for him was emotionally significant. In other words we treat his story precisely as we would a dream, and we often find that it begins to yield important and significant information. Or again, if our patient is badly stuck and unable to get going, we may ask him to think of a number, and with that as our starting point, by means of his 'free associations', endeavour to penetrate to some incident which has significant psychological value, for him. In such ways we are able in most cases to get the analysis moving.

I have already mentioned in this book the value of drawings and paintings and how we encourage the patient to express himself by such means. These too can be analysed and interpreted just as one would analyse and interpret a dream, and such pictures can often be not only very informative to the analyst, but tremendously helpful in enabling the person to find some release from his inner tensions. Indeed, the pictures drawn and painted in this way can sometimes be of diagnostic value, and cases have come my way where I was led to suspect an underlying psychotic condition, not from the behaviour of the person, or his manner of speech but from the execution of his art, and in such cases was able to advise against analysis. But if pictures fail and dreams dry up, the individual can be encouraged to talk of either the present or the past, and before long one is brought to some problem which can serve to set the analysis in motion.

On the day on which this is being written, for example, I have seen a person who brought no dream, had failed to make up one as requested, and had done no drawing, while when asked to relax and allow a picture to form in her mind, she produced something that was patently 'thought up' and useless. With so great resistance it was impossible to get anywhere, and so the resistance barrier had to be dealt with by explaining what was taking place. Then I started her talking. At first she was not inclined to say much, except blame her husband who seemed to be the author of all villainies in her estimation, but bit by bit the conversation was turned back to her childhood, of which she seems to have a complete blank in her mind, revealing much buried mental pain from which she is hiding by forgetting. Several incidents came into her mind, and before we had finished the session small tears appeared when she thought of an incident relating to her father: I hope by this to have stirred her unconscious sufficiently to release dreams, and I hope what I have said has removed some of the resistance. Another way in which difficult people can be loosened up is by setting them the task of writing down their troubles, and whatever else they would like to say about their life: this often is the only course open when words completely fail them at the sessions, and it is interesting to note how the writing changes in character, frequently becoming infantile in information as well as in idea.

But when all the techniques of analysis have been considered, the dream remains the most important instrument of all, and its interpretation is by far the most difficult part of the analysis. It is an art which can only be learnt by training and experience. The modern scientific mind may have little

patience with what is 'only a dream', and may regard the
dream as containing merely the stuff that fairy-tales are made
of, which is true enough, for fairy-tales have value as
expressions of the unconscious, and are used frequently in our
sessions. For long the Church has shared this scepticism, in
spite of dreams playing a definite part in the Bible, and the fact
that history was turned upon the interpretation of dreams.
We sometimes wonder, humanly speaking, what would have
happened if the Magi had not interpreted their warning dream
correctly, or if Pilate's wife had been given her way with
her interpretation of her dream, viz. 'Have nothing to do with
that just man: for I have suffered many things this day in
a dream because of him' (MATTHEW xxvii. 19). Indeed it
appears in the light of present knowledge that the Church
has been too quick to agree with Nebuchadnezzar's 'wise men,
the astrologers, the magicians, the soothsayers' (DANIEL xi. 27),
who found dream interpretation difficult, and she has been
too impatient to learn Daniel's art.

Every dream is saying something important about ourselves,
for it is an expression of the hidden part of the Self. As Jung
says 'the dream is a divine voice and messenger', but the
message is disguised by what Freud called 'the Censor', that
function of the Self that prevents the deep secrets from
coming into consciousness, and so effectively does it do its
work by turning the dream material inside out and upside
down, and by distorting it in most subtle ways, that, more
often than not, the one thing we can be quite certain is that
what the dream appears to be saying is not its true meaning.

The Jungian and Freudian interpretations of dreams are
very different; both can be true revelations of the unconscious,
i.e. both interpretations can be saying the same thing in different ways, or the dream material may be expressing, at one
and the same time, different aspects of the unconscious. This
may sound irrational, but if we are ruled by the rational we
shall not learn much about the unconscious, for we are dealing,
in the main, with levels of life other than rational, which are
part of our experience, and the direct cause of the illness.

I have recently read a book by a neo-Freudian in which
were set forth various possible interpretations of a difficult
dream, and for one reason or another each interpretation was
rejected until the last was reached; the working out of the

material was very complex, but had the dream been approached first from a Jungian angle the interpretation would have been immediately obvious, and it would have agreed with the conclusion of the neo-Freudian. On the other hand, there are dreams of which the Jungian can make no sense at all, but which the Freudian immediately understands.

The amazing thing is the effect of dream interpretation upon the patient. As the dream is discussed, and this is particularly true of the Jungian approach, the person is obviously stirred to the very foundations, and I have seen energy drained away from consciousness by the working of the unconscious, that the person has every appearance of being asleep, and when he 'comes to' he is as tired as if he had done two days' work. One man yawned at the rate of one yawn per minute for half-an-hour! It is impossible to say what is happening save that 'the Spirit is moving upon the face of the waters', and the intellect is completely out of its depth.

Some dreams are described as 'big dreams' in that they are critical, and have an importance that can often be sensed by the dreamer. It may be that they bring out the unconscious material that has never been brought forth before, and such dreams, often marking a critical point in the person's development, are worthy of the most thorough examination. In this connection two important points must be made.

First, dreams indicate a pattern and may reveal, often in a heavily disguised form, a series of successive stages in the person's development. Thus, for example, if such a dream can be broken up into three sections A, B and C, it may be found that B recalls an incident that has been repressed. Section A recalls a particular set of circumstances that were operative in the person's life, at a much earlier age than the incident B, but the incident B occurred because of the circumstances A. The incident B resulted in the person orientating his life in such a way that a certain pattern of behaviour, represented in the dream by C, became established. It needs little imagination to visualize the therapeutic value of interpreting such a dream, especially if the pattern of behaviour represented by C is part of the trouble with the individual's present day living. Moreover, such a chronological pattern, A, B, C, can be found not only within a single dream, but also within a series of dreams recorded, for example, in a single night.

Secondly, in the same way that a thermometer reading tells a physician about a person's physical condition at the time that the reading was taken, so a dream is indicative of a person's state at the time when the dream was recorded. Moreover, just as a temperature chart records a patient's physical progress, or regress, so a series of dreams, recorded in chronological order, tells a psychotherapist how a person is progressing along the road to Wholeness. It is vital to realize that a dream, far from being a purely random event, bearing no relation to a person's state of well-being, is what it is because the person is what he is at that particular time, and used creatively, with understanding, it can help the person to achieve the Wholeness that should be his. Some considerable experience of this work convinces me that, through the dream, one is often brought into relationship with the operation of the Holy Spirit in human personality.

In order to show something of the value of dream interpretation I shall outline a number of dreams of a very ordinary kind, omitting the analytical details. The first dream, presented by a woman, is as follows:

'An old china cabinet was given to me, I did not want it, so I took it to a dealer: I thought it was worth a few shillings, but he gave me £2,000. He took a piece of sandpaper, rubbed off the gaudy paint, and to my amazement there was gold underneath. He gave me the money. I tried to find the person who gave me the cabinet, but he was gone.'

china cabinet—This represented the dreamer herself, particularly in her feminine aspect, and she regarded herself as worth but a few shillings. Her unconscious valuation of herself was very low.
the dealer—She identified the dealer with our Lord, Who saw her real worth. He was revealing the gold, her real treasure.
gaudy paint—This was her conscious approach to life. She had dressed herself up in ways which would catch the eye. She knew of no other way in which to find her significance and value. She did not understand why she was trying to impress the world.
£2,000—She felt that this was not for her, which meant that

she did not want to accept her true value. Two is the feminine number, and she was being shown what great worth she held as feminine. She would have given the money back to the man who gave her the cabinet, but he had gone, with the result that she has to accept the place and value God had given her.

The second dream provided by a different person ran:

'The animals of a circus had escaped along a road. I ran very fast to escape from them, and finally I ran into a shop and feverishly tried to close the door, but whilst I was doing this the tiger, of gigantic proportions, which chased me, was pawing at the door. I was not sure whether I should be able to close it in time.'

This is an anxiety dream. You may see that it carries a Freudian interpretation of sexual significance, so that if one had been hasty that interpretation would have been supplied, in which case the chief importance of the dream, which was other than sexual, would have been missed. On asking for associations, the road brought into consciousness a forgotten incident. Her parents had told her, when a small girl, by way of punishment and threat, that the coalman would take her away in his black bag, so that she had visions of being driven away, to a 'nasty' black coalman at that! She recalled, more-over, how she had run upstairs and hidden under her bed, sobbing for hours, while her parents had just laughed. She felt the terror of it for years, and whenever she saw a coal-man in the street she would run. What was buried in the incident was the rejection of her by her parents, and the feeling that they did not want her as they did the other children in the family. She felt that if any terrible thing happened, her father and mother would do nothing to save her.

The third dream was as follows:

'I went into a room where men were sitting: the man in charge had white hair, he asked me my name. I told him various names, which seemed to me to be ancient names, and they did not make sense. The chief man said: "The time is up, and you must go." I nearly reached the door when I shouted out my proper name: then I was called back. I felt most tranquil.'

This woman, from early times, had been posing, putting on one act after another. She had given herself many 'names' which did not make sense, and we recall from the Bible that a name can mean a person's character (cf. Simon now called Peter, the rock-man). The 'ancient names', which 'did not make sense', also have a reference to the Collective Unconscious, so that the patterned behaviour of the ancient past is being repeated in her life. The fantasy life is a dangerous thing when we allow ourselves to exchange it for reality, and we sense in the dream that the situation was critical. Had she left the room without giving her name she would have lost her sanity, but fortunately, at the last moment, she chose reality. Thus the dream, at a critical phase of the treatment, indicated the wisdom of pressing forward with the analysis. In spite of the real danger, the prognosis was good.

The man with the white hair we shall meet again in this chapter, for he is the archetypal good father, who in the last analysis is God, the wise and loving Father. We are reminded of the beginning of the Catechism, where the question 'What is your name?' is asked, and which, you may remember, has to do with being 'a member of Christ, a child of God and an inheritor of the kingdom of heaven'. This is the fundamental question which faces Everyman. The surrogate of the man with the white hair was the analyst who, through the analysis, had been bringing the person face to face with her real and true value. The dream set out the issue most vividly, and once again the prognosis was good.

A fourth dream, again the dream of a woman, was:

'I was walking across the lawns and past rose beds of a country mansion; it was dark and I could only just see the shapes of things. I came to the door of the great house, which was mine, and entered. I felt very much out of place for I was shabbily dressed. I opened a door on the left of the entrance hall and within the rooms were many ladies, dressed in period costume: they looked at me disdainfully, and I closed the door. The same thing happened on the other side where were the men in the dress of the same period. Finally, I decided to go upstairs; there I changed my clothes and I came downstairs dressed in blue. I felt now I could take possession of my house.'

The fact that it 'was dark', and she 'could only just see the shapes of things', indicates that her unconscious was casting a gloom over her life, so that nothing could be seen clearly. The gardens were her adornment, while the green of her feminine nature was not visible, since her spirit burnt so low that it gave insufficient light. The mansion was herself, it was hers, yet she could not use her life, for she was not in possession of it, but rather was a stranger to it. Her clothes represented her shabby self-regard. The men and the women were strictly separated, that is the feminine and masculine parts of her personality were divided by a bad inheritance, to which the 'period costume' referred. She had closed the door upon both the masculine and feminine aspects of her life. Fortunately she decided to rise to a higher level, where the third spiritual body resides, and here she obtained 'a new look' in the blue, which represents the spiritual, dress. With this new outlook she descends to the normal level upon which life must be lived, and as a result the old guilty darkness vanishes, a clear sense of direction in life is experienced, and she enters upon the inheritance of a life rich and spacious.

These interpretations may sound somewhat prosaic to the reader, but to the persons who made these discoveries about themselves they were full of meaning and power to transform life.

A Modern Traveller's Tale

I now turn to a series of fantasies produced by James (page 90) which I have called 'A Modern Traveller's Tale'. They were not written as we should write a story, knowing broadly what we were going to write, but were written by an inner compulsion, the writer not knowing what was going to be written; we may liken it to a literary doodling. From the analyst's point of view they can be treated in exactly the same way as dreams, and the comments made regarding dreams would be equally applicable here. Thus there is a progression through the series, each fantasy indicating a stage of James's progress at the time that the particular fantasy was written. The fourth fantasy, for example, is charged with great danger, and when James produced it his situation was perilous. In fact he has since won through to a level integration (which Jung would call 'individuation') and purposeful living hitherto unknown in his experience, and he would not produce a fantasy of that kind today. I have followed each fantasy with short notes on the interpretation. If the interpretations seem too highly imaginative then two factors should be remembered. First, the story outlined by them is consistent with James's general background, and secondly, the interpretations, which were worked out by James with only questions and promptings from me, had a profound and transforming effect upon James, which would indicate that they were 'ringing true' at a very deep level.

I shall divide the first story into two parts, which will make it easier to follow.

'I made my way through the market place of an eastern city, and as I passed by I noticed the stalls loaded with all sorts of merchandise, olives, grapes, melons, and all sorts of food brought by the country folk. I looked at them enviously, but since I had no means of buying them, I passed on. I walked rapidly from the market place, down the winding lane which led me to the walls of the city. I reached the gate, and passing the beggars who sat there asking for alms, I went out into the open country. As I walked the vineyards and the olive groves were visible on the hillsides, the sun shining over them brought out the beautiful greenness of them all.

'The desert lay in front of me, presenting a barren picture; it lay silent and yet awe-inspiring. The sun, as I staggered on, was merciless; and my tongue was parched, my feet sore from the hot sand of the desert.'

An eastern city represents mystery, wonder, enchantment; that is, the enchantments of life. The market was laden with the good things, the luscious foods, but they were not for him, for he had no money. In infancy he had seen the good things but they were not for him, though he looked at them longingly. 'How badly life is treating me; I should be treated better than this!' was his feeling. He hurried past the beggars, probably thinking only of his sad condition, and as he passed on he saw all the good life around in the sunshine, but again it was not for him. Soon he was footsore and parched, weary of life which had treated him so badly. Was this journey really necessary? Would he not have been better off if he had stayed with the beggars or sought the shelter of the olive groves? The answer to the second question is Yes, but he journeyed on because he wanted the world to see his misery, and how unjustly life was treating him!

The story continued:

'I felt I could go on no longer, and then as if it were a miracle, I saw an oasis in front of me with palms: a number of men were there watering their camels, and filling their bottles against the next stage of the journey. I stumbled on, and reaching the well I fell to the ground and lost consciousness. When I came round I perceived an old man standing over me, holding to my parched lips a water bottle. The water that issued from the neck of the bottle was so sweet and refreshing that it restored me.

'The old man spoke to me. "My son, why are you wandering in the desert like this?" I replied: "I am an outcast from my brethren, abandoned from my youth, and left to fend for myself. I have nowhere to go, and yet I seek a habitation." He smiled at me and said: "You must come with us and help us to sell our merchandise in the next city, which is several days' journey from here." He lifted me upon his camel and we rode off across the desert, and at last I was at peace and in good hands. The old man rode at my side, and as we journeyed he told me tales of the wonders in the next city. I was happier than I had been all my life, and I felt no longer alone and afraid.'

This man, saturated with self-pity because he had been deprived of the good things he wanted, found himself in his self-made desert, and it was only when his pride was utterly exhausted and he was abject that he could be helped. A prodigal son of another kind, he had to come to himself and realize his plight, but he was amazed to find so much help at hand upon the instant of his abasement. What a spoiled child he had been, even to the extent of hurting himself in order to be sorry for himself! He had gone through life demanding his rights, too proud to beg, seeking a habitation which was beyond the realms of reality, until he met the old man, the archetypal Good Father. He refreshed him with the water of life, a theme which is important in both the Old and New Testaments. In fact, upon discussing the fantasy its writer at once brought to mind by association the incident of the rock which was struck by Moses in the wilderness (EXODUS xvii), the incident of our Lord at the well of Samaria (JOHN iv), and the Marriage in Cana of Galilee (JOHN ii).

When the old man suggested that he might help them to sell their merchandise, the author of the fantasy thought of 'being saved to serve', which represented the turning of himself outwards, from love of himself to the outer-body. He thought also of the Parable of the Labourers in the Vineyard, and especially of the man who at the last moment was called to serve (MATTHEW xx). The Parable of the Good Samaritan also came to mind (LUKE x. 30). The travelling company he associated with the Church. The old man who travelled with him was now that 'aspect' of the Deity known as the Paraclete, i.e. the One Who is called to one's side as helper (Greek), Who guides and teaches many things, and Who 'leads us into all truth'.

This rich material, with its vast and deep religious associations, could have nothing but a profound effect upon him after the meaning of the fantasy had been explored. It showed that we should have to follow him into the wilderness of his soul and relive the hurts which he had repressed ('lost consciousness'), and open up what had led him to retreat from life and wallow in self-pity and self-punishment. The second fantasy, of a different nature, began this task; however, it will soon be apparent that the final assurances of the first fantasy were fully needed for it seemed that the Holy Spirit, the Paraclete, had at once been taken from him.

'The courtroom was crowded, this I saw clearly as I stood in the dock. I recognized so many of my friends, and the look on their faces was so condemning, that I wanted to hide my face to blot out their stares.

'I listened to the Prosecuting Counsel bringing out all my crimes, hate, envy, and the most fearful of them all—murder. I had murdered so many people in my life, and destroyed the happiness which was theirs.

'The Prosecuting Counsel finally presented his case, and the Jury retired to consider the verdict. I was taken below to await their decision. I knew what it would be because the list of my crimes was so formidable that no verdict other than "Guilty" was possible. At last I was taken upstairs into the dock, and stood to face the Judge. The Jury were asked by the Clerk: "What is your verdict?" The Foreman rose to his feet and said: "We find the prisoner guilty of the crimes set out against him." The Judge looked sternly at me and said: "Prisoner, you have heard the verdict of your fellow men; have you anything to say?"

'I could not speak, but shook my head. The Judge then said: "You have been found guilty by your fellow men, and it is my duty to condemn you to life imprisonment. You will spend the rest of your days in solitary confinement where you can think about your crimes against humanity." I was led below, with the looks of the people torturing me, and I was seen no more.'

Until this point in his development James had only known that he was afraid of his work, of people, of life itself, and that he felt that people were looking at him critically wherever he went. Now, for the first time, he begins to realize what has been lying deep within his soul, and why it is that he has been running away from life, and living under such nervous tension.

His crimes were hate, envy and, above all, murder. He hated because all his life he was made to do what he did not want; he was forced into a profession he would never have chosen, he was made to learn to play the piano, which he detested, he was made to do his homework whilst other boys played in the street, he was made to go to church. He hated those who had robbed him of his childhood, who imposed upon him unfair competition, 'making him do at nine what could only have been expected of him at nineteen'. He hated because of his physical deficiencies—his being small, his face which he regarded as ugly, and his bow legs. Above all he hated God for leaving him unprotected in life, for taking his father and mother from him, for allowing his big brother to have such power over him.

He envied other children for what they had, they had fathers, they had love whereas he was alone and, starved and cold, they had everything and he had nothing. He envied children their straight legs and their big bodies; he envied their health, for he was sure he would die of tuberculosis as did his father. He envied other people their success, he marvelled at the way in which they had got on in the world whilst he had never had a chance.

He murdered, in his fantasies, all the people he had hated: 'I could murder the lot of them,' he said, and he would include God among them. He had been taught much about Hell as a child, and he said, 'I can sense the punishment of God, and that I am sent to Hell and punished unmercifully.' It was his hates and envies, and above all his murderings that made him feel such a colossal sinner, and turned him into his own Prosecuting Counsel and Judge, and led him to banish himself to solitary confinement and his self-made Hell.

It is worse to fall into the hands of men than into the hands of God, but worse than the hands of men are our own hands when we have turned them against ourselves. In this picture is seen the dreadful reality of self-punishment, which marked James's conscious life with repeated acts of atonement. He was not consciously aware of the crimes he had committed: his punishment was taking place in the cell of his unconscious thought.

In this fantasy there are various very dangerous elements. He wanted to hide his face from the stares of people, he had nothing at all to say in self-defence, and he accepted every charge declared against him by humanity. He was condemning himself to life imprisonment, and what was most sinister of all, to solitary confinement. He was 'led below' and was seen no more. Here is the picture of a man retreating from the life of man into the death of solitariness. His consciousness was in the gravest danger of being drawn below into the dark prison of the underworld. The analysis at this point was standing on very thin ice indeed.

The third fantasy brings us once again to the archetypal father:

'I went into a bookshop, and as I approached the counter a man came in from the back room who bade me "Good morning," and I replied in the same words. He asked me what he could do for me, and although I tried my hardest I could not think why I had gone into the bookshop. I gazed round the shelves, hoping desperately to bring my memory back to the book I required. As I stood there, speechless, the man's face was suddenly transformed, as his expression softened from the severity it had when he came first into the shop. He said: "Can I help you by suggesting a book you require? Do you want a book on travel, or adventure, or poetry?" None of these appealed to my mind, and then suddenly, with a blinding flash, I knew what I wanted. I said to the man: "I want a book on knowledge, a book in which I can read how to find out how to live."

'He smiled kindly at me, and shaking his head, he said: "My son, no such book exists. Knowledge is not found in the books I have in my shop. If you want to have knowledge you must find it through the bitter experiences of life, through the soul-searing events which have taken place, and will take place in the time we spend on this earth."

'I was somewhat put about by this, and, seeing my expression, he said, with a most comforting smile: "My son, be not dismayed; but go on your way and you will find that the bitterness of your experience will be turned into that peace that passeth all understanding, and which, when it comes to you, will possess your whole being." I thanked him for his kindness, and I left the shop to take up my life, and to wait for the coming of that knowledge.'

We note the kind of shop into which he had gone, a bookshop with its intellectual emphasis: feeling physically inferior he tried to win status by intellectual achievement. Basically he did not know why he was in the realm of books, hence his bewilderment in the shop: he could not think what he wanted, and in this respect was so much like the child who does not know what he wants and is restless until he finds it. At last he realized what he wanted to know, and that was the knowledge of life without which he could not live.

The man who appeared from the hidden recesses of his mind was the wise old man, the wise, guiding Father-figure who holds the wisdom of the ages and the depths of man's experience, Whom we recognize as the Good Shepherd. At first he thought he was rather severe and un-cooperative, something like the Judge in the previous fantasy, stern and condemning: but soon he realized that he was very kindly, and only wanted to help someone who had gone into the wrong shop so blindly. The man suggested to him what books he needed to consider: first, one on travel. The traveller friend of ours should never have locked himself up in solitary confinement, and have lived a life of the narrowest experiences: he must go out into the wider spaces of life, fill his lungs with invigorating air, enjoy new scenes, increase his pleasure and widen his interests. Then he suggested that the second kind of book to consider was one on adventure, for our friend could have lived no less adventurous a life: he had retreated from every highway into that cramped shop where he was completely lost. His paralysis must be overcome, his fears of movement must be replaced by a feeling that all the world was his to enjoy. The third kind of book was poetry. Life had nothing of the rhythm it should have, nothing of the sheer joy of perception. In fact, he could not perceive any of its beauty, and on lovely days he would tell me that he could see no beauty anywhere, even though he had travelled to the sessions by road, from a neighbouring county, through scenes of great beauty. The wise old man was saying that 'bookishness' can be a hindrance to true life and perception: there is a wisdom that cannot be had from books, and the only way in which it can be had is in the hard and bitter school of experience, with its 'soul-searing events'. Like all children he was wanting to know without toil, and sweat, and tears. Had he not appreciated the man's wise counsel he might have remained in the shop in confusion, but on the positive side we note that he did go out into the wide life of the affairs of men, even though some lack of resolution can be detected in that he waited for the coming of the necessary knowledge. He seemed already to have forgotten about the travel, the adventure and the poetry.

The next fantasy reveals again the very great dangers that awaited him:

'Out of the black mouth of the cave issued three creatures with

M

the faces of devils, their eyes gleaming, their mouths twisted in evil snarls, and their cloven hooves pounding the ground in fury. They approached and stood before me, leering at me. The first spoke: "I am Envy, the first part of your being." The second one said: "I am Hate, the second part of your being." The third one spoke: "I am the greatest of my brother devils: I am Pride and all uncharitableness, and the whole of the remaining sins of the world are in me. I am the greatest part of yourself."

'These three devils joined in chorus: "Come with us into the darkness of the cave, and there we will make plans to enter into other beings and persuade them to join forces with us." I was powerless under the evil influences of these devils, and I was impelled to walk towards the opening of the cave when I heard a voice, coming down from the sky, which spoke in loud tones: "Do not go with those devils, my son, and have nothing to do with them. You can never live with them in your being, and you cannot help them to destroy your fellow beings."

'I was amazed, and trembled in fear. I spoke to the sky: "How can I help but go with these devils, since they are so strong?" The voice of the sky continued: "You cannot throw them out of your being in your own strength, but I will help you, even though you do not think I can." The sky darkened, the voice from it faded, and I was left alone with the three devils. My companions spoke to me: "Do not listen to that voice from the sky, it will promise you so much, and it will not give it to you." Even as they uttered these words, the sky lightened, and the storm and the lightning flashed, and the voice from the sky spoke again: "Devils, take yourselves from this my child, and leave him in the peace he has never seen or felt. You have been part of him too long, and now you must go."

'As the voice spoke a flash of lightning came down and struck the three devils, and they were burnt up until nothing was left of them. The voice from the sky said: "See, my son, how strong I am, that I can destroy these devils. Go your way in peace, free from these devils: henceforth dwell with me and I will dwell with you, and I will be with you always."

'I turned from the open mouth of the cave, and walked into the bright sunlight which had replaced the storms and tempests. I felt clean and whole, and ready to live a new life.'

The black mouth of the cave, which represents his unconscious with its great dangers, threatens to overpower him, and it is a moment of the greatest peril. The primitive aspects of himself threaten to gain supremacy and destroy his conscious self. We can see very clearly a personality split, divided by its many voices which come from a kingdom divided from the Self, which Jung would describe as the Autonomous Complex. The three devils are reminiscent of the Temptation of our Lord, the agony of Gethsemane with the gravest conflict raging between light and darkness, life and death, Heaven and Hell: it was as though He entered through the gates of Hell so that He might prevail against them on our behalf. The traveller must settle this conflict, his future depends upon the issue before him. The voice is that of the ideal self, the true conscience, which in this case was to him the voice of God. His inner conflict is felt to be as a contest between God and the Devil, they are fighting for his soul.

We have already seen something of the Devil Hate, but it is realized now that Pride is the chief of the devils, ever the first of sins. This pride represents his inability to accept his lot in life, his smallness, the way in which he has been treated, and because he cannot accept them he compensates for them with his intellectualism. He is seeking mastery over all things, in his own strength, through his method, and he is reluctant to recognize his own weakness. Moreover, his fantasy world has great value to him, for within it he is omnipotent and omniscient, while his intellectualism is a mask that he wears before men, and which hides his true self from God and man, but he chooses to wear it. The hurt of the fantasy lay in the fact that he was compelled to realize his powerlessness to cope with the evil forces within himself, even though he had set himself up as almighty. It was his pride which led him to believe he could save himself by his own efforts, and which resulted in humiliation and pain and brought upon him his own undoing. He must believe that his 'sufficiency is of God'. Happily he listens to the voice of God, and in that is the promise of final victory. He must learn the secret of the holy communion:

'I am the vine, ye are the branches: he that abideth in me, and I in him, the same bringeth forth much fruit: for without me ye can do nothing' (JOHN XV, 5).

The next of these fantasies which I shall quote is as follows:

'The streets of the city were busy; buses, cars, lorries and other forms of transport moved ceaselessly, with great noise, passing me as I stood on the pavement, looking on without seeing. As I stood on the pavement edge, an old man came to me and bade me "Good morning." I hardly answered him, because I was feeling sad and lonely in the busy city. He looked at me reproachfully and, sensing my mood, he spoke to me: "Why are you so miserable, my son?" I answered him: "I am a stranger in this big city, and I have no friends with whom I can talk, and with whom I can enjoy my life." He put his hand upon my arm and said: "Come with me, my son."

'He steered me safely across the street to the other pavement, and propelled me along several other streets until we came to a very quiet street, where the noise and bustle of the city did not penetrate. In this street stood a church, which we entered; it was empty, but at the east end stood the altar, its candles burning brightly, and the light of the sanctuary lamp flickered. He led me to a pew at the back of the church and made me kneel down. He said: "My son, weary though you are, bewildered, afraid and tired of life, I will still be with you, and if you will follow me I will show you the way to a far better life than you have experienced up to now: but you must be willing to suffer, and even to die, before you can glimpse at the joys that will come to you."

'These words filled me with awe, and I trembled exceedingly. I turned to see the old man at my side, but he had gone. Had he spoken these words, or was it my imagination? I could not reason, but I found I was no longer afraid. I left the church and as I went through the porch I saw a text written there:

'"He that exalteth himself shall be abased, but he that humbleth himself shall be exalted. Hear ye, ye of little faith."'

We notice again how withdrawn from life he was, his interest was burning very low and he was scarcely aware of the outer-body. He seemed to be helpless, merely standing and allowing life to pass him by. He was so wrapped up in himself that he had ears for nothing, but his own inner words, 'Poor me! My life is so sad, so lonely, no one takes any notice of me: no one understands me', and he could barely hear the old man speaking to him. He did not know how to cross the road, which symbolizes the fact that he needed the help of the old man to make the necessary change, and to go over to the other side of life. The church, to which he was led by the good Father-figure, was the symbolic good Mother who ever cares for her lost and bewildered children.

This coming together of the Good Father and the Good Mother images was of the greatest importance to his sense of Being. James, as you may remember, had never known his father, and a large part of his intense mental pain, and the splitting of his personality, had resulted, in part from this absence of a good Father-figure, particularly in his earliest years. He would have been conscious of this absence long before he could accept the position intellectually and, moreover, the absence of an earthly father would have made it difficult for him to accept the idea of a Heavenly Father. The meeting of the Good Father and the Good Mother was the answer to the deepest, and unformed, questions regarding his existence. He said: 'I cannot see or hear my father,' and he asked: 'Who am I? for I am utterly formless.' The meeting of the parents would correspond to the coming together of the masculine and feminine parts of his own soul, the spiritual and the earthly, and would provide an essential integration. In that meeting he would have experienced for the first time the infinite compassion and care to be associated with spiritual parenthood. This would then have opened the door to the discovery of the third, spiritual body, without which there can be no wholeness.

The church is very dark, and there is an inner sanctuary, a most sacred place, for it is the place of re-birth. The sacrificial altar is there, upon which the old life must be placed, and from which will be received the cleansing and renewed power of the Eternal Sacrifice. His place must first be at the back of the church, for he must come in humility and reverence or not at all. How difficult it is for him to understand this, for he needs to be told to kneel! We see the grip which his self-love has upon his soul; it has very nearly destroyed him, and he is confronted with one of life's most difficult tasks, which is to turn that love outwards. The outer-body has treated him so cruelly, he feels, that there is no use living in the world at all; he is angry, deeply hurt, insecure, afraid, life is too much for him: so in order to make himself insensitive to it all he has retreated almost entirely within his inner-body. His one contact seemed to be through his proud endeavour, but that had failed him in middle-age, and his over-planned life had fallen to pieces. He summed up the position in a brief dream in which he saw a man (representing himself) sitting at a table (by association taking him back to his mother's breasts), in a daze, with many good things around him; but none of them could he take. The reason for this was that if he did, he would no longer be able to be sorry for himself. In his vision he does not go up to the altar, which implies that he is not ready for the sacrifice of his pride. And, in his retreat from the price to be paid, he is shown in the porch the truth that only 'he that humbleth himself shall be exalted'.

Our traveller added some further comment upon the fact that he was taken to the back row of the church, and he made the observation: 'I was born on the back row; when it came to my turn there was nothing left!'; nevertheless he felt that just as much was expected of him in life as if he had been fully equipped, which made him very angry with God, Who was to him a great Pharaoh demanding bricks without straw. Although he hated God for this, he could do no other than comply. He believed that he was expected to place much upon the altar but, he asked: 'How can I make my offering when I have been given nothing to offer?' and from this he reasoned, 'Because I am not making my offering, God is extremely angry with me, and He will destroy me. God has no use for me or else He would have given me brains, and yet He expects me to use brains in my profession.' He feels that God angrily insists that he proves his worthiness in His sight, which to him is an outrage. The Law's demands are absolute, therefore, against his feelings and his will, he must feverishly seek to satisfy these demands, and pile upon the altar his sacrifices, scrupulous religious observances, deeds of which any Pharisee would be proud, yet they are 'as filthy rags'. This 'bondage to the Law', of which St Paul spoke on many occasions with considerable emphasis, is something from which Christ came to set us free, for it is ever empty and worthless, in that so little of man goes into it, and it is bred of cold obligation and is performed under duress, with an accompaniment of pride, and hidden rebellion because it is imposed. Thus the altar is empty in spite of so great striving, and our traveller has to be humbled and taught the very beginnings of love. For love is free, and it is a thousand leagues removed from calculation and contract, obligation or bargain; and since our friend saw life only in terms of imposition and duty devoid of love, he had nothing to place upon the altar of love.

The last of these fantasies was one in which the traveller enters the winter of his soul before the promise of the re-birth can be fulfilled.

'As I walked down a country lane I saw the rust of autumn, the leaves of the trees were turning brown, and many had fallen on the ground, making a carpet which darkened my footsteps. I thought to myself that autumn, the forerunner of winter, was a wonderful time. The trees which in spring and summer had been so green, so beautiful, had now been stripped of their beauty. But I realized that even when the leaves had gone, there was a stark beauty remaining. It was as if the trees had gone to sleep as some animal hibernates until the warmth of the spring returned.

'As I walked along I caught up with an old man and, joining forces, we walked along, talking of the seasons, the prospects of the winter, and the rush and bustle of life. When I asked him how he felt about being old, he replied: "My son, I do not think that I ever grow very old, at least so far as my soul is concerned. It takes me a long time to do my work, but I accept this as being quite natural. I am quite content to live each day as it comes, to thank God for His goodness in giving me my health and strength to do my work, humble though it be."

'Presently he stopped and, pointing to a cottage hidden amongst the trees, he said goodbye to me. His parting words were: "Go in peace, my son, and may the grace of God be with you in your life.' I waved to him as he went through his door, and went on my journey with his words ringing in my ears. The winter of discontent was at hand, but the hope of spring was before me.'

This was the last in his series of fantasies, and it contained a warning of the hard winter ahead. It is not unusual for the unconscious to forewarn in this manner: it enables the person to feel that, when the storm breaks, nothing is really out of hand, and that a plan is being worked out by the Spirit. The subsequent story of the analysis fully showed the terrifying severity of that winter, but the hope of spring never really died.

It is interesting to note that this man who in his conscious attitude, constantly asserted that he was unable to appreciate the beauty of the world around him, nevertheless in his fantasies, which were largely a product of his unconscious, showed a remarkable appreciation of the beauty of nature.

For the traveller, Time itself was a problem, since he was middle-aged; the falling leaves of his life presented to him a sombre picture, for the spring and the summer had passed, and 'his footsteps were darkened by the leaves'. Although he was aware of the stark beauty of winter, it was too cold for him and his thoughts turned to hibernation, as though he would have hidden himself away from the rigours before him in the body of the great mother Nature. His heart was full of foreboding, when he met his good friend, the Old Man, once again; their conversation was about that which lay so heavily upon the traveller's heart—the coming winter and the coldness which chilled his soul. Death has its terrors for the guilt-stricken soul, for it brings one to judgment; time is that which bears all her sons away and presents them before the Throne of God. It was not surprising, therefore, that he was concerned with the passage of time and the approach of winter.

The Old Man spoke of the folly of the rush and bustle which showed the feverish anxiety 'to eat, drink and be merry, for tomorrow we die', as though life were becoming quickly spent. The neurotic person is as impatient of the present as any discontented baby, and he looks back upon the good old days when he was cosy with his mother who saw to his every need. The Old Man, who has at his command the wisdom of the ages, pointed out that the real values do not suffer by the passage of time; his soul never grew old, for it is ever refreshed by the spiritual-body.

The time of departure had come, and the Old Man bade the traveller farewell as he passed into his cottage, the dwelling of the humble soul. The cottage had not been seen by the traveller, since it was hidden from him by the spreading branches of the trees which were to him the enveloping arms of the mother, whose protection he sought against every hardship of life. The loss of that mother protection was to be his great hurt in the many months of the winter before him, as he won his way to independent manhood. It was amongst the trees of the Garden that the sweat of blood flowed, and it was on a tree that the Lord of Life was crucified, when it was as night. The tree can also symbolize the instinctual urges of life, which crucify us anew as we both accept and transform them. The hope of the Resurrection of Life never died, and as he faced the darkness he received the promise of Divine peace and grace.

This ends the quotations from his fantasies; I hope you have appreciated their value as a means of renewal of life. After a time our friend turned to the writing of poetry, and each morning before his session he would quickly write his verse.

I close this chapter with some verses he wrote which are appropriate to our theme.

> O Heavenly Lord, teach me to know,
> That by Thy love divine,
> I'll find in time the love I need,
> That will my heart refine.
>
> Help me to cast away my hates,
> The envy, and the strife,
> That healed, forgiven, and restored,
> I'll find a better life.
>
> O take my heart in Thy dear hands,
> O enter in with grace,
> That in my mended heart I find
> The power to win the race.
>
> Restore my sight, open my ears,
> Break down my foolish pride,
> That I may live, and truly live,
> And never from Thee hide.
>
> And as the Passion of Thy Son
> Is getting near its end,
> I pray my journey will go on,
> With help that Thou dost send.

O may I look upon the Cross,
As being for me a sign,
Not as a thing of torture, Lord,
But just Thy grace divine.

And as my poor bewildered soul,
Foretells its coming death,
Let me not grieve, nor still lament,
New life *is* coming with Thy breath.

NINE

WHOLENESS

WE ENDED the last chapter by referring to the whole Self, and we have come to assume health to be synonymous with wholeness. This requires some examination. Dr R. Lambourne[1] is critical of this assumption, and he says it is high time we gave the idea an honourable burial. He points out that wholeness is usually related to 'form', and he instances Chinese vases and Greek sculpture. This is something different from what is meant by wholeness in the Bible. We can appreciate his point when we visualize him on his rounds seeing many saintly people, who are anything but whole in the Greek sense, and who are yet whole as the Bible would see them. It is a point which needs to be made; however, we would suggest in psychological practice the Greek notion of wholeness has more relevance.

Exactly what is meant by wholeness in the Bible is something which I must hand over to the theologians to settle, for the idea is by no means clear. As with other ideas in the Bible, there is discernible a development in the concept of wholeness. It is made all the more difficult in this case since the notion not only includes a relationship with God and the community, but also physical and, what we should call, 'mental' sickness. A psychosomatic relationship is involved. The people of our Lord's day regarded sickness as a punishment for sin, which belief our Lord went out of His way to deny at least on one occasion, and mental sickness was believed to be the work of demoniacal influences. It seems to me that we shall never know exactly how our Lord viewed the causation of sickness. However, we do know the power He had to heal both the physical and mental aspects of illness, and that this power operated by something passing as 'virtue' from Him into the sick person; the sick person was influenced, he was

[1] A. A. Jones (Ed.)—*The Wonder of Divine Healing*, Arthur James, 1958.

made 'whole'. The incident of the Ten Lepers (LUKE xvii. 12) suggests that such healings did not always establish a new relationship with God, yet within the men something happened in the direction of wholeness.

Our everyday language speaks of 'an unbalanced person', and in our psychological jargon there is the 'integrated personality'. Here we are using the idea of wholeness in the Greek sense, it presents the notion of a personality of symmetrical form, with proportion and balance, something which we should all desire for ourselves. Moreover, we feel that our religion has an essential part to play in the attainment of the highest measure of integration. Jung has made this search for wholeness a central feature of his psychology. It is the four-sidedness of the square where the opposites balance one another, the four quarters of the soul's universe with the basic elements of Intellect and Emotion, Sensation and Intuition. This is no invention but has been presented to us by Jung as a scientific discovery within the realm of the psyche. This personal four-sidedness is frequently brought to our notice in the dreams and drawings which people bring to the analytic session, without having any idea at all of the significance of what they have done; it may be a picture of a walled garden or town, usually with its centre piece, or they may produce a perfectly patterned square, or sometimes a circle, the chief feature of which is the symmetry or the movement towards it. I have many scores of such drawings.

The discovery of wholeness, what Jung calls Individuation, is what we work for in the analysis, and we see it taking place as by an inner movement of the Spirit as the work proceeds. The wonder of it is that it takes place outside conscious control. We see people ill just because they lack this balance and symmetry. Perhaps it is because they are all head and no heart, or all earth and no heaven; there is too much of the sky's blue or the flaming red of the passion, but when these two meet we have the royal purple; the healing comes as the opposite parts are married, and the new Self is the product of that marriage. Around these meeting points considerable tension is experienced, and the pain of birth may even be found to be too much, in which case wholeness is never achieved; yet it is just at the point where the opposites meet that growth and new life take place. The Cross was firmly embedded in the earth yet it reached high into the heaven. Thus healing is a bringing together into a new or greater state of relatedness of the many parts of our three bodies in which our life is lived.

The unique personality of our Lord, expressed fully in each of the three bodies, through drawing into itself the life of man as well as by His supreme outpouring love, effected new levels of integration in the people who responded to Him. He brought reconciliation and transformation which nowhere else could be found. In the inner oppositions between light and darkness, the good and the evil, where there is an ever present tension, He brought, through the very conflict, a higher level of being. Even failure to achieve a transformation was not wasted in the economy of spiritual growth: the Saul who persecuted the Christian Church was transformed into the Paul who established the Church more than any other person, the denials of Peter were transformed into the very spearhead of the first Church. By sin, grace abounds. The hate, and the hurts born of it, by reconciliation through forgiveness raised man to a new glory, bondage gave freedom greater value, 'the thorn in the flesh' and many other infirmities led the Apostle to give glory to God, for out of weakness comes so great strength. It is in this very context of suffering that the neurotic has his growing point for he, to regain any measure of wholeness, must cease to wallow in his self-pity and hates and grievances, and learn to take his sufferings as the points from which life will blossom as the rose. The hurts of the past are used creatively. However, this transformation is effected not only on the conscious level but in the deeper levels of the unconscious mind. So long as we are caught up in these conflicts of life passively and negatively there can be no wholeness and healing. The Cross is never something merely to be borne. Our Lord, with utmost clarity, presented to men these growing points, He made them face the issue, the utmost choices in life in all their stark opposition, and in the working out of a reconciliation they discovered they were whole. He showed how their anger should be used when he drove out of the Temple the money changers, He showed how the publicans and sinners could be brought into the service of God. It is no wonder that the common people heard Him gladly. He gave them hope for He took their 'down-to-earthness', which the pious despised and condemned, and reconciled it with

Heaven. His great love redirected hate into hate of the evil, self-love into self-respect, and the whole burden of guilt was removed because He took it upon Himself; thus they took up their beds and walked, and it was because they had in part become whole. For perfect wholeness they would have to wait until they reached the Heavenly City, but this was at least 'a day's march nearer Home'.

It may be along these lines that we can better understand William James's 'Once Born' and 'Twice Born' souls. The Once Born are they who, from the beginning of their lives, have been caught up, to a far smaller extent that the average person, in the play of opposites; within their inner-body they have known no real problem of feeding in their infancy, and the successive stages of the development have gone forward with unusual ease. All the time they have enjoyed an outer-body which has been bathed in sunshine, although there have been difficulties to overcome. Irenic influences have surrounded them, for the mother gave them all the love and security they needed, without excess or stint. The relationship between father and mother was happy and duly proportionate, the rivalries of other children were at a minimum, and there was a natural outlook upon all things natural. Religion was that of the Good Shepherd, where holiness and love were blended, and duty was love's expression set within a framework of living which was no more disciplined than it was kind. In a home where the sunshine of God bathes happiness and suffering alike, and where the family life is daily renewed in Him, the child has the conditions set for his being of the Once Born, although even then it is not guaranteed for the unconscious must be taken into account, and some chance happening in life may stir its deep waters and create great problems. Such a person as we have been describing will never have known a time when God was unreal to him. He will be a well integrated personality in which his unfettered energies will be expended freely and happily in the service of God and man.

The Once Born person is obviously living satisfactorily in all three bodies. He is 'at home' in each of them and they are for him bound together in a unity of experience. Such a picture of the person who has a good measure of wholeness shows that what we might describe as the value of the soul, measured by our standards, rests upon a multiplicity of factors drawn together in a single direction. It humbles that pride which regards man as being capable of working out his own salvation without the aid of a Saviour. This attitude may be found in much Jungian practice. God's ways of working are wider than the measure of man's mind, and in His scheme, He doubtless has a place for the discoveries of the Spirit which man has made along many devious paths. I believe that the non-religious Jungian therapist is working by the Holy Spirit unwittingly, and without Him he would achieve nothing. A Jungian therapy works within the depths of the soul, and it is here where we are closest to God; we should not think of God as operating entirely from without. We need to recall the parable of the leaven working secretly; the seed growing secretly finally produces maturity within the Kingdom of God. Jung uses extensively all religious symbolism in a scientific context, but when we fill this symbolism with its rich spiritual content it has added therapeutic potency as we well know from our own experience.

Each one of us may have within him a small corner of his soul protected from the rest, and dearly prized, which belongs to the experience of the Once Born; at least we hope so, for it enables us to appreciate their experience. However, most of us belong to the Twice Born, for our lot has not been cast in so fair a ground as the Once Born. We have been caught up in violent tensions of the opposites, grim fantasies of infancy haunt us still and our outer body has been like the troubled sea or the desolate wastes, and the third body has been remote. We have had, or we need to have, a shattering experience of conversion. There can be no wholeness so long as we live with the old hates and resentments, the jealousy and envy, the murderous rage, the ruthless fight for superiority, the indulgence of self-pity or frightened flight from responsibility. All this, and much more besides, needs to be transformed and nothing but an experience which shakes us to the very foundations can effect it. A mighty act of redemption is the only hope. The most eschatological language is no exaggeration of the experience.

To make my point clearer in regard to Jung's use of symbolism in dealing with the sick personality, I would say a little from his point of view upon the necessity of this great experience of conversion or transformation. The raw material of life has to be placed in the crucible before the fine gold of life is known, which is like the Psalmist's being purified seven times in the fire, seven being the perfect number; it is this tribulation which brings forth the gold of the New Jerusalem. The vital experience hurts greatly, and is most costly. It contains all the terror of the Jonah motif, where the fugitive and frightened soul has to descend into the monster's belly, that great Leviathan, in order to be reborn a new man. This is much the same experience as that of the Virgilian journey into the underworld of evil odours and frightening shapes. The same essential theme may be presented as a Pilgrim's Progress of many trials and threatenings, such as the monster on the path which must be passed. A very frequent presentation is that of the dark cavern which must be entered and passed through if the light beyond is to be reached. That cavern holds ghastly monsters. These are but variants in expression of the supreme theme of Calvary, the tomb, the Descent into Hell, and the Rising on the third day. The Twice Born, from the scientific Jungian standpoint, must bear this bitter, terrifying and most painful experience before the new life can be known. Such are the experiences through which the Spirit takes the Soul on its dark night journey to the land of everlasting light. It is catastrophic, and to be near to someone passing through such an experience is to be filled with a holy fear, for one is witnessing things which cannot be spoken. The Twice Born Soul is a reality and he is seen by his measure of wholeness which engages life at a new level both in the inner and the outer bodies and, whether realized or not, also in the third body of the Spirit. New and better relationships are the obvious reward.

On the physical level an illness usually breaks down relationships with the outer-body, for it takes a man from his work, sometimes from his home. It prevents the wholesome service to fellow man being made, betrays self-esteem which is an important item in human relatedness, and tends to make him run away from life and hide himself like a sick animal. If in one case the fault may seem to be due to the weakness in the inner-body, so in another the responsibility for the breakdown of satisfactory relationships may be due to the attitude of the outer-body because it has appeared to be too unresponsive to the infant, it withheld its protective love, the child was frozen stiff by psychic coldness, terrified at being left to face life alone, panic stricken by hunger, ousted by rivals from the living space, and made to feel that Nature is unnatural and unclean. That outer-body was first known as the breast, it grew into mother, into father, brothers and sisters, playmates and finally the total material and personal universe. The first experiences are bound to colour those that follow. So when the breast is hostile and unresponsive, a whole chain of experiences of rejectedness and unrelatedness follow; subsequent experience may just go to prove that first impressions were correct. Not being able to come to happy terms with the outer-body is one of the major causes of mental sickness and loss of wholeness. A man's adjustment to the third-body is something which belongs to later life and may easily become, though unrecognized, the major issue of his adult life. Things happen to us, in life, which are powerful enough to destroy our ideas of God and the spiritual world—ideas which all too often have never grown beyond our infantile outlook. At an early stage of life God carries the projection of the bad mother and bad father images when the parents appear to be more bad than good; God may be presented as a policeman, and He becomes identified with the vicious Super-Ego in so many cases. All this may happen within the inner-body, but there comes from without the crude unloving presentation of God, the God Who is more interested in seeing that His commandments are kept than the wellbeing of His children, the God whose punishments are out of all proportion to the sin and Who is made to be more vindictive than any mortal. God also may be presented as the Utterly Unknowable or Utterly Other One with Whom there can obviously be no relatedness; out of a desire to give Him the glory due to Him He becomes so high and lifted up that no man can ever reach Him. Indeed He is presented as the Great Opposite, for all that we are and feel and think is finite, and He is the Infinite One, necessarily out of relationship in any living sense of the word. All this is taking away an essential part of the Soul which must live and move and have its being in the spiritual-body, as it does in the other two bodies. An initial mistaken and bad response on the part of the infant and older child to the outer, and the third spiritual-body, sets a course which

N

can lead to ever widening divergence as the years pass on, and with that divergence comes weakening and loss of relationship with its consequent mental sickness.

The task before us is to help that frightened and isolated Self back into a condition of relatedness to its outer and spiritual-body. This work is anything but easy to effect because, as we have said, it needs must, in the case of a seriously ill person, take us into the unconscious mind where the terrors and the hurts of the past are buried. Merely to inform the conscious mind is hopelessly inadequate; a real measure of reliving the past experiences is needed. The psycho-therapeutic ministry, in reaching these deep levels and re-enacting them takes the Self out of its isolation by building up a new relationship with the therapist himself, which will expand into ever wider relationships. It is the experience of a new kingdom in which life can be exercised in service. It is significant that our Lord spoke so often about the King-dom; in fact to enter His Kingdom was to pass from death into life, from sickness into health. He brought to people a new sense of belonging; the lost were found, those who deemed themselves as outcasts found themselves taken into a relationship pulsating with the warmth of love, the hopeless took up again their courage, sinners their self-respect; it was because they were given a place in life, because they were wanted after all and were believed in. Love-starvation was their common complaint, which is to say their loss of relation-ship. The depth of our Lord's personality with its love, strong and devoid of sentimentality, reached the hidden depths of the sick soul and, through His relationship, effected, with one glance and word, what we effect so slowly and haltingly, if at all.

The secret of our Lord's work was infinitely more than His sublime teaching. That has inspired mankind as no other ever has, yet it was always the relationship which He established that sent men away praising God for what He had done for them in healing their sickness. In some same way we know the effect upon us of a friend, especially of a friend in need; there is a mystery of fellowship, an intercourse which has no lan-guage which still is spoken, and by which there comes to us new life. This taken to the nth degree is what our Lord did for people. This same unutterable word of healing He meant to go forth from the body He left behind, His Church. We, as a Church, were commissioned to heal in His Name. This healing work consists of the establishing of loving relationships. Our ministry must be exercised corporately.

Before we pass on further, to say something about the group or fellowship as being an important instrument in our ministry of healing, we must say something about the greatest of all instruments of transformation, the Cross. This is the greatest act of healing ever enacted. Like Moses' serpent lifted up in the wilderness, it has brought salvation to many sick souls lost in their private wilderness. Nothing ever looked so desperate as Calvary, therefore it can deal with the deepest despair; never was there one so outcast and despised of men, no figure so lonely, no pain of mind and body so great as in Him Who was so sensitive. Further, no demonstration of care like that has ever been seen, the great Shepherd of the sheep laying down His life for the lost. There the Cross stands, whether we look at it or not, declaring the out-reaching and out-pouring love of God to all sorts and conditions of men, so that those who feel themselves to be nobody's child, forsaken and unjustly treated by the world, can know that the One Who matters most of all understands and cares. But even this is not all, for however we seek to explain it, it was a saving act, effecting reconciliation and restoring us to fellowship with God and man. Christ there was taking into Himself our shame, the very depths of our guilt, the bitterest hates and resentments, the jealousy and the intolerant pride, the greed and coldest indifference; He embraced with His outstretched arms the whole burden of our sin and let it die with Him, and thus being set free we can rise with Him into the Resurrection life. This has immense therapeutic value when people, stricken by the full bitterness of their guilt, lay their burdens in His arms. It is 'the old, old story of Jesus and His love' which, in the analytic situation, we see before our eyes taking away the sins of the world. In that scene are drawn together the heights of Heaven and the depths of earth, the utmost hate and the utmost love, pride and humility, strength and weakness, shame and glory, life and death. Just as these opposites are made to face one another and in their tension give rise to a new integration, so the broken relationship with God is raised to a new level of experience, and our broken-down relationships with one another are built up into a new community of the forgiven and the forgiving. We are received back into the life of the world, and we live in the fellowship of the Holy Spirit.

The Cross draws us to Him in Whom we all meet; He is the fountain head of our fellowship with one another, for the closer we draw to Him the closer we are caught up in His Church. As St Paul says:

'(ye) are built upon the foundation of the apostles and prophets, Jesus Christ being the chief cornerstone; in Whom all the building fitly framed together groweth unto an holy temple in the Lord: in Whom ye also are builded together for an habitation of God through the Spirit.' EPHESIANS ii. 20, 22.

Like the stones in our ancient churches, all shapes and sizes, we fit together making that which is whole; it is the relatedness of the many differences which makes the fair temple of the Lord. An even more striking illustration is given by the Apostle in the fourth chapter of the same epistle, where he refers to the many parts of the body with diversity of function and comeliness making a whole. There is the organic wholeness in which all share in the wholesomeness of the parts or in their ineffectiveness. All this emphasizes the importance of being related in the right way. We can sense here something of the Greek idea of wholeness as 'form', for the many members of body, as also the many different parts of the temple, form into a harmonious and symmetrical whole; the stresses are contained and balanced; the needs of the whole are overruling. The Biblical idea of wholeness, it seems to me, is mainly that of relatedness—it is being 'right with God' and 'right with one's neighbour'. This wholeness is inseparable from the religious community. It would therefore seem that the Greek and Biblical ideas of wholeness are aspects of the same thing, they are inseparable. Right relationships make for beauty of 'form', the fair beauty of the Lord.

In our concept of the outer body we have been showing that our surround, personal and material, is an essential part of life. The wider are our interests and personal contacts with this outer-body the better it is for us, but these contacts will bring frustrations and pains for they will multiply the tensions of the opposites; nevertheless, as we have said, these are growing points and by meeting them new levels of experience will emerge. We shall find through our life in the outer-body that we are caught up in the corporate sin of man, and in an even greater degree in the moral sickness of other people. If we were saved from sharing the sin and sickness of other people, we should not have the incomparable gain of sharing their good and the benefits we derive from this extension of our life into the outer-body. Perhaps we have never been so much aware of our outer-body as in these days of the atomic bomb, the intense pressure of international affairs with its cold war, the impersonalization of work through mechanization, the impact of the wireless and particularly the television, the sallies into outer space, the unprecedented rate of advance in scientific knowledge and technology. The result of all this is that the part of us which is the outer-body is moving at a pace with which the inner-body cannot keep up, so that there is a real feeling of insecurity which contrasts with the stability, for example, of Cranford and Barchester. But, however important this material side of the outer-body may be, it is not to be compared with the value of personal relationships.

Time after time the way back to health is the way back into the full life of the outer-body. This is being demonstrated by Group Therapy. This therapy is being increasingly used in our hospitals and it has much to commend it, as the results show. A small group of mentally sick people meet with a leader, and their tasks together are verbal in character; the patients are expected to keep the group discussion going. They are expected to be candid in the discussion of their troubles, problems, symptoms, etc.; they turn personal problems into group problems, where it is a great help to discover that other people have chips on their shoulder similar to one's own, and thus people within the group help one another out of their own experiences; and they also help each other in sorting out the tangles of each member's life. There is considerable value in feeling that other people are after all interested in one, or that one is not the only pebble on the beach. The Church has long used this idea of public confession, although our normal congregation is far too large for the therapeutic work of Group Therapy. Besides this, as was felt about the Oxford Group, over-much publicity of private life is not a good thing, except when it is confined to a small circle of people who have become a fellowship and entity amongst themselves.

Nevertheless, the confession of 'sin' within the small group helps the patient to realize that he is not the biggest criminal in all the world, by hearing that others in the group are the same as he. Thus there is a sharing out of the guilt, and it is seen in better proportions. The emotional environment of the group is more important than the rational contributions, and when it comes to the expression of the intense emotions, such as anger and jealousy, the feeling of the group on the matter is often more effective than that of a single person.

Healing work is of the nature of a change in the personality of the patient, with the result that the symptoms are alleviated or cured. It is possible to produce these effects without an enrichment of the personality, as in the case of leucotomy, where the personality deteriorates, or where a smothering effect is produced. In the therapy we envisage and use, there is a considerable movement towards greater wholeness, so that the person becomes a better person in himself. This is definitely effected in many cases by means of Group Therapy, as it is by individual analysis. An advantage of Group Therapy, besides being able to deal with larger numbers than the individual therapy can, is that there are wider forces operating for good—the individual therapist has become the group, and it is a short step from the group to the outside world. However, there are patients who cannot obtain the benefit they should from the group treatment; somehow they cannot play, or they may be so seriously ill that a full-scale analysis is imperative. I have helped various people who either gained nothing from Group Therapy, or who were improved by it but not sufficiently.

The emphasis in all this is upon the value of being taken back into the outer-body, and the consequent enlargement of the Self. Perhaps in some quarters Group Therapy is regarded as an entirely new idea, but the principle of it is adumbrated in the Old Testament, where Israel is a spiritual community, and in the New Testament, where so much emphasis is laid upon the Kingdom of God, and the Church as the Body of Christ, where all the members have an organic unity. Group Therapy is the fulfilment of St Paul's injunction to the Galatians:

'Brethren, if a man be overtaken in a fault, ye which are spiritual, restore such a one in the spirit of meekness. Bear ye one another's burdens, and so fulfil the law of Christ.' vi., 1,2.

In the Gospel there is the instruction, when dealing with an offender who is proving difficult, to 'take with thee one or two more, that in the mouth of two or three witnesses every word may be established. And if he neglect to hear them, tell it unto the church. . . .' The intimate communal life of the Primitive Church is entirely in line with modern Group Therapy, and as Dr Frank Lake insists, we shall have to break up our church-life into smaller units along such lines if the larger life of the Church is to become more effective. It is often the call of the psychiatrists of our hospitals, to the Church, to provide small groups of loving friendship into which their patients may be directed upon leaving hospital. When we can meet such a request we are doing a therapeutic work of great importance.

Finally, there is the greater body in which we live, the spiritual-body. However rich the outer-body may be in human relationships, it is inadequate to satisfy all the requirements of the Self. The value which the humanist sets upon life has but man's own authority, and in times of stress the question will rise 'What is man?' If we can give the Psalmist's answer to this question: 'Thou madest him a little lower than the angels, to crown him with glory and honour,' we are raising the status of man into another dimension. Without that valuation few will be able to escape the depression born of futility. We all need self-respect, but what self-respect is there so long as we see ourselves like the grass? 'The days of man are but as grass: for he flourisheth as a flower of the field. For as soon as the wind goeth over it, it is gone: and the place thereof shall know it no more'. (PSALM ciii. 15, 16).

Another fundamental need of man is to feel secure, and the only abiding security is that of 'the Everlasting Arms' and the Divine promise to be with us always. Our deepest need of all is love, but as the years pass by and friends are no more, when the children have forsaken us and love is left to the National Insurance, how poor has become that outer-body! But if we have been lifted up into a body which was before everlasting, and which is not contained by time and space, whose life is the Divine Love, nothing more is left to be desired, for we can trust all that we care for into its keeping. Man's spirit needs this dimension, and it is through a sense of relatedness at this deepest level that we shall draw closest to the perfect wholeness.

Whether the fellowship of the Church be strong or weak, there is this provision. She is on the side of wholeness so long as she proclaims the love of God. One way of combating disease is to keep the body strong; this is true of the sickness which threatens the mind. A positive view of life must be kept before us, even when it is necessary to retrace our steps into the dark past. I cannot think of anywhere where so positive a view of life is to be found as within the Church of Jesus Christ. Even if our organizations are not what they should be, and may we never be content with that, they are providing some degree of relationship. Clubs for rock 'n' rollers, and for other rebellious young people, all serve their purpose in so far as they are helping them to discover the rudiments of the personal outer-body. The Church would fail them if she did not take them beyond this stage. From all this they may come to find an answer to their existential questionings and discover what is the meaning of their Being.

The third-body brings before us the full significance of relationships. The summary was given by our Lord when He said:

'Thou shalt love the Lord thy God with all thy heart, and with all thy soul, and with all thy mind, and with all thy strength. This is the first and great commandment. And the second is like, namely this: Thou shalt love thy neighbour as thyself.'

This is the last word on the matter, it gathers together all the law and the prophets. This third body is the fellowship of the Holy Spirit which penetrates the inner and the outer bodies at every point.

We see in the Jungian scheme that relatedness is the key to the problem of the Self, and in so far as the inner-body is concerned it is expressed by the balance of the square, or the symmetry of the circle. These themselves, like the outer- and the inner-bodies, are related to the centre-piece. You will remember the drawings I mentioned previously, where the garden has its central fountain—not far removed from the well and from Him Who sat there and discussed the water of eternal life—or the city with its centre—Jerusalem with its temple is doubtless in our minds. There is a relatedness to the centre. I have had brought to me, from time to time, drawings of arrows being shot at a target where the person is trying to find his own centre. It is a spiritual exercise, for at that centre is God.

When we turn to the Freudian picture of life we are immediately confronted with a supremely important system of relationships, where the mother is first and father second, with a wide range of family relationships following. Once again, the all important thing is relationship. The religions of the world deal with relationships in some way or another. Relationships are the central factor in experience and this is confirmed by the fact of clinical experience, that when relationships go wrong a person becomes ill; the collapsed edifice of life is rebuilt as the relationships are restored. On the political and international scene the same fact is revealed, relationships are the beginning and the end of the matter. The philosophy of relationships is the philosophy of life.

It is here where we see the third spiritual-body to be the key to the whole, for the spiritual realm is nothing if it is not made up of relationships. The Godhead is even seen to be a Trinity. The Christian religion establishes relationships, in its great reconciling function, both vertically and horizontally. Where the four arms of the Cross meet there is a figure, Person or persons, and it is He Who effects the relatedness. Our mystical union with Him in prayer, sacrament and meditation is our being caught up into the realm where all things have their place and are made one single whole. The Many and the One are reconciled, not by loss of identity as in a universal sea of being, but by each one sharing in the fullness of all, and the means by which this relationship is achieved is Love.

Love is nothing if it is not a relationship, and it implies at least two beings; as long as love remains we feel secure and fear is overcome. God is love; and to live within that body is to know an eternal security and joy. Those people who have a living experience of life in this body have a great power for health of mind. The Christian ministry to those sick folk of whom we have been thinking is to help them to discover this spiritual-body so that they live within their own trinity.

TEN

PROSPECT

In this concluding chapter I shall discuss what seem to me to be the practical possibilities before the Church of a less detailed knowledge of psychotherapeutic procedure than here set forth, in general, and of this specialist ministry, in particular, At the outset it is obvious that if the clergy had a better understanding of this subject, which always takes them to the heart of human behaviour, first of all they would benefit themselves in many ways, and this would give an added effectiveness to all their ministry. People would find that the clergy had more to contribute than they imagined, and that the parson would be discovered to be down-to-earth, as well as up in the sky, where sometimes they feel him to be out of reach.

A second gain would be an almost entirely new awareness of what constitutes sickness of the soul. The trained priest would find the neurotic condition, which we all share in some degree, related to what he calls Original Sin. Those who are deeply entangled in mental illness will reveal what is happening in the less seriously afflicted. He may find that he has to make some change in the labels he puts upon himself and other people. He will gain a profounder understanding of what lies behind Isaiah's words:

'Why should ye be stricken any more? Ye will revolt more and more: the whole head is sick, and the whole heart faint. From the sole of your foot even unto the head there is no soundness in it; but wounds, and bruises, and putrifying sores: they have not been closed, neither bound up, neither mollified with ointment.' i, 5, 6.

This new awareness would be of the part which the unconscious mind plays in life, and of the patterns of behaviour which a man will follow outside the control of consciousness and as by an inner law. It will save him the labour of spending fruitless hours over people's problems, for a psychological understanding would at once lead to his making a very different and more successful approach than he had ever dared to hope for by a purely rational handling of the situation.

The knowledge of psychological functioning would in many cases revolutionize our personal approach to people, and the reactions they cause in us. Often we should find ourselves asking: Why am I reacting in this particular way when dealing with certain difficult people? and an honest answer, aided by our psychological insight, might well change the whole relationship. We find that one of the great gains of an analysis is an altogether new ability to suffer 'fools' and psychological knaves gladly. The difficult person may remain difficult because he is following unconsciously his infantile pattern, but our seeing through this makes us tolerant and even profoundly sympathetic. We can visualize many transformed Parochial Church Council meetings as a result!

Apart from this, although we may realize there are many more personal dustbins than we ever imagined, we should be less weighed down by the 'sin' of the world because much of it would be seen to be moral sickness. We should be far less worried by the militant atheists, for we see them sending their defiance to the wrong address. We should be no longer horrified at the most lurid confessions people have to make, because no longer should we view such as the products of a person with full conscious control of his life. We should at once realize the sickness and thus avoid great hurt and further damage as the result of misunderstanding; whereas before we should have blamed, now we give hope through understanding and encouragement. This is the more difficult way by far, for it is a simple matter to distribute labels from the sin box and plaster them down hard on all and sundry. Surely it is this kind of thing which makes people feel we lack understanding, and say it is of no use going to the parson for he will only blame and have pious words to say. It is a fact of experience that, as the result of being known to have psychological understanding, many people have come to me who otherwise would never have dreamed of coming to me or of going to any other parson. This alone should commend such a ministry to the

Church which by the old methods leaves the multitudes unmoved in the wilderness.

So far we have spoken about the gain to be had from an overall psychological understanding. There will be, and in fact there are, many clergy who want to have more than a general awareness of so important a field of intimate personal knowledge so that they can better serve their Lord. For them the future holds unspeakable joys and satisfactions, although at times a sword will pierce their own souls. New life can be given for old to many sick, distressed folk by means of sanctified common sense informed by a reasonable amount of psychological knowledge. This will have to be a main objective of the Church, for there are not sufficient clergy to allow for a large number of them to be withdrawn from the depleted ranks to engage in specialist activity. However, one would not doubt that when such a specialist ministry became recognized and provided for in some way it would meet with a very considerable response from young men, and possibly women also, who otherwise would not consider the ordinary ministry of the Church. It might well raise the whole status of the ministry in the eyes of the undergraduate class, and they might undertake psychiatric training to that end for their university course. But this is to hurry on too fast with my theme.

We have been considering the many people who are not sufficiently ill to require special aid but who are distressed persons, and who could be made whole by the average psychologically enlightened parish priest. There remain the more seriously ill persons. In view of the many examples given in the previous pages, it is clear that here is a special task to perform in the Name of Jesus Christ. But this requires much reading and training, yet it is clear that a number of clergy to act as specialists is indispensable, for the clergyman in the G.P. category will always have a number of people coming to him with whom he cannot and should not deal. One practical difficulty is that although, generally, one has a good idea of the seriousness of a person's disorder in the first few interviews, something hidden in the unconscious may present itself after some time and this may demand immediate action and a psychic operation of a major order may have to be undertaken calling for considerable skill and understanding. This is quite likely to happen in hysterical cases. Sometimes the most indefinite symptoms demand the longest and most difficult analysis. Such was the case of a young man whose main complaint was his failure to come to grips with things. He could do his work moderately well, but all the time he knew he was not living as he should no matter how hard he tried. No one would ever have suspected anything was wrong with him and he would have merited, by all appearances, a prize for virile manhood. His problem was most obdurate, ever remaining unexciting and uneventful, though we never felt ourselves to be in a position of stalemate. The analysis dragged on for two years and the demands it made were quite considerable; the conclusion was well worth all the expenditure of time. His analytical story was well summed up in one of his closing dreams in which he was visiting a doctor for treatment upon his knee, but it turned out that he required a major operation on his spine. In such a case there was no fear of matters passing out of control, but in other cases it is sometimes otherwise.

The most remarkable instance I have had of the simple case becoming complex was that of a young man who found his stammer to be a handicap in his professional work. He had obtained a very good degree at Oxford, and in a highly competitive examination in his profession he came near to the top of the list out of a thousand entrants. His considerable acumen was brought to play upon his problem and for a month or two all went well, with a marked improvement. Then the trouble began. It was Lent and his vicar was preaching a course of sermons on Sacrifice and Paying the Price. He went on a Monday evening during this penitential season to hear Odette Churchill give a lecture upon her wartime experiences. On his way home from the lecture he asked himself: Should I have been able to have gone through all that? In the early hours of the morning he woke up with acute appendix pains; the doctor was called and on the Thursday he was admitted to hospital. Information as to the medical side of the story is lacking at this point, save that he was regarded by the staff as a strange kind of patient. He had his operation and when he was coming round from the anaesthetic he asked a nurse: When is it Good Friday? He was enacting an atonement by his suffering. Odette Churchill was screening his mother, towards whom he had sadistic fantasies buried in his unconscious. For these he must atone on the strict principle of 'an eye for an eye, and a tooth for a tooth'. Good Friday would mark the completion of his sufferings. But the Good Friday he sought was still far distant from him.

The stay in the hospital was protracted to a month, during which time numerous complications developed, for he was still unsatisfied in his mind that he had paid a sufficient price of suffering. Shortly after his discharge from the hospital I happened to return to my Vicarage, which is beside St Margaret's church, when I saw Edmund coming out of the church in a semi-collapsed state. He had only just returned to work at his office, but this was in the middle of the morning. I have never seen anyone look so green; he was ghastly. He managed to blurt out that he had a gastric ulcer and that he was dying. His chest was heaving violently and he was sweating with the pain. I assisted him into the Vicarge, where we took stock of the situation; under the circumstances the normal procedure would have been to summon an ambulance, but knowing Edmund I looked for something other than a physical disorder. We soon discovered that his mind was working upon his father, who had died as the result of stomach complaints, including a gastric ulcer. Once again the atonement pattern was in operation; he had wished, in his infantile fantasies, his father dead. Thus he must suffer to the same degree, and in the same way, as his father suffered in his final illness. He at once became easier on a discussion of all this, and the heaving subsided and he looked generally better; in the afternoon he was back at his office. Following upon these two incidents the analytical pressure ran very high and he was acutely ill. At last the time came when he could do his work reasonably well and an opening came along to join an important firm. This he took and, although he was far from what he should be, for his various hysterical symptoms were still operative, he left Leicester to make this new start in life. I passed him on to a well-known psychiatrist, who treated him for a further eighteen months.

The moral of this story is that if the Church is going to take this work in hand it is essential that there should be some clergy who could cope with such an experience as this. Perhaps kindly disposed psychiatrists could give assistance? but where are they, outside London, who not only would have the time, but also experience in analytical therapy? Such a therapy is incredibly difficult to obtain. Nevertheless, the experienced clergy must have someone to whom they can go for advice, and in such cases as this, to whom they can pass on 'their headaches'.

At the risk of repetition I would stress the need for clerical therapists learned and trained in these matters. It is impossible to over-emphasize the necessity for extensive study of psycho-therapeutic literature, as well as for special training, if such work as is outlined in this book is to be undertaken. No one should enter upon it without being fully aware of the complexities of the task, and of the possible risks entailed. One unsuitable person treading where angels fear to tread could bring this ministry into disrepute, and counteract the good-will gained by many priest-therapists fully adequate to the work. What has come to be known as 'Counselling', which is the assisting of people by means of a psychological approach, is one thing, and depth psychotherapy is another, and these two should never be confused. Never for a moment should it be imagined that Counselling is all that a Church is called upon to perform; were this so, almost all the people mentioned in this book, and many more who could have been mentioned, would still be in bondage to the worst of all pain, and would be outside the fold of the Church; and, further, our Lord's commission to heal the sick would, to that extent, have been left unfulfilled.

The mention of psychiatrists brings us to the financial aspects of the work. Doctors have to live, and the psychiatrists who are most likely to help, because they have the time, are those outside the mental hospital service. Such psychiatrists— and there are few enough outside London—have to make their living by charging fees. They could not be expected to fill their lists, which they could easily do, with people passed on to them from the Church, who are not usually in a position to afford their fees. They could not be expected to take on this long list of patients who, without exception, would be diffi-cult, and who would, therefore, be on their books for many months. The truth of the matter is that such psychiatrists are just not there, so we shall have to fall back upon the resources available within the Church.

The question of the payment of the specialist priest-therapist remains. He, like the doctor, must live and this service must have a practical foundation. I personally have never made a charge for my services. I like to think of the Church, and He Who is the Head of the Church and Who gave commission to heal, as being the only One to Whom thanks should be given and the thank-offerings be made. As part of the priest's ministry, this help that we are able to bring should be the free gift of God to his Children, for it is only one of the unnumbered mercies with which He surrounds us. It seems to me that if fees were paid to the priest-therapist it would look as though the account had been settled, and the person might well go away feeling satisfied with himself for having found something on the cheap! There is also the feeling I have, doubtless a legacy of having been brought up in a clerical family, that one cannot send in a bill for preaching the Gospel—of which healing is so integral a part. Further, it looks like trading upon the infirmities of people. This must sound very strange to a medical man, and he has every right to quote the Scriptures and say 'The labourer is worthy of his hire'. The psychiatrists also might add that the payment of a fee is part of the treatment. The neurotic is self-centred by nature of his disorder, and it is necessary to turn his attention to the outer-body, and the people who belong to it, who have their rights. He is far too ready to expect the world to come running to him, and to take all that is given without so much as a thank you, as it was in the case of the nine lepers in the Gospel. Thus the psychiatrist may say that the payment of a fee does the patient good (as it does the psychiatrist!); it helps the patient to realize that he has received services and that there are obligations, and that he must begin to look away from himself and see things from the other's point of view. There is good sense in this. Further, there are the people who would unduly cling to the therapist; this is all the more likely if they do not have to pay anything for it!

Thus there are two sides to the question. Perhaps the squeamishness of the priest could be overcome by the work being a department of diocesan organization. In this way the diocese could collect a fee as a contribution to the work of the Church, and some of it could come back to the therapist as salary. But when all has been said on the subject of fees I am still of the opinion that the clergy in particular, and the Church in general, should not make a charge, save possibly the merest token, for their services. Thankofferings—yes; fees—no; and the thankofferings to go to the Church rather than to the therapist. However, if the priest-therapist should not make money out of his ministry, neither should he be out of pocket by it. There are expenses over and above those of the ordinary parish priest, such as books which are necessary for frequent reference and which, in this specialist sphere, are expensive; telephone calls and correspondence may be considerable charges. I have made reference to the Vicarage furniture, which at times receives very rough handling; and an abnormal amount of fuel is used, since one is confined to the house most of the day.

This brings us to the other half of the problem. When there were such things as redundant churches in our towns and cities, with the barest minimum of parochial responsibility, some of them could have been set aside as centres for this specialist activity; they would have provided a house and a basic salary, they also would have to be central. But today this is unfortunately a crying over spilt milk, for with the schemes for the re-organization of manpower under redundancy, and the utilization of the money locked up in the endowments of these churches, there now remain very few indeed of such churches available for our purpose. It is asking too much of any man to fulfil his ordinary parochial responsibilities and to do this work as well; it would be neither fair to the parochial system, so badly understaffed, nor to the parish priest, for he would see so few people in the available time that it would not justify his special training, nor would he be able to build up sufficient experience to enable him to cope with the great diversity of problems effectively. The only way seems to be for the Church to make room for this ministry in a central way, that is as part of the diocesan life, if it is to function properly. It means the work will have to be undertaken much more seriously, and all the necessary provisions for its exercise will have to be borne at diocesan level. Those of us who, through experience, have been forced to recognize the value of this work for the Church and have a real sense of the magnitude of the task involved in the Church's ministry to the sick, feel so strong that it should be given authoritative encouragement and should have a high place in the list of diocesan priorities.

An alternative suggestion sometimes made is that the thera-

o

pist should hold a very small parish and function from there. This would be a possibility if a one-church-parish of minute proportions could be found within easy access of a large centre of population. The therapist must be accessible, with frequent transport services to his place for those people who are dependent upon them. This practical factor will rule out many a small village, which usually has bus services on only two days of the week, and they very limited. The obvious answer is for the therapist to go to the people. A town consulting-room would have to be provided, and here a city Vicarage might be used for some consideration to cover the expenses. Care would have to be exercised, for although this sounds all so simple there is a practical difficulty in regard to the therapist himself; unless he has some safeguards he would soon require to be treated himself. He would scarcely ever see his home, for the demands upon him would be very considerable. For example, my first person comes at 8.30 a.m. and only occasionally, through a cancellation, am I free before 10 p.m. On occasions I have had as much as between eleven and twelve hours of case work alone in a day, and besides this I have done work relating to St Margaret's, which is an important city church, and to my Rural Deanery, in which I am responsible for much administrative work as deputy Rural Dean. This is done single-handed. I only mention this to show that an almost impossible situation confronts the future of this great therapeutic ministry unless something is done about it centrally in the diocese. But to return to what I am saying about the therapist and his timetable, he will find himself working until 10 p.m. in the evenings, for the majority of people can only come to a session after 6 p.m. on account of their work. If travelling were added to the therapist's early and late hours it would be more than any man or family could stand. On the whole the suggestion of a country parish seems to have more against it than for it.

Another possibility would be for the therapist to be attached to a church as a kind of Curate available on Sundays. It would provide a little income, and also it would be a welcome change for the therapist who does need to keep his contacts with a more balanced outer-body.

The next problem is that of training. This is at the present difficult on account of the heavy commitments of the parochial clergy. It is no use a man in charge of a parish of 20,000 people contemplating therapeutic work at the deeper level. A place might be provided for the therapist where there is a staff of clergy, but it would mean that he would not have to be moved for many years. Care should be taken not to waste the therapist's training by giving him work which other people could do just as well.

The Theological College should be the place where the prospect is opened out before those training for the Ministry, and if a man seems suitable in every way to be a specialist therapist he should be excused much of the usual syllabus in order to have experience in mental hospital and other detailed therapeutic training. Apart from the training of such people I would make a plea that psychology should be one of the main subjects taught to all the students; that it is not taken seriously passes comprehension, for what is psychology but 'the study of the soul'!

For those priests who have a special leaning towards a therapeutic ministry training presents a real problem. When the Church is well supplied with clergy of the specialist class of therapist this will cease to be a problem for their services will be available as teachers. The difficulty lies in the period when only a very few clergy are available to train others. At present various psychiatrists will give a training-analysis to those who can afford it; Dr Graham Howe, for example, holds seminars for the training of lay analysts.[1] Those of us who have experience in these matters are always ready to train suitable people. Training also may be had at St Augustine's College, Canterbury, where at the time of writing it is given by the Sub-warden, the Reverend C. D. Kelley, D.D. I only wish we had in this country the thoroughness of the American Episcopal Church in providing systematic training. The Roman Catholic Church is fully alive, at least in certain quarters, to the great value of psychotherapy; I have been told of a priest who has been sent to Switzerland to be trained by C. G. Jung. Dr Frank Lake is exercising his mind very much upon the training of the clergy in these matters, and he is actively engaged in giving most valuable instruction in psychotherapy to the clergy. He is doing more than anyone has ever done to bring home to the Church the tremendous opportunity before her. He gives systematic instruction in

[1] The Open Way, 57 Queen Anne Street, London, W.1.

O*

his seminars, which he holds in fifteen dioceses in the Midlands and the North. In a number of cases bishops are giving him every encouragement, which is of fine promise for the future. Although this has been taking place but for a year, at the time of writing there are now clergy who are advertising the fact that they welcome people with problems, and they give them opportunities to receive their 'Counselling'. Besides this pioneer work of the seminars Dr Lake is in great demand for conferences of clergy, and he is beginning to penetrate the Theological Colleges. His former missionary experience is being put to this new enterprise which, aided by his outstanding teaching ability, may mark a turning point in the life of the Church of England.

It will serve the two purposes of showing how lacking is the Church of England in this approach to life, and of outlining what is being done elsewhere if I say something about the training which is given to interested clergy in the United States. A theological student or pastor is trained at a centre which combines both theory and practice. There is always a period of training in a hospital or clinical centre, which is supervised by a qualified chaplain-supervisor; full collaboration with the medical staff takes place.

The chaplain-supervisor must be a graduate of a university and a theological college, he must have had a reasonable amount of ordinary pastoral experience, one year at least must be spent in clinical pastoral education and a further three months of clinical experience under supervision. There is required a high standard of personal qualification which is appraised by an accrediting committee. Such a person is set over the training, theoretical and clinical, of the students from the theological college and other clergy. The hospital fully co-operates, and at the end of the course a man is deemed qualified by the medical profession to deal adequately with the average emotional problem. Thus the misgivings of the medical profession are removed.

A register of all the clergy in this country doing therapeutic work of this kind is badly needed, for at the moment the handful of clergy carry on their work often unknown to one another. Such a register would be capable of becoming something like the doctors' register, and it would bring the necessary degree of supervision and qualification. The most

interested person is not always the right person to be a
therapist, and some form of selection is necessary.

This brings us to a brief consideration of our relationship
with the medical profession. If a doctor has practical proof
of the value of the services given he will be grateful to the
Church for the help she can give. He may not go so far as
to send his patients along to the priest-therapist, because he is
afraid of giving 'cover' to the non-professional person, but he
may be very glad indeed when his difficult neurotic patients
find their own way there. Eventually when the doctor has
sufficient confidence in the therapist he may occasionally send
his patients to him, and this is more likely to happen when
the Church has established the ministry on a proper basis
as in America. Apart from all this it is most important to have
co-operation with the psychiatrists of the local mental hospital
who will deal with the psychotics who come to the clergy for
help, and who also will give advice in the case of border-line
psychotics and stand by in case of need. I should like to put
on record here my profound personal appreciation of a certain
psychiatrist of repute who has acted as Consultant to the St
Margaret's Clinic. Without such a person in the background
the effectiveness of the work would be diminished.

We have mentioned E.C.T. already and something more
needs to be said about this very common treatment in our
hospitals. My first observation is that almost all the people
I help have had this treatment at some time. There are many
people who are helped by it, some of them for a short time,
others for a long time. There are times when, apart from
the use of drugs which the doctor alone can give, E.C.T. is
necessary in order to calm down the anxiety attack in which
the person is too disturbed in mind to be dealt with in analysis;
when he is more settled the analysis can proceed. With
hysterical persons in particular, considerable anxiety storms
blow up and then drugs will help; the same is true of deep
depressions; the closest co-operation with the psychiatrist is
required on such occasions.

The time has come to end these pages. I am convinced that
the Church is being offered a new instrument with which to
exercise the ministry which her Lord laid upon her from the
beginning. It will bring a new effectiveness to the whole
Ministry through the gaining by the clergy of a new view-

point of the people to whom they minister in so many different ways, and also it will win for the Church a new appreciation and devotion from the people of our country.

This is the general gain to be had by these psychological insights; a far greater gain is the restoration to the Church of a real healing ministry, both spiritual and scientific. In times past she has allowed the healing function to slip out of her hands to her own great weakening and to the continuing hurt of those in need. I have sought with the ability at my disposal to make clear that psychotherapy is readily baptized into the Christian Ministry to its great enrichment; further, I would declare it to be a God-given instrument without which many people will remain sick in soul. A demonstration has been made by St Margaret's Clinic that the Church can meet a need for healing. This need is of prodigious proportions, for people are crying out of their despair for help and they hear 'no voice, nor any that answered'; but when they hear an answering voice from the Church they flock to her in their numbers. The smallest imagination will see what this could mean to the Church were the clinics multiplied and set up in our towns and cities. I have shown that the work can be done, as it must needs be to be really effective, at a specialist level by ordinary clergy who have submitted themselves to the disciplines of psychological theory and practice.

My last word is a plea that the Church will not throw away this immense opportunity out of prejudice or partisanship, fear or ignorance, but that she will see in this work a movement of the Spirit in our broken and bewildered age. We seek from the highest level of the Church's life every possible encouragement, and this not only in word. Provision should be made for the training of clergy in psychotherapy, and the many hindrances and encumbrances now laid upon men able to perform this task should be swept away. Given the will, financial considerations will be found no hindrance, for mental suffering is so widespread that an appeal for funds for the establishment of a ministry to the emotionally sick would, I believe, meet with an immediate and generous response. I can see no difficulty before the Church but what can be overcome. We ask for fearless leadership and imaginative direction in a matter so full of promise and so much in accord with the mind of Christ.

These pages will have failed their purpose if they are read as setting forth the work of someone who is very exceptional and endowed with special gifts which he is using within the framework of the Church. I hasten to affirm that I am no different from many hundreds of my fellow clergy who could, given the opportunity, do better work than I have done. I have no diplomas, no medical qualifications, but what I have attempted to show is the practical worth of my labours. 'By their fruits ye shall know them.' I ask for no other test than this, indeed this must ever remain the Church's qualification in these matters. By the grace of God I have been allowed to assist in the bringing to birth of new lives for old more times than I can remember; these children in the Spirit are the reward which awaits a Church which realizes her opportunity and takes it.

APPENDIX

LSD

by

FRANK LAKE

LSD-25, or lysergic acid diethylamide tartrate is a mescaline-like drug whose effects were discovered by accident in Switzerland. Apart from some physiological changes in perception which result in hallucinations, of lovely designs, shapes and colours, the main effect of LSD is to lift the areas of repression which cover infantile memories. This effect occurs most favourably where the subject is a patient in need of treatment and already within a good relationship with a therapist.

A minute dose of this medicine is drunk in plain water and after about half an hour its effects begin to be manifest. The ordinary world appears to be seen in an unreal way and the deeper world of past emotions begins to come to the surface of consciousness. It is impossible to forecast which memories will appear first. Sometimes they are extremely happy memories of infancy and the blessedness of life in the first year. On other occasions patients begin to giggle, but the character of the laughter may change into something more hysterical and frightened. This is likely to herald the emergence of the memory of some infantile emotional anguish, usually of separation from the mother within the first nine months of life.

At other times the grown person, even if by now at the age of 50, may relive vividly the anger with which weaning came as an unacceptable experience. The patient under LSD is quite convinced of the reality of these experiences, which are reported often with detail which the patient had no later means of knowing but which can be confirmed from independent observers who were adult at the time.

It is also characteristic that the patient remembers the way in which he reacted to this early emotional stress. The interesting fact is that throughout the rest of life he has tended to react to emotional stress in the same way, that is, for example, by an hysterical clamouring for attention, or a 'schizoid' detachment from relationships which have become too painful to bear, or a depressive defence, whereby the infantile anger is controlled inwardly so that it does not manifest itself. We see here the roots of the psychoneuroses of adult life developing surely and permanently from events in the first year.

One characteristic which seems of major importance is this: many of the most severe sufferers from infantile deprivation within the first six months of life are quite certain that though they were lying in dread and panic because the mother was not there, they made no outward cry of pain or anguish by which the average mother could know that her child needed her desperately. These people were often regarded as unusually good babies because they never cried, and could be left for long periods unattended. If the baby shows an unnatural independence of maternal attention it is doubtful whether this should be matter for maternal congratulation.

One thing is certain, the human infant in the first nine months after birth is incapable of conceiving of itself as existing for very long without the visible presence of its mother. To leave any child too long without attention, or in the dark without company, can lead to severe emotional shocks which give rise later to the psychoneuroses, which manifest themselves in anxiety, phobias, emotional disabilities, depressions, persecutory delusions and the like.

Since the patient is under LSD for about four hours and needs the presence of some understanding person all the time, preferably the therapist, its use is very rare in the busy mental hospitals. On the other hand analysts have not taken it up as yet since their often rigid orthodoxy demands a much slower approach lasting many years to reach the same experience. Even then, in orthodox analysis, the infantile experiences are dealt with by inference from dream experiences and the analysis of the transference, whereas with LSD the recall of the memory is direct and needs very little, if any, interpretation from the therapist.

GLOSSARY

of technical terms not defined in the text

Abreaction—the re-living of repressed emotion.

Agoraphobia—a dread of enclosure.

Libido—psychic energy, desire, longing urge. Freudians see it as mainly sexual, whereas Jungians regard it as general psychic energy, and not as a force: it is seen in the play between opposites, where the degree of tension produces the strength of the libido.

Masochism—the converse of sadism. A perversion of a sexual nature which derives pleasure from self-inflicted pain.

Neurosis—a functional mental disorder.

Phobia—an unreasonable fear, arising from infantile experiences and of considerable intensity.

Psychosis—an insanity where the Ego has to some measure broken with reality.

Repression—an unconscious rejection of painful material, concepts and feelings, which remain active in the unconscious. Jung speaks of the region of the repression as 'the Personal Unconscious'. No effort of will can recall what is repressed. Whereas Freud regarded the repression as an automatic shutting off, Jung sees a repression as possibly taking place through a series of suppressive acts. A suppression is a conscious pushing out of consciousness of anything undesirable.

Sadism—the erotic pleasure caused by the infliction of pain upon objects other than oneself.

Schizoid—a shut-in type of personality manifesting some of the characteristics of schizophrenia. It featured by seclusiveness, social inefficiency, inability to become warmly and emotionally involved in people and situations, tending to eccentricity and a high degree of subjectivism.

Tic—an involuntary muscular spasm.

BIBLIOGRAPHY

a. BOOKS OF FIRST IMPORTANCE

The works of Freud, Jung, Adler, Stekel.

Alexander, F. *Psychosomatic Medicine*. London, Allen & Unwin, 1952.

Berg, Charles. *Clinical Psychology: A Case-Book of the Neuroses and their Treatment*. London, Allen & Unwin, 1948.

Deutsch, Helen. *Psychology of Women*, 2 vols. London, Research Books, 1947.

English, O. Spurgeon, and Constance J. Foster. *Emotional Problems of Living*. London, Allen & Unwin, 1947.

Fairbairn, W. R. D. *Psychoanalytic Studies of the Personality*. London, Tavistock, 1952.

Guntrip, H. *Mental Pain and the Cure of Souls*. London, Independent Press, 1956.

Hadfield, J. A. *Psychology and Mental Health*. London, Allen & Unwin, 1950.

Klein, Melanie. *The Psychoanalysis of Children*. London, Hogarth, 1932. *Contributions to Psychoanalysis*, London, Hogarth, 1948. *Envy and Gratitude*, London, Hogarth.

and J. Riviere. *Love, Hate and Reparation*. London, Hogarth, 1937.

Laing, R. D. *The Divided Self*. London, Tavistock, 1960.

Maeder, A. *Ways to Psychic Health*. London, Hodder & Stoughton, 1954.

Suttie, I. D. *Origins of Love and Hate*. London, Routledge, 1935.

b. GENERAL BOOKS

Alexander, F. *Psychoanalysis and Psychotherapy*. London, Allen & Unwin, 1957.

Barker, C. E. *Nerves and their Cure*. London, Allen & Unwin, 1960.

Baynes, H. G. *The Mythology of the Soul*. London, Methuen, 1949.

Berg, Charles. *Deep Analysis: The Clinical Study of an Individual Case*. London, Allen & Unwin, 1947.

Fordham, F. *Introduction to Jung's Psychology*. London, Penguin, 1953.

Jacobi, J. *The Psychology of C. G. Jung*. London, Routledge, 1942.

Roberts, D. E. *Psychotherapy and a Christian View of Man.* London, Scribner, 1950.

Schaer, H. *Religion and the Cure of Souls in Jung's Psychology.* London, Routledge, 1951.

Way, Lewis. *Adler's Place in Psychology.* London, Allen & Unwin, 1950.

Wexberg, E. *Individual Psychology.* London, Allen & Unwin, 1930. *Individual Psychology Treatment.* London, C. W. Daniel, 1929.

White, V. *God and the Unconscious.* London, Harvill, 1952.

c. VALUABLE BOOKS FOR LIMITED PURPOSES

Berg, Charles. *The Unconscious Significance of Hair.* London, Allen & Unwin, 1951.

Flugel, J. C. *The Psychology of Clothes.* London, Hogarth, 1950.

Foulkes & Anthony. *Group Psychotherapy.* Pelican Book.

Groddeck, G. *Exploring the Unconscious.* London, Vision, 1950, Chap iii.

Hadfield, J. A. *Psychology and Morals.* London, Methuen, 1949. *Dreams and Nightmares.* London, Penguin, 1954.

Horney, Karen. *Our Inner Conflicts.* London, Routledge, 1946.

Kraupl-Taylor. 'Therapeutic Factors of Group Analytical Treatment', *J. Ment. Sc.,* Oct. 1950.

Layard, J. *The Lady of the Hare.* London, Faber, 1944.

Sokoloff, Boris. *Jealousy—A Psychological Study.* London, Carroll, 1948.

GENERAL INDEX

INDEX OF CASES DESCRIBED

INDEX OF SCRIPTURE REFERENCES

GEORGE ALLEN & UNWIN LTD
London: 40 Museum Street, W.C.1

Auckland: 24 Wyndham Street
Bombay: 15 Graham Road, Ballard Estate, Bombay 1
Buenos Aires: Escritorio 454-459, Florida 165
Calcutta: 17 Chittaranjan Avenue, Calcutta 13
Cape Town: 109 Long Street
Hong Kong: F1/12 Mirador Mansions, Kowloon
Karachi: Karachi Chambers, McLeod Road
Mexico: Villalongin 32-10, Piso, Mexico 5, D.F.
New Delhi: 13-14 Ajmeri Gate Extension, New Delhi 1
São Paulo: Avenida 9 de Julho 1138-Ap. 51
Singapore: 36c Princep Street, Singapore 7
Sydney, N.S.W.: Bradbury House, 55 York Street
Toronto: 91 Wellington Street West

ANXIETY IN CHRISTIAN EXPERIENCE

WAYNE E. OATES   *Demy 8vo. 15s. net*

The Christian doctrine of the cross bears a significant relationship to the everyday anxieties of men and women in their search for integrity and redemption. This relationship is brought out clearly and forcefully in this book by a leading counsellor and teacher of pastoral psychology.

Anxieties have been a burden to men and women for centuries. They have a particularly far-reaching effect in our own day because of the underlying conflict and tension that emphasize the crucial problems peculiar to our time.

There is a detailed analysis in each chapter of a different shade of anxiety: economic anxiety, finitude anxiety, the anxiety of grief, the anxiety of sin, legalistic anxiety, the anxiety reactions of the morally indifferent, the anxiety of the cross, holy dread related to the anxiety of the cross, and in conclusion, anxiety and the fellowship of concern.

GOD, CHRIST AND PAGAN

M. I. BOAS   *Demy 8vo. 25s. net*

Dr Boas achieves a well-argued case for the difference between 'pure religion' and the 'paganism' by which conventional ideas and the practice of religion are all too often obscured. Writing with the authority of his experience as a psychiatrist and physician, Dr Boas is able to separate genuine religious experience from its substitutes.

He describes first what man seeks in religion, how primitive religion satisfies man's aims and the extent to which superstition is a component of cult. Subsequent chapters set forth the Hebrew and the Christian solutions to the problems of religion versus cult and lastly the author achieves a radical valuation of the data in the Old and New Testaments.

CHRISTIANITY AND FEAR

OSCAR PFISTER   *30s. net*

'The present book,' as the author states in his preface, 'is designed to set out the results of thirty-six years of study dealing with the nature and history of Christian love as applied to a single but exceedingly important problem, that of fear,' and thus to solve the problem of religious fear on psychological lines. Pfister resolves the paradox of Christianity—the supreme religion of love—alienating men terrified by its dogma, or by the surrounding dangers of the temporal world, enforced by the stake and hell fire. In other words, theologians had failed to make intelligible the processes of salvation, regeneration and sanctification because they dealt not with the living faith but with the theoretical by-products, and failed to satisfy profound human longing and needs.

Pfister removes the neurotic traits from religion by the method employed in the cure of non-religious neuroticism, by the restoration of love and its elevation as the dominant factor in life. Scholarly and profound, with the wide sweep of the historian and the intimate depth of the true psychologist, and deeply stimulating in its conclusions, it is a human and, in the best sense, religious study.

BAY WINDOWS INTO ETERNITY

A. GRAHAM IKIN   *Demy 8vo. 15s. net*

This book is written as simply as possible for all who seek to deepen their own spiritual lives and to play their part constructively in this critical period of human history. Today mankind is challenged by the very destructiveness brought into being by man to find the way of the spirit, which involves harmony and peace in the fullness of living in true fellowship with God and man.

Glimpses into this way of life are given in this book which enrich our daily living. They are not mirages in a cloud, says the author, but experiences of a more spacious and gracious mode of living.

GEORGE ALLEN & UNWIN LTD